P. E. LUKIN
GREENSLEEVES
6 HOBART ROAD
HIGH WYCOMBE, BUCKS HP13 6UD
TEL. (0494) 520357

BIG WING

BIG WING

The biography of Air Chief Marshal
Sir Trafford Leigh-Mallory
KCB, DSO and Bar

Bill Newton Dunn

Airlife
England

Copyright © Bill Newton Dunn, 1992

First published in 1992 by
Airlife Publishing Ltd.

British Library Cataloguing in Publication Data

A catalogue record for this book is
available from the British Library.

ISBN 1 85310 240 7

Printed in England by Livesey Ltd., Shrewsbury.

Airlife Publishing Ltd.

101 Longden Road, Shrewsbury SY3 9EB, England.

Contents

Acknowledgements

The author is most grateful to the following for their help in the preparation of this book:

Air Historical Branch, Ministry of Defence (especially Air Commodore H. A. Probert)

Air Chief Marshal Sir Harry Broadhurst GCB, KBE, DSO, DFC, AFC

late Mrs Mary H. Brooke (née Leigh-Mallory)

Major R. P. Chaworth-Musters (re Annesley)

County Archivist, Cheshire County Council

Sergeant E. G. Cockings

Librarian of Christ Church, Oxford

Air Chief Marshal Sir Kenneth Cross KCB, CBE, DSO, DFC

Guy Dodgson

Mrs Jacqueline Doherty (née Leigh-Mallory)

'HTF Coventry'

Reverend Group Captain A. Haslam MC, DFC

Air Vice-Marshal J. E. Johnson CB, CBE, DSO, DFC

Mrs Kay Leigh-Mallory

Mrs Avie Longridge (née Leigh-Mallory)

Dr R. Luckett, Magdalene College, Cambridge

John Mallory

Mrs Jeanette Maxwell-Brown

Air Chief Marshal Sir Theodore McEvoy KCB, CBE

Mrs Clare Millikan (née Leigh-Mallory) Reverend and Mrs

Mr Roger Miles of Thames Television

F. D. Moss, Rector of Mobberley

Colonel B. J. R. Murphy

My parents, Owen (Lt Col) and Barbara Newton Dunn

the late Lord Philip Noel-Baker

Mrs Alison Pearson

Mrs Jeane Pollard (née Dodgson)

Air Vice Marshal Sir Cedric Porter CBE

Lieutenant General Harold Redman KCB, CBE

Hugh Sawbridge, Haileybury School

M. G. Sims, Librarian of the Staff College, Camberley

Air Commodore F. M. F. 'Freddie' West VC, CBE, MC

Lieutenant General Sir John Woodall KCMG, KBE, CB, MC

Chapter 1
Off to Pastures New

On 14 November 1944, a British military York aircraft stood ready to leave from Northolt airfield near London. Everything appeared to be perfect with the plane although not all its paint had yet dried. It was about to carry a very important passenger, Air Chief Marshal Sir Trafford Leigh-Mallory, accompanied by his wife en route for Ceylon. He was going out to command all the Allied Air Forces in the war against the Japanese in South East Asia.

To his colleagues Leigh-Mallory was known simply as 'L-M'. Many important people were there to see him leave, among them his daughter Jacqueline and his son Tom. As he stepped aboard he was followed by his chauffeur, Cockings, carrying his briefcase. One of the painters warned him to keep the briefcase away from the wet paint. The chauffeur handed the briefcase carefully to L-M, who said: 'Well, cheerio Cockings! Best of luck.' Cockings said goodbye to his chief and expected to see him back in England the following February.

The plane took off and flew southwards, accompanied by an escort of Spitfires. Reaching the coast of France, Leigh-Mallory's crew sent a radio message to the escorting Spitfires thanking and dismissing them. They turned and flew back to England. L-M's plane flew on alone across France.

Next day, L-M's mother wrote a description of the departure to her daughter Mary:

> 'I had such a nice message last night from Jacqueline to say that the start had gone off perfectly, and they went away escorted by Spitfires — rather thrilling! Yes indeed, it would have been nice to have been there. Trafford rang me up on Sunday and sounded in excellent spirits — just his strong, *happy* voice. I do trust all will go well with them! Doris, he said, had had some tummy pain — but very natural with poor Sam having been put away, which would try her sorely, but the change and warmer climate will help her, I hope.'

Leigh-Mallory's first scheduled stop was near Naples in Italy. But the plane did not arrive there. There was no trace of it. No wireless SOS messages had been received. Search planes were sent out — but no clues were found. The German enemy did not boast of having captured Leigh-Mallory. It had to be presumed that the plane had crashed and that L-M was dead. Sixteen days later on 1 December, L-M's personal assistant, Lady Freeman, wrote to his mother:

> 'I have purposely postponed writing to you because I hoped that by waiting I might have better news, or at least some definite news to

give you. But now it seems we must abandon hope, since the official search, both from the air and on the ground has been abandoned.

The fate of the plane remains a mystery, and there is positively no clue to what might have happened. From the time the escorting fighters left (which was within an hour of their departure from Northolt) there was silence, and no wireless message was received from the plane. Nor has it been substantiated that the machine was seen after having crossed the French coast.

For the RAF, and indeed for the whole country, it is a catastrophe which we can ill afford. For his family and for his friends it is an irreparable loss. But for him I can only think of it as a grand ending to a very fine and distinguished career. There is no doubt it is how he would have liked to go, for he often told me that he looked with horror on the prospect of growing old and outliving his usefulness to the Air Force, to which he devoted all the best years of his life. Of course, he still had many years in front of him before he would have quitted the Service but I believe (and he believed) that in his command of the Allied Expeditionary Air Force, he had touched the peak of his career.

Never before in history had one man commanded so vast an air armada, engaged on so momentous an enterprise. There is no possible doubt that the success of the invasion of Europe was due in no small measure to the brains, organising power, tremendous industry and iron determination of your son.

It has been my privilege to work for him for nearly two years — all through the planning, preparation, launching and subsequent development of the invasion of France. During that period I learned to know him, as I suppose few of his friends have known him and I speak from the heart when I say that his loss is the most grievous I have had to suffer.

I have worked for many people as secretary, and since I joined the Service have come across all sorts and conditions of men. But I have never known anyone with greater capacity for hard work, with more meticulous care for detail, who took greater pains to master his job than L-M. Nor have I known anyone more loyal to those he served, or to those who served under him, or who inspired greater devotion and loyalty in his subordinates, than he.

He was a striking example of the human paradox. At once forceful and diffident; ruthless (if need be), but kindly; dictatorial, almost inclined to be pompous, yet essentially simple of heart. It was this innate contradiction in character, which made him sometimes liable to be misunderstood, and I think only those who knew him really well appreciated his true worth. That was sterling; for he had one aim only in life — to serve his country and to do his job to the best of his ability and to the limit of his strength. Only one thing mattered to him — the immediate task in hand — and into that he would throw himself with untiring energy and unflagging zeal.

The circumstances of his departure from this country to take up his new Command are typical of the man. Always impatient of delay, anxious to be off with the old and on with the new, utterly fearless of flying in weather which might well have daunted a less bold spirit, thinking only of getting started on his new task and throwing into it that immense strength and boundless energy which made such a success of anything he undertook — he left on his last journey.'

Lady Freeman was the second wife of Air Chief Marshal Sir Wilfrid Freeman, who had served as Chief Executive at the Ministry of Aircraft Production since 1942.

Many other tributes were made. General Montgomery wrote to *The Times* on 3 December:

'I should like to pay tribute to two great friends who have recently been killed in the service of the allies: Bertie Ramsay and L-M. And, indeed, this tribute might well come from the whole Army, since both were firm friends of many soldiers, and both had worked whole-heartedly to establish and to maintain those friendly relations between the fighting services which are so vital at all times.

I had known both of them for many years and worked with them at various times . . . I have the most happy recollections of the planning period from January to June (1944), then the assault on June 6, and the subsequent operations. Difficulties and differences sometimes arose, as they often will: but they were always overcome, and we knit together as a team of three, owing personal loyalty and devotion to Eisenhower, our Chief, who held us all together, all the time . . . And now I am the only one left of that British team of three; and I feel that it is right and proper that I should pay a tribute to my two comrades. They were not to live to see the fruits of their labours; but when this business is over, and the world is once more at peace, we must not forget the part that was played by Bertie Ramsay and L-M: a great sailor and a great airman: both great friends of the Army and both great English gentlemen.'

Air Marshal H. E. P. Wigglesworth (who had worked for L-M and was subsequently said to be a model for the fictional hero Biggles) wrote to L-M's mother from the headquarters of Fighter Command at Bentley Priory:

'For the last year I was his Chief Staff Officer, and was in constant touch with him throughout the trying days prior to and since the invasion of the Continent and was his confidant in many things . . . May I offer to you, on behalf of myself and other members of his staff, heartfelt sympathies . . . We mourn a friend and great commander. Believe me, he was esteemed by all for his fine character, kindliness, and thoughtfulness for others. His particular anxiety was to look after his pilots and junior officers. We were all extremely proud to serve with him and under him — he was certainly an inspiration to us all. The loss of Sir Trafford goes even further than our immediate circle for not only the Royal Air Force but also the nation have lost a great servant, officer and man. You will have seen ample evidence in the papers during the past year of the very high opinion of him which was, and always will be, held by the whole country as well as by those who worked closely with him.'

A long obituary appeared in *The Times* on 14 December 1944. It described L-M as 'one of the most capable and talented air commanders of the war'.

Who was L-M? Why is there no popular memory of the Englishman who commanded the greatest air armada in history? What forces create two men like him and his legendary brother?

Chapter 2
Childhood

'The time will come when thou shalt lift thine eyes
To watch a longdrawn battle in the skies,
While aged peasants, too amazed for words,
Stare at the flying fleets of wond'rous birds.'
Thomas Gray 1737

As we have seen, L-M was destined to exercise operational command over history's greatest ever 'flying fleet of wond'rous birds'. It is said that human characteristics are partly inherited and partly acquired from their surroundings, so it is interesting, within the bounds of available knowledge, to examine L-M's ancestry and environment during his formative years, and to trace the development of this 'human paradox — forceful and diffident; ruthless but kindly; dictatorial but essentially simple hearted' — who was to be selected to plan the air support for Operation OVERLORD and to execute it so effectively.

L-M was born on 11 July 1892, in the village of Mobberley, Cheshire, where his father was rector of the Anglican church. As L-M was destined to play a leading role in one of the greatest events of our history, it is perhaps worth recording that his birth coincided with the election victory of another man to leave his mark, the eminent Victorian politician, Gladstone.

L-M was the youngest of four children, of whom Mary was the oldest, being seven and a half at the time of his birth; George was just six and Avie (a contraction of Annie Victoria) was four and a half. So L-M was not only the youngest but he also faced the biggest age gap. Indeed, Mary was later to regard him as a very 'uppity' small boy, always trying to catch up with the three much older children. All four children were subsequently to prove their strength in different ways, George becoming a legendary mountaineer who vanished almost at the summit of Mount Everest in 1924, and Mary and Avie achieving the ages of 95 and 101 respectively. The three elder children had been born in the same village, but at a different house, Newton Hall, further from the village railway station. Their paternal grandparents also lived in the same village at the Manor House next to the church. Their ancestral inheritance was from the prosperous but unexceptional upper middle classes.

L-M was christened on 5 September 1892 by his own father at Mobberley church. He was given the names Trafford Leigh Mallory. His godfather was Sir Lees Knowles, a wealthy bachelor and local

Member of Parliament. The name of Trafford was chosen from his father's mother. Her maiden name had been Henrietta Trafford, and she had died the same year. The Traffords had traditionally been prosperous landowners. In College Church in Manchester there is a memorial of 1513 to Sir Edmund Trafford and the industrial estate outside Manchester called Trafford Park was once part of the family's estates.

The village of Mobberley had been the home of the Mallory family for several centuries. This was probably because the gift of the village rectorship lay in their own hands. According to local history 'in 1359 Sir Ralph Mobberley estated all his lands on John Leycester with the advowson of the Church of Mobberley. Thomas Mallory, Dean of Chester, purchased the advowson to whose posterity it yet remaineth'. This far-sighted Thomas Mallory became rector of Mobberley in 1621. Ever since then, the Mallory family had decided who would be the next occupant of the post. Trafford's father Herbert was the sixth Mallory rector at Mobberley.

But this continuity was not what it appeared to be. Trafford's father had no Mallory blood in his veins. Trafford's grandfather had started life as George Leigh: he had courted a Miss Julia Mallory whose father was the Rector of Mobberley and who lived at its Manor House. She had no brother so her father, the Revd John Mallory, insisted that Julia could only marry George Leigh providing the latter changed his surname to Mallory — in order that any children should be born as Mallorys. George Leigh readily agreed and married Julia in 1832. The same year he became the Rector of Mobberley.

His young wife, Julia, died in 1835. However after her death, George remained as Rector of Mobberley, continued to use the surname Mallory and continued to live in the Manor House. The following year George married his first cousin Henrietta Trafford, the daughter of Trafford Trafford Esquire of Oughtrington Park. Curiously the latter's father had also been born a Leigh and had changed his own surname when he had married a Trafford heiress in 1762. Our Trafford's ancestors were decisive and practical men!

George and Henrietta Mallory had ten children. Their last child, Herbert was born in Mobberley in 1856, and would be the father of our subject Trafford. Thus, Herbert was born as the youngest of ten children from middle-aged parents who were first cousins. This could have led to a less than healthy constitution. But Herbert grew up normal and intelligent. He took a degree at Trinity College, Cambridge, and set out to follow his ancestral footsteps by entering theological college. And this was how he met Annie Jebb, his future wife, Trafford's mother.

Annie Jebb was an only child. Her mother was the daughter of a clergyman and became the second wife of an elderly clergyman, the Revd John Jebb. Her husband died after only two years of marriage and their only child, Annie, was born posthumously in 1862. They were left far from destitute: her mother inherited the Jebb family's Walton Lodge estate at Chesterfield to the exclusion of her husband's first family.

Annie grew up fearless, lively, wilful and fun-loving but she was untrained and undisciplined. Before Annie was eighteen years old, her mother was inspecting the young trainees at the local theological college. Her mother selected one of them, Herbert Mallory, as a suitable husband for Annie. Peaceful Herbert had little chance of escape. When he showed signs of faintheartedness over Annie, he was accused of 'trifling with her affections'. Herbert's family raised objections that Annie was too young and frivolous. But the couple were married in June 1882 when Annie was nineteen years old, shortly after Herbert had been ordained.

Annie became an enthusiastic but unreliable parson's wife for Herbert. The same traits appeared in her attitude to motherhood. Though she loved her four children, she was not prepared to put herself out for them. When bored or unwell or feeling in need of 'taking the waters' at a spa, she would take herself off for cures or holidays for weeks at a time. She left her family in the charge of a succession of bewildered governesses who were quite unable to control the nest of four lively children.

Neither Herbert nor Annie had the least idea how to handle money. They were hopelessly extravagant and were constantly in difficulties. Annie always bought the latest devices as soon as they appeared on the market — such as an ice-cream making machine and a device called a vacuum cleaner. There was no thought of being economical. Both Mary and Avie recalled that at home they never saw the same piece of meat on the table for a second time. Instead, half-eaten joints were to be seen decaying in the larder. This extravagance made all four children careful with money in their adult lives. Later on there were times when the four children had to get together to rescue their parents from the consequences of the latters' improvidence.

Annie was equally hopeless at managing servants. The household was permanently in a state of crisis and flux. She was a great 'stirrer up', possibly because a calm and orderly existence bored her. Mary, Trafford's sister, remembered their brother George asking her: 'Why is it that whenever Mother comes into the schoolroom a row starts?'

To the end of her long life Annie retained a child-like sense of adventure and fun: self-centred and unselfconscious, she did exactly what she wanted without consideration for anyone else, organising people and bending them to her will. Her appetite for life, even in old age, earned her great affection from her grandchildren, to whom she was a constant source of amusement and wonder. As a mother she caused endless embarrassment and exasperation.

As a father, Herbert counted for less in every way, opting out of this household frenzy and preferring to retreat into the calm of his study. The children were fond of him and sorry for him in his trials with their mother. But he — no more than her — was not someone to be depended upon and to be turned to in a time of need. Annie in later years enjoyed claiming that her sons inherited her forcefulness. It is reasonable to assume that they also inherited something from their father and, with parents of such diverse character, it is perhaps not surprising that L-M became the paradox described by Lady Freeman.

With such unsupportive parents and a lively and dashing trio of older siblings always ahead of him, young Trafford was very much on his own. Nor did he have a permanent loved nanny-figure on whom to depend in that restless and unstable household. He was often left with the servants, who changed as frequently as did his nursery governesses. Indeed, one of Trafford's playmates was the gardener's son. One day Annie found the gardener's son wearing Trafford's hat and she was very angry:

'That's his best hat,' she remonstrated.

'Well, I'm glad it's not mine,' the gardener's son answered back cheekily.

That this incident was vividly recalled by Mary eighty years later suggests that the four children did not often dare to cheek their mother themselves. Anything for peace and quiet, or taking avoiding action, was more likely to be their response to her storms and drama. It is not surprising that Trafford eventually married a gentle, sweet and subservient girl, entirely unlike his mother, and that he organised their money and servants himself.

Trafford had one companion of his own age — named Oliver Jenkinson. Oliver was a second cousin who had been abandoned by his own parents; his mother had vanished and his father had remarried. His uncle, Sir Edward Jenkinson, had raised two separate families simultan-eously — who first discovered each other at his graveside! According to Mary, Annie 'in her sour way' did not bother with Oliver.

Mary recalls Trafford and Oliver fishing together in the village pond. She also remembers Trafford at the age of five being afraid of geese at a farm which lay between their home and the village railway station: but Trafford solved that difficulty by standing at his garden gate and getting rides from a passing carriage or milkcart.

The children were all sent away to boarding schools. In 1900, when Trafford was aged eight and still at home, he sent his sister Mary a birthday present at her boarding school. She replied:

'My dearest Trafford

Thank you very much indeed for the nice present you sent. I am sure my hair will be quite tidy and I shall be absolutely neat now I have a little looking-glass and comb. Thank you very much for your letter. You are getting to write quite well now aren't you.

Have you found your guinea-pig yet poor little wretch, is the other one quite well?

Do you always remember to feed the doves; give them a little cheese in their seed sometimes they like it so much. Mind you write and tell me when they begin to lay.

I hope you are keeping Father in good order, and not letting him get too naughty.

Please give my love to Bryan, Bridget and Gertrude.

If you haven't taken the negative of Boxer to Ted yet mind you do soon as he asked me for it the last day of the hols, and I hadn't time to take it to him. When you go give my love to Miss Whitelegg.

With my love I am your loving sister Mary.'

Later that year in October, Trafford was mentioned in a letter to their mother from his brother George who was away at Winchester College:

'Please tell Trafford from me that he must buck up and become a Mathematician and if he can't read decently by next hols I shall kick him.'

All four children were required to learn to play the piano. None was very good at it. Mary recalls being made to practise downstairs while her mother dressed herself in the room above. Each time Mary played a wrong note, her mother banged her stick on the floor above. Eventually, Mary slammed down the piano lid and refused to learn the piano ever again. Annie left the four children to their own devices a great deal and it is not surprising that they got into a few scrapes. Mary recalled with pleasure going to the farm nearby and climbing the haystack and George, who was blessed with an astonishing gift of balance, once climbed alone onto the roof of Mobberley church and walked round the top of the parapet of the tower to the terror of those watching below. Trafford watched but did not follow him. On another occasion both boys climbed onto the roof of their house: their father was very fussed, but their mother, herself a keen climber and rider in her youth, was not at all bothered. George descended from the roof by himself but Trafford, being six years younger, needed a ladder.

'We were frightful children,' Mary recalled. 'Mother was very strict but Father egged us on. Usually he was very occupied with his duties.'

The three older children enjoyed playing cards together. On the way to visit other houses, they travelled in a brougham and played cards to while away the time. Their father, as the local clergyman, was much embarrassed by this — and insisted that they pull down the blinds of the brougham before they played.

Meanwhile, important changes were affecting the world outside. In 1901 Queen Victoria died after a reign of sixty-three years. In 1903 the first non-experimental radio-telegraph conversation took place across the Atlantic between King Edward VII and President Theodore Roosevelt and on 17 December an event took place in North Carolina which was to dominate the subsequent life of eleven-year-old Trafford. Two brothers, Wilbur and Orville Wright, made the first ever reported power-driven flight of a heavier-than-air machine. Their first flight lasted for twelve seconds; their fourth for fifty-two seconds. Their machine's average speed was thirty-one miles per hour.

Trafford in his turn was sent to boarding school, St Leonard's in Sussex. In April 1904, when he was nearly twelve years old, he was at home at Mobberley for the holidays. Mary wrote to their mother who was away from home convalescing from an operation, to the effect that he was very busy mowing the tennis lawn, seemed to be very well and was getting quite fat. It was apparent that the young Trafford's enjoyment of his food was an occasion for merriment within the family, who claimed to be able to tell when he had eaten too much — his eyes turned pink!

Not much is known about Trafford's progress at St Leonard's, but a postcard survives dated 21 November 1904, to his Aunt Harriet at Malvern:

'I hope that George will get his exam. Please give my love to Aunt Ellen and the cousins. Last Wednesday we went to see a football match between St Leonards and Tonbridge. When we left St Leonards were one ahead. With best love, Trafford.'

In quiet Mobberley, village life apparently continued as usual. In August 1904 Herbert chaired the committee which organised the thirteenth annual Mobberley Fruit, Flower and Vegetable Show. The Show was highly successful, attracting 483 contestants. Then, unexpectedly, the family's routine changed. At the beginning of October, the Mallory family suddenly moved away from Mobberley. The children were appalled. The cause was that their mother had become 'over friendly' with another male in the neighbourhood. Not surprisingly, no record of this episode survives for a biographer.

After growing up and spending his whole working life at Mobberley, their father exchanged his rural church living with the vicar of St John's Church, Birkenhead, in the nearby city of Liverpool. He did not surrender ownership of the Manor House at Mobberley nor the right to nominate the next rector — because he hoped his family would return there in due time.

At a farewell ceremony the villagers of Mobberley presented Herbert with 'a handsome testimonial' and an illuminated vellum address. There was also a gift of 'a handsome revolving bookcase' from the members of the choir and 'a useful dressing case' from the children and teachers of the village school. In his farewell sermon in the church Herbert described the past twenty years as one of 'many great changes', commenting that: 'There is not now residing in Mobberley one of the gentry who were here in January 1885.'

When he was nearly fourteen it was time for Trafford to move on to public school. His parents could not afford the fees for Winchester College where his brother George had been, so on 4 May 1906 he was sent instead to Haileybury in Hertfordshire. There he joined Melville House and was placed in the Lower Remove Class. His parents chose for him to be put on the Classical Side as opposed to the Modern Side or the Army Class.

In his first term he did well in mathematics, being placed third out of twenty, but less so in Modern Languages being only eleventh out of thirteen. The list of 'Books to be Read Next Term' were 'Rivington's Single Term Latin Readers, Fourth Term Book II' and 'Morice's Stories in Attic Greek'.

Next term in September 1906 he was moved up a class to the Upper Remove, still on the Classical Side. He achieved fourth of twenty in Maths but twelfth of eighteen in Modern Languages. Reading included 'Caesar Book I, Ovid, and Selections From Xenophon'. He became athletic — and competed in the school gymnastics competition on 13 December 1906: the school magazine records that 'Mallory did a good quick turn'.

In January 1907, he went up another form to Lower Middle 2 Class where he excelled. He won the Form Prize, being top in Maths and eighth out of twenty-three in Modern Languages. New reading was 'Virgil's Aenied, Walford's Extracts from Cicero, and Tales from Herodotus'. In school gymnastics on 15 March, 'Mallory worked remarkably well'; on 28 March, competing as second string for Melville House in the inter-house Jullundur Cup contest, he won the Passing-Out Prize. He then represented the school — as George had done at Winchester — as the junior half of the third gymnastics pair.

In the summer of 1907, Trafford was moved up another form for the third successive term. This time in U.M. II and L.M. I, he achieved second place in Maths. In the winter term he moved up again into U.M. I, achieving a second in Maths and third in Modern Languages. In January 1908 he rose to the L.V. form — his sixth new class in six successive terms! But this proved to be an academic peak. He was still on the Classical Side but apparently started to lose interest and motivation. He achieved less good placings, only fourth and nineteenth respectively. The Summer term was the same. He moved with his friends up to the U.V. form in September 1908, but there he stayed for five terms. At the same time his sporting prowess continued and he represented the school at gymnastics and his House rugby team as a prop forward.

On holiday in August 1908 George and Trafford, now sixteen, went together to climb in North Wales. On the 9th they jointly wrote in indelible pencil to their mother at St John's Vicarage, Birkenhead. It can only be described as a glorious letter. Trafford wrote first:

'Cowsleigh
Capel Curig
Sunday
My dear Mother,
We are having a glorious time here. We went up Tryfarn (the central butress) [sic] yesterday and an excellent climb. Thank you for sending the silver [underlined] spoons and forks. We are very comfortable now. We are in a cow [thinly crossed out] kind of hut, which has a cowstall at one end, which is used for cows only during the winter; all the other part is used for hay. It is situated just beside a stream in which there is the most glorious bathing among

the rocks, there being one place in which one can sit and it is as smooth and comfortable to sit in as a bath and the water comes up to the middle of one's chest. It is so absolutely glorious here that I cannot find words to express it, so George is going to have a turn at the pencil.'

George continued on the next line:

'Trafford really wants to have what he calls a bed rehearsal! And oh! what beds! Some feet of hay covered with blankets — no mattresses can beat that. If Mary and Avie will come (we intend to stay indefinitely) we can partition the hut. Or we could probably find rooms for them in some farm house near by: there is a small cottage not far off which I think we ought to take en famille next year.

It is not properly raining yet and I'm afraid it will be wet tomorrow.

We have had a peaceful Sunday — and rather a pious one beginning with an 8 a.m. service.

When you send the shirts we should like a second tin mug (4½d) which we can't procure here. The Welsh people are most kind and hospitable and we can get most things very easily. A home-made CAKE would be very pleasant.

I hope this will be posted in L'pool tomorrow morning.

Yr. loving sons, George and Trafford.'

Another letter from Trafford to his mother from Haileybury survives; it was dated only 'Sunday', but was probably written at about this time, because on the back is 'I do not think Trafford's report specially good this time do you? Please me (sic) on any news you get of George.'

'My dear Mother,

I was so glad and not a little surprised, to see your writing again so soon. It is splendid that you will be able to go home at the end of three weeks. I expect I shall find you quite altered in appearance, when I get back. I am so glad you are getting on quite well and that nearly all the pain is over.

Will you please try and impress very deeply on that Father of mine, that I very much want the collars I asked him to get last Sunday.

About three weeks ago I bought one of those large art proofs 30 by 20 in, and I have just had it framed in London, in a dark oak frame, three inches deep. It is awfully nice, it is called "the Sunlit Mere".

I am going to write to George and try to persuade him to come and have tea with me next Saturday, I do so hope he will come. There is nothing really exciting on here just now.

Please give my love to all the family.

I suppose you see Emily every day. What? Il va sans dire. With much best love, ever your loving son Trafford.'

Mary recalled watching Trafford at a school cricket match: she said that she thought that he pulled on his batting gloves as if he was the greatest cricketer in the world.

Avie remembered Trafford as 'a very efficient person always'. The family used to go and picnic up the River Dee every year: Avie recalls Trafford aged about fourteen 'offering to carve the birds and he did it most efficiently'.

Back at school, in his third U.V. term, Trafford changed from the Classical Side to the Modern Side where he stayed for a year. For his final two terms he joined the new History Set and finished in the second-highest Form, the M. VI. While there he may have read a newspaper which recorded, on 16 October 1908, the first powered flight in Great Britain. This took place when Samuel F. Cody flew for 1390 feet at Farnborough.

In June 1909, aged nearly seventeen, Trafford played for his house cricket team. In the inter-house semi-finals, he batted eighth: according to the *Haileyburian* 'Mallory was the only other batsman to make any score, and his 19 runs was a fine effort to save the side'. But the following year he is recorded as playing in only one of his house's three cricket matches, batting and scoring only one and ten in the two innings.

In October 1909, he played at prop forward in inter-house rugby. The *Haileyburian* magazine records:
'The Melville forwards, with some good dribbling, and one or two rushes, especially one headed by Mallory, kept Colvin house back for a considerable time.'

After this match, he was awarded his House Badge. The following year he played again and was also place-kicker for his team.

On 19 February 1910, he represented Haileybury in gymnastics against Cambridge University:
'Mallory worked consistently throughout, and showed up particularly well on the rings. The rest of our team were outclassed.'

The following term, on 22 May, Trafford led his three-man house team to win the school's Jullundur Cup for gymnastics. George sent him a postcard from Milan:
'My dear Trafford, Congratulations on your gym success. I was delighted to hear about it this morning. When are you going to Aldershot? I am leaving Florence for Basel tonight, and thence to Paris. G.H.L.M.'

Meanwhile on the family front, George was away at Cambridge University and Avie got married to Harry Longridge. Trafford took time off from Haileybury to attend the wedding, which was at Mobberley on 20 June 1910. It was evident that Trafford admired the freedom which was being enjoyed by his elder brother at university. George was able to travel during the holidays around the continent of Europe seeing the sights. Trafford preserved a postcard which George sent him in March 1910 which simply stated: 'Leaving for Basel tonight and thence to Paris'. During the summer holidays when George was away climbing in Switzerland, he wrote to their mother on 10 August exulting in having climbed the Jungfrau the previous morning, and ending his letter: 'It is very sad news that Trafford has mumps. I'm afraid that he'll be rather miserable after spending a few days in bed'.

Trafford was made a School Prefect in September 1910. He also took part in the school Debating Society. According to the *Haileyburian* on 31 October he was seconder to the Opposer of the Motion 'That the modern generation mistakes comfort for progress'. The school magazine records that:

'T. L. Mallory rose to talk about morality. It was obvious that for a man to go and do his work like a machine no moral thought was needed. However, when a man had leisure he had time to think over the moral issues of life. It was comfort that gave a man this time for moral reflection. Hence comfort was necessary for moral progress. He then proceeded to give several examples from history.'

In his final term, Spring 1911, Trafford played hockey for the school: on 25 February he played centre-half against Norwood Third Eleven: the *Haileyburian* recorded that 'Mallory defended well'. In the school gymnastics competition on 14 March 1911 he finished third.

On 26 March 1911 L-M learnt that he had won an Exhibition scholarship to Magdalene College at Cambridge University. It is difficult to reconcile this achievement with the family opinion, recalled by Mary, that Trafford had been idle and had freewheeled his way through school. Looking back on his schooldays it really seems that he had made the most of them, playing a full part in every aspect of school life. We can see him developing self-confidence, demonstrating an ability to be a good team member, with plenty of initiative, and occasional glimpses of leadership. He also showed his innate strength of character by determining his own goals and working towards them while keeping his own counsel. A manifestation of this was the quietly determined, almost unobtrusive, way in which he pursued his objective of following his brother to Cambridge. Could it be that while he was apparently coasting along, he was in fact hiding his light under a bushel, more intent on acquiring knowledge than demonstrating it — a sign of growing self-sufficiency?

When he left Haileybury in April 1911, it might have been difficult to predict that L-M would become the great leader that he eventually did, but the boy had undoubtedly laid the foundation of the man.

Chapter 3
Cambridge, War, Wife and Flying

Trafford went up to Magdalene College at Cambridge in September 1911 when he was nineteen. There he read History. His brother George had left an indelible mark at Magdalene. So much so that after his death in dramatic circumstances, one of the courts at Magdalene was named after him. George had excelled at sport, having been Captain of the Magdalene First Boat in the rowing races in the summer of 1908, when they did so well. He had been a member of the Fabian Society — a new group of socialist thinkers — from December 1908 to September 1911, when he resigned. More relevant however was George's membership of the Kingsley Club: the circumstances of his membership reveal his character.

The Kingsley Club — named after the Victorian novelist Charles Kingsley — had been revived in Magdalene College by undergraduates including George Mallory in 1906. Its members, originally restricted to ten, were to meet weekly and in strict sequence each would read a literary paper to the others followed by a discussion.

The Minutes of the October 1907 term read: 'There being no secretary, a spontaneous meeting was held in Hall during dinner: this was arranged at the request of the late secretary Mr (George) Mallory, who having previously decided that no other member of the club was likely to perform so well as himself the duties of a secretary, instigated his own election to that office.'

Trafford wisely did not attempt to follow slavishly in his brother's footsteps, either at Magdalene or during the holidays, when although he accompanied George rock climbing, he pursued his own interest, which was sailing boats. He bought his first dinghy on 5 September 1912, for eleven pounds sterling at Liverpool. He named it Doris — although he had not yet met his future wife who bore the same name. At Magdalene Trafford did not excel at sport, nor did he join the Fabian Society. But as well as participating in many other College activities, he did follow his brother into the Kingsley Club. He was invited to attend as a guest on 28 November 1911 when, prophetically, the topic to be discussed was 'War and Germany'. At the start of his second year at Magdalene in 1912, Trafford was elected to the Kingsley Club as a full member. One other Magdalene undergraduate, who was one year senior to Trafford, was elected to the Club on the same day: his name was Arthur W. Tedder.

Both Trafford Mallory and Arthur Tedder were regular attenders at the weekly meetings of the Kingsley Club. Subjects discussed included: 'Reality and Joy', 'J. A. Symonds', 'Culture', 'Stevenson's Letters', 'Autobiographical Intention', 'Poetry, its meaning and uses', and 'Sufism'. Those who were not experienced in Sufism already, learned that it is concentrative meditation, one branch of which is the whirling dervishes.

On 3 March 1913, Tedder read what, according to the minutes, was 'an extremely interesting paper on Beethoven'. Tedder left Cambridge in 1913, a year before Trafford, and sailed east to join the Civil Service in Fiji — but not for long, as we shall see.

In due course, it was Trafford's turn to prepare and to read a paper. The 1914 minutes give the following account:

'At a meeting of the Society in Mr Benson's rooms on Monday 9 February, Mr T. L. Mallory read a paper on the Annesley Case. A brief and comprehensive summary of the events as alleged by each side and of issues at stake was followed by a comment on the difficulties with which each side was faced in proving its points. These difficulties were owing to a variety of reasons chief among which was the fact that thirty years had elapsed between many of the alleged incidents and the trial: other reasons were the nature of the witnesses called and the delightful and bewildering freedom with which they had in most cases perjured themselves. The reader dealt with much of the evidence, little of which was not germane to the case. An hour and a quarter, however, is too long for any paper, and the time might have been shortened, if more of the evidence had been summarised and less read. The summing up with which the reader concluded was of a convincing nature, and it was evident that he carried the whole case — and that no short one — with remarkable clearness in his head. In the discussion several points — and among them that of the reader's verdict — were criticised.'

The Annesley Case was a famous set of four trials between 1743 and 1745. They concerned whether an attractive young male who had recently returned from the American colonies was, or was not, the rightful heir to a dead Irish Earl, instead of the Earl's unpopular brother who had assumed the title. It turned on whether the Earl's wife had, or had not, given birth to a son in 1715, there being convincing witnesses and evidence both for and against such a happening. That Trafford was able to give a summary which was understood by his friends speaks well of his emerging ability to grasp and to explain a complicated set of facts.

Among the ten others present at that meeting was an Honorary Member, A. C. Benson. Benson was a don who became Master of Magdalene in 1916. He was a particular friend of George Mallory, and is popularly remembered for having written the words of 'Land of Hope and Glory'. He too had a court at Magdalene named after him.

This was almost the final meeting of the Kingsley Club. Their last gathering took place on 12 March 1914. The next entry in the Minutes is for 19 November 1914 and states simply:
> 'At a business meeting it was determined that no more meetings should be held until a more favourable time.'

Trafford was approached by fellow undergraduates at Magdalene in his final year to become the first President of the College's new Debating Society. Political subjects were to be taboo. Despite this ban, the first motion to be debated was 'Equality of opportunity is undesirable'. The average attendance in the society's first year was twenty, out of the college's total membership of fifty undergraduates.

After taking the intermediate Tripos examinations of 1913, when he achieved only the minimum necessary of a Third Class Pass, Trafford decided to change to law and his final degree, Bachelor of Law, was better. The decision was made, law was to be his profession. Like his brother before him, he had chosen not to follow his father into the church and so, together, they ended the centuries-long tradition of self-appointed Mallory rectors at Mobberley village church.

On 1 November 1912 Trafford had paid a one guinea fee in order to obtain the application form for the Inner Temple in London. He had been admitted to membership there on 22 November 1912. He planned to 'devil' there for his godfather, Sir Lees Knowles, in order to become a barrister himself. One of his certificates of good character on entry was signed by A. C. Benson.

Trafford 'kept' seven terms at the Inner Temple from Michaelmas 1912 to Easter 1914. He ate the requisite number of dinners. On leaving university Trafford had intended to continue his legal training. Trafford had little money of his own although the four brothers and sisters were each left one thousand pounds in 1914 by their aunt, Mrs Alice Greig. Trafford also received two silver candlesticks and was the 'residuatory legatee' of her estate.

All this time Trafford's father had pursued a non-clerical obsession. In 1914 his labours were crowned with a very small success. He had fought an unsuccessful case right up to the House of Lords for the right to be able to take the peerage of Lord Leigh of Stonelagh. This was refused. But instead he obtained Royal Assent to add Leigh onto his surname — although he and his family had already been using it.

On Wednesday 22 July 1914, Trafford's sister Mary was married at Claughton near Lancaster. Trafford was one of eight stewards together with his brother. She married Ralph Brooke, a Lieutenant in the Royal Artillery who also kept wicket for the Lancashire county cricket team. A reception with a refreshment marquee for two hundred guests was held on the lawn at the Vicarage.

Just one week later on 29 July Trafford attended the marriage of his brother George at Godalming. The bride was Ruth Turner, and Herbert Leigh-Mallory presided at the church service. Trafford's very practical gift to George was a night-marching compass. Trafford was then the only one left unmarried, but as usual, he was planning to catch up. According to his sister Mary he used to make notes at parties about the girls he met, assessing them as potential mates. It is interesting to speculate what his criteria might have been. Given his methodical way of doing things, he probably compiled a manual 'spreadsheet analysis'; if so, he most likely pencilled in his mother's characteristics as column heads and then inked in the opposite.

World events moved apace. At a distant place called Sarajevo, Archduke Ferdinand was assassinated on 28 June 1914, and on 3 August, the British government issued an ultimatum to Germany on the subject of Belgian neutrality. The ultimatum expired at midnight. At 11 p.m. on Tuesday 4 August 1914, Great Britain declared war against Germany.

It was widely expected that the war would be over before Christmas and therefore nobody wanted to miss the fun. Trafford's father recorded the excitement on 6 August in a letter to his wife, who was staying with friends after the two family weddings. He wrote that Birkenhead was 'seething with soldiers and excitement — motors, horses, cycles and even ordinary bicycles all commandeered for the troops . . .' Trafford, he remarked, seemed very contented at home and had 'just gone off to play tennis with friends . . .'

He was wrong. Trafford had gone off in his private way to enlist in the army as a private soldier. That day he joined the 10th (Territorial) Battalion of The King's Liverpool Regiment of the Territorial Army. He was number 3121 Private Mallory. The regiment was known familiarly as the Liverpool Scottish. The backbone of the regiment was the local rugby club for whom Trafford played.

At ten o'clock the next evening an urgent call was sent out to all enlisted soldiers in Birkenhead to parade immediately at 5 Fraser Street. They were billeted that night in the Shakespeare Theatre. Next day they each received an 'embodiment' grant of five pounds and a ten shillings kit-allowance. George's reaction to Trafford having joined the army is recorded in a letter to their mother on 18 August:

'Excellent news of Trafford — it will be very good for him and he will enjoy himself too.'

Army training began immediately, being route marches and parades in Sefton Park. On 13 August they went by train to Edinburgh where their Battalion formed part of the Forth Defence. Training became serious. A typical day started at 6.45 a.m. with an hour's physical drill which frequently took the form of company races to the top of Arthur's Seat. After breakfast training continued until 4.30 p.m., sometimes with lectures afterwards. There were rumours that they might be sent abroad to India, Egypt or Malta.

The historian of the Liverpool Scottish regiment, A. M. McGilchrist, wrote in retrospect:

'All who served with the Liverpool Scottish in Edinburgh will look back to those days with pleasure and a wistful longing that the clock could be put back and that they might camp again in the King's Park and re-live the old life. But of all the memories of that time the one which will stand out in the minds of many is that of the Church Parades in St Giles' Cathedral. The noble setting, the almost overpowering weight of tone in the singing of the soldiers' hymns by the huge congregation led by the splendid brass band of the Battalion, and the ever-present thought at the back of everyone's mind of the future and what it might hold, combined to make these services both moving and memorable.'

One of Trafford's companions in the regiment, although a little older, was the Battalion's Medical Officer, Lieutenant Noel G. Chavasse. He was to win a Victoria Cross in August 1916 at the Battle of the Somme — and an unprecedented second Victoria Cross posthumously after he died of wounds in the Third Battle of Ypres in August 1917 aged 32.

Only a week after joining the army as a private soldier, Trafford was promoted to be a Second Lieutenant 'on probation'. On 3 October 1914 he was formally commissioned as an officer. At this point he was moved from the Liverpool Scottish regiment. The colleagues whom he left behind sailed to Le Havre with the British Expeditionary Force on 1 November and quickly went into the front line. Their strength in November of 885 officers and men was reduced to 370 by the start of January — due to battle casualties and to the disease of trench-foot. The Liverpool Scottish were later involved in the First Action at Bellewaarde on 16 June 1915 when seventy-five per cent of them were casualties.

Trafford, now Second Lieutenant T. L. Mallory, was transferred to the Fourth Battalion (Extra Reserve) of the Lancashire Fusiliers, stationed at Barrow in Furness. For Christmas 1914 he was able to return home on leave to St John's Vicarage, Birkenhead. What happened immediately afterwards is best recounted by the series of telegrams which he retained all his life. On New Year's Day 1915 a telegram arrived for Trafford at Birkenhead from Norwood in South London:

'Arrive 10.25 Sunday Victoria L Doris.' (Doris was Miss Doris Sawyer. L for love?)

Two days later on Sunday 3 January 1915, Trafford reached London and stayed at his sister Mary's house at 117 Herbert Road, Woolwich, where he signed the visitor's book. Mary's husband Ralph was an army instructor at the Royal Military Academy at Woolwich. Perhaps Trafford confided his intentions to them, but there is no record of this.

Two days later, on 5 January, Trafford received a telegram from the army Adjutant at Barrow addressed to 'Mallory Caversham, Upper Norwood' which simply said:

'You May Leave London By Midnight Train'.

Two more days later, on 7 January, Trafford, back with his military unit at Roa Island, Barrow, received a telegram from his mother:

'Love and Congratulations Await More Details Anxiously Mother.'
Next day, Trafford received the following telegrams from, respectively, Mobberley, Staleybridge and Betws-y-coed, Wales:
'Heartiest Congratulations. To Whom. Avie.'
'Hearty Congratulations. Is It Doris. Father.'
'Excellent News. Our Ferventest Congratulations. George.'
It does not take much to deduce that Trafford had proposed marriage to Doris and that she had accepted him. In a fit of understandable but uncharacteristic opaqueness, Trafford had sent telegrams to his family announcing his engagement but omitting to mention his fiancée's name! And on 7 January Mary wrote in her diary:
'Got a wire from Trafford announcing his engagement to Doris Sawyer. Wrote to him.'
On 8 January Mary wrote to Doris inviting her and her mother to lunch. They came on the 15th. Mary commented in her diary:
'Like Doris very much. She is a sweet-looking girl and seems very nice.'
The differing characters of the family come out in the exchanges: Father and Avie humorous and teasing, Mother worrying and intense, George wholehearted and serious, Mary practical.
Trafford wrote with photographs of his fiancée to one of his father's devoted church ladies, Helen Kissel, who lived at Tanneby near Malvern. She wrote back warmly and charmingly and ended her letter '. . . . and accept much yourself from your affectionate friend Helen Kissel.' Trafford kept her letter all his life.
Doris was the second of three daughters of E. Stratton Sawyer, who lived at 7 Beulah Hill, Upper Norwood. Her family was said to be descended from the famous Dutch Admiral, Van Tromp, who had sailed up the River Thames with a broom at his masthead 'to sweep the English from the Channel'. She was tall, dark and gentle, entirely unlike Trafford's mother in looks and character. Not in the least self assertive, she was perhaps more artistic than practical. But she must have had a determination of her own, because in the previous April, she had gained an MRCM degree at the Royal College of Music.
The manner of L-M's courtship was wholly in keeping with what we have learned about him so far. We have already seen that he was making notes about the various young ladies he was meeting. In Doris, whom he met at a dance, he had found someone who met all the criteria. But he did not at the time try to make any impression, because when, a few days later, he turned up uninvited at her house to begin his campaign of courtship, she did not even remember him. However, as we have seen, his campaign was successful and it was not long before he was engaged. *Vidi, veni, vinci* — to reorder Caesar's dictum. Was this process of bride selection a model for campaigns to come? To use the military idiom which was to become his own, he had conducted his reconnaissance — the dances — evaluated the intelligence gathered — the notes — made his decision, and acted

swiftly and effectively without, it seems, consulting anyone about his plans.

His strategy, if such it was, seems to have been successful. His marriage was to be a happy one. He dominated Doris right from the start and such was her devotion to him that she deferred to him in practically everything, even to the matter of choosing and dismissing the servants. They were blessed with two children, a boy and a girl. Doris was very sweet and gentle with them, but Trafford was always her number one priority, so she never found time to discipline them. For his part, Trafford was always too preoccupied with his work.

But the war continued. Trafford's Battalion but not him was embarked on 12 February 1915 at Southampton on two cross-channel steamers, *Queen Alexandra* and *Trafford Hall*. After forty-eight hours in a rest camp his battalion went by train to Bailleul on the Franco-Belgian border. From there it marched to La Clytte to start training in trench warfare. As part of the 3rd Division of the 7th Infantry Brigade it defended a sector on the lower slope of the Messines Ridge. The February weather was cold and miserable — alternate frost and rain. The Battalion's first casualties were on 26 February 1915.

However, Trafford had been kept in England for further officer training. On 3 March, George wrote to his mother:

'Great news about Trafford! I'm very glad you have him so near now. It's a great feather in his cap that he's been picked out in the way he has. A smart young officer — I suppose they say. Much love to yourselves and Trafford — Please tell T, in case I don't write, that I'll meet him in London any Wednesday or Thursday for preference: for any other day he must negotiate.'

On 21 March 1915, Trafford and Doris motored over for lunch with his sister Mary. Trafford said that he was expecting 'go to the Front' shortly. By 3 April he was there with the Third Battalion (Reserve) of the South Lancashire Regiment.

Contrary to expectation the war had not ended by Christmas 1914. Instead no end was in sight. Each side dug in, and the struggle intensified. Early in 1915 the Germans announced they felt free to torpedo unarmed passenger ships: the *Lusitania*, an American passenger ship, was torpedoed by a German submarine on 7 May. Of the 1906 passengers aboard only 764 survived.

On 1 May Trafford's Battalion was moved into the front line near Elzenwalle Chateau. Next day they had their first experience of gas, giving sore eyes but no casualties. On 5 June they were moved into the Salient in order to relieve others on the south edge of Sanctuary Wood near Hooge.

On 16 June the Battalion took part in the assault of the Bellewaarde Ridge. The Germans held the Ridge and were able to overlook the greater part of the ground east of Ypres. The attack was carried out at dawn, preceded by an intense bombardment. The first line of German trenches was overrun with little resistance. But mist and smoke caused the leading British soldiers to run into shells of their own barrage. The remainder of the Battalion held on to its assembly position and suffered casualties from German artillery fire. By evening the new British line had been consolidated.

The Battalion was relieved at midnight. One officer and 29 other ranks had been killed: nine officers and 237 other ranks were wounded. Trafford was wounded in a leg and was brought back to England — on what happened to be the one hundredth anniversary of the Battle of Waterloo. Just as the Battle of Waterloo had enormous consequences for Europe, so did Trafford's enforced homecoming have enormous consequences for him: indeed, it might not be too much to say, for Europe, for Trafford was to play a leading role in two great battles to come.

His family, of course, were relieved to have him home safe and relatively sound. Mary wrote in her diary that it was 'great thing to hear he is safely back and only slightly wounded'. His mother went to stay with Mary on 19 June and on the 21st — the very day on which Trafford's promotion to Lieutenant, in the 4th Battalion (Extra Reserve), was announced — she was able to visit him in hospital in Oxford. On the 23rd, he was home in London with Doris, entertaining Mary to lunch; she recorded 'He is lame but looking well'.

During the period while he was recovering Doris and Trafford decided to get married. The marriage took place quietly at All Saints Church, Upper Norwood, on Wednesday 18 August 1915. His father officiated. The best man was Lieutenant W. Everard Dickson of the 4th Lancashire Fusiliers. But once again Trafford seems to have been economical with information, because on 19 September 1915 George wrote to their mother asking for the address of 'the newly-weds'.

He had time to think and reappreciate his situation. He had seen something of the war at first hand. With his enquiring mind and logical thought processes he had probably understood it more than most. Be that as it may, it was during this period of enforced inaction that he made a momentous decision.

Trafford did not allow the marriage to divert his attention from the war, and how best to make his 'come-back' to the field of battle. It was during this period of rehabilitation from his wound that he decided to answer the call for volunteers for the Royal Flying Corps. Initially the call was aimed at Gunner subalterns, who would have the specialist knowledge to act as Observers, 'spotting and ranging' for the Artillery. This was a service normally provided by Forward Observation Officers, located in the front line. Trafford, of course, was not a Gunner but as the RFC expanded, Infantry subalterns were also invited to apply.

After Trafford's experience during the assault on Bellewaarde Ridge on 16 June, when the leading soldiers had run into the shells from their own barrage, he would certainly have appreciated the limitations of artillery fire directed from the ground. There is nothing like a bit of violence to impress an experience on a man's memory. Also in his memory would have been his first hand knowledge of the advantages of a bird's eye view, gained from his rock climbing adventures with his brother, George.

One probably needs to look no further than that to understand Trafford's motives, and indeed his daughter was later to say that young men joined the RFC because they felt there was no future for them in the trenches unless they 'could see over the other side of the hill'. She must almost certainly have heard that from her father. But added to all that was the appeal to the adventurous spirit, which Trafford undoubtedly possessed.

Public interest in flying had grown rapidly in the years before the war. The first flight in Europe had been made in 1906 by a Brazilian living in Paris and the first flight by any Englishman on 8 June 1908 by Mr A. Verdon Roe, who later designed the Avro aeroplanes. Wilbur Wright had made a tour of Europe in 1908-9. On 25 July 1909, the first heavier-than-air flight had been made across the English Channel. Louis Bleriot had taken off from the dunes near Calais and thirty-seven minutes later landed beside Dover Castle. His average speed had been 47 miles per hour. The flight had had a striking effect on public opinion, convincing millions that flying had a practical future, and that Britain could no longer totally rely on the Royal Navy to defend it.

There had been an 'International Aviation' meeting at Bournemouth from 6-16 April 1910. But the dangers of flying had been heavily emphasised when the Honourable Charles S. Rolls became the first Englishman to be killed in a powered-aeroplane crash. Three years previously he had founded a motor-car company with a Mr Frederick Royce.

The year 1912 had been an important year for aviation in Britain. The Royal Flying Corps had been formed in April 1912. Flying exploits had caught the imagination of the British public. The long London-to-Manchester air race in 1912 had been an epic. Louis Porlin had won but Britain's Claude Grahame-White had made a gallant and popular effort to catch him by flying through the night and the fog.

As soon as he was fit, Trafford applied to join the Royal Flying Corps. Mary noted in her diary for 3 November 1915: 'Trafford comes up (to London) for the night. He is up to try to get into the Flying Corps. He seems very well and cheery.' Next day she noted: 'He goes off early, hoping to come back, but doesn't appear again.' (Which seems typical of one side of the Trafford we are coming to know.)

There were height and weight limits for the Royal Flying Corps but Trafford, who was five feet, nine and a half inches tall and weighed about 145 pounds, was accepted. He asked to be a pilot. There was some delay, as his papers were mislaid, and it was not until 4 January 1916 that he was posted to the No. 1 School of Aeronautics, at Reading, for training as a pilot. Trafford left no record of his motives and was not a man to confide in others, so his reasons for joining the RFC can only be guessed. But there are records from men who later served with him, which suggest the truth.

An expression used by Trafford's daughter 'the other side of the hill' was much heard in those days. Indeed, it still is, whenever land forces are locked together in battle. Alec Haslam, who later became an Observer in Trafford's squadron in 1918, explained:

'It was sticking out that Air Observation was the thing. As a gunner in the trenches you could only judge your success by the cotton wool bursts.'

Another early pilot, Freddie West, who also transferred from the army, explained:

'We lived in trenches in mud up to there,' gesticulating. 'We could see these chaps' pointing upwards, 'having the vastness of the sky at their disposal, and the comforts of their bases back there. But above all, we were shot at morning, noon and night without ever seeing the enemy. Every night you went out to the barbed wire. You can only walk ten feet to and fro, in mud up to your bloody eyebrows, and you see the chaps in the blue sky up there. When you're young, there's an animal fighting instinct: the fact you could see your opponent must have appealed to many people, and it certainly did to me.'

A private soldier, H. T. Farquhar, who also joined the·RFC in 1916 and was later with No. 8 Squadron under Trafford's command, explained:

'I went over the top twice in 1915. It was a horrible experience. They came round asking for people to work on munitions. Once you were out of the trenches, you could see clearly you were well out. After the infantry, the RFC was a piece of cake.'

Trafford spent seven weeks at the Aeronautics School before graduating on 22 February 1916. While under training there, he and Doris went to tea with his sister Mary: there they inspected Mary's first child, Barbara, who had been born on 26 January. After graduating, Trafford was posted to Number 12 Reserve Squadron and then, on 31 March, to Number 20 Reserve Squadron. He was sent on a gunnery course for ten days at Hythe on 15 May.

Trafford had plenty to learn as a pilot. Although the Royal Flying Corps was only a few years old, developments in aeroplane technology were happening fast. At the start of the war, planes were used purely for reconnaissance. In this way, during the first sweep by the Germans through Belgium and north France, RFC operations helped the British army to escape from the German trap by providing sufficient advance warning of German movements. The RFC's job became to identify and map enemy railheads, airfields, ammunition dumps and batteries.

It soon became vital to be able to clearly identify friendly planes from the enemy's. Initially British planes were unmarked. But after some had been shot at by British rifles from the ground, a Union Jack was painted on the underside. However at a greater height only the red cross was visible which often became confused with the German markings. So, in late October 1914, the Royal Flying Corps instead adopted the French design but in reverse order: three concentric circles of red, white, and blue.

To begin with, aircraft did not have fixed guns. Pilots and observers carried handguns and a few hand grenades which were sometimes used in the very difficult and rarely successful attempt to attack enemy aircraft. Later machine-guns were mounted forward of the front cockpit of the pusher aircraft, such as the Maurice Farmans, which had their propellers behind the cockpits; these guns had limited freedom of fire in azimuth and elevation, and were operated by the observer.

Then, in July 1915, the Germans introduced the Fokker fighter plane, which was superior to anything British. The Fokker was a single-seater monoplane: it was extremely manoeuvrable, could dive vertically, and mounted a belt-fed machine-gun which was synchronised with the plane's propeller so that the bullets missed the rotating blades. This technological development was to revolutionize air combat.

The German air tactics were to cruise at a height then dive onto their targets, preferably out of the sun. Victory usually went to the pilot with the greatest skill or daring. In January 1916 an order was issued that British planes must fly in formation and not alone.

Meanwhile his brother George was also in the army. He wrote to his mother 'from France' on 21 May 1916:

'My dear Mother, I'm sorry I didn't manage after all to write you a letter yesterday. I was in a state of collapse all the morning and afternoon till I had to take charge of the guns for a long shoot after tea and after the captain came around and spent the evening — and so bed-time came after going round the guard and hoped I would write early this morning: but this morning was spent in waiting about to shoot, which after all we did not do. And then came a colonel and major in a car with their satellite from Headquarters and I was told of my new job of which I have just written some brief notes to Ruth [his wife]. All the afternoon I have spent finding out about this new work: first some miles on motor bike (incidentally I missed my way); no horse exercise would compare with this; and then on from Hqrs by car to a dressing station and thence much walking about to inspect various persons and things and I feeling ready to drop with fatigue all the time. On my way back here the back tyre of the motor bike went pop! And here I am in the billet with only a few minutes to go before dinner; and after that I start off again to spend the night out or at least the greater part of the hours of darkness.

I'm very happy out here. They are such a pleasant lot of men in the battery — many of them Scottish Territorials brought from his shipbuilding works in Glasgow by our Captain Lithgow. This is a great blessing in one way; they can literally turn their hands to any job you can think of. They seem to be highly willing — amenable and I expect to get on with them quite well — though alas! I fear I shall have little to do with the working of the battery for some time now. I have been hoping to hear from you for some time, but my letters have stuck somewhere it appears. It was a great satisfaction to have a sight of you and Father before coming out. You will enjoy having Ruth and Clare (his daughter) I expect. Is it as hot with you I wonder as it is here?

Much love. Yr. loving son George.'

George was a far better correspondent than Trafford and we shall have to rely on him to a large extent for a Mallory view of the war, which the two brothers fought, each in his own way. George in the mud, a gunner officer, but Trafford out of the trenches, out of the mud, out of the ever present threat of artillery fire. He lived in relative comfort, but, and it was a big but, he had committed himself to becoming an RFC pilot when the Germans had superior planes. And the average life expectancy for a novice British pilot in the front line was being numbered in days rather than weeks.

Chapter 4
Command in Flanders

Trafford graduated from the Central Flying School on 8 June 1916 and was awarded his pilot's wings. He was seconded to the Royal Flying Corps for flying duties on 7 July and was posted to Number 5 Squadron and travelled immediately to the continent to join it.

Much had happened during the thirteen months since he had been wounded. The German attack in 1915 had petered out at the Battle of the Marne. Each side had increased the depth of its defences, and the struggle had turned into dogged trench warfare.

In the air, Germany had concentrated chiefly on the development of Zeppelin airships rather than on heavier-than-air craft. Zeppelins were able to stay up in the air for a longer time and were more reliable than aeroplanes which, being in their experimental stage, frequently broke down. Airships could remain over one place. However they were more costly to build and to run; they moved more slowly and they were more vulnerable, because they contained inflammable hydrogen gas.

The British had also tried to develop airships. The 'Mayfly' was 512 feet long and 48 feet in diameter with a gas capacity of 700,000 cubic feet. She had failed to get off the ground in her first trial in May 1911: when she was tried again in September she broke her back through structural weakness. Airship development in Britain was therefore abandoned.

Another new development was bombing from the air. German airships had made a number of bombing raids during 1915 over England including London. On 31 January 1916 nine German airships had flown to the Midlands: together they had dropped 379 bombs, killing 70 people and injuring 113. All had left England safely.

The British had already tried to bomb from aeroplanes. On 22 September 1914 four British aeroplanes had set out from Antwerp to try to bomb the Zeppelin sheds at Düsseldorf and Cologne. But thick mist had prevented all but one aircraft from reaching the target. It had glided down and dropped its bombs but had done no damage. On 21 December 1914 the first German aeroplane had appeared off Dover and dropped one bomb into the sea. Three days later another German aeroplane had dropped the first bomb to explode on English soil. By the time Trafford joined No. 5 Squadron, bombing was common practice.

Other new technologies were being developed. Photography had proved to be useful. Before that, enemy defences had been mapped by hand-sketching. Most fliers now used their own cameras but new lenses had to be designed.

The importance of Wireless had been quickly appreciated because it could be utilised in all weather conditions: the alternative was flashing light signals but these were often obscured. Initially few aircraft had been fitted with wireless sets. Although Marconi had first succeeded in 1899 in transmitting wireless messages across the English Channel, the noise and vibration of aircraft engines seriously interfered with the radio signals.

In December 1915 Sir Douglas Haig had succeeded Sir John French as Commander-in-Chief of the British Army. Working with the French commander, Joffre, Haig had planned a great offensive. But the Germans had attacked first — on a nine-mile front opposite Verdun on 21 February 1916.

A British counter-offensive had been planned for the summer of 1916 in the area north of the River Somme. Secrecy was essential. The Royal Flying Corps' task was to deny to the enemy any prior knowledge of the British preparations. Not a single German plane must be allowed to come within visual range of the British lines. The German Air Service was very active but they worked on the principle of patrols flying up and down their own front line. British machines were not interfered with until they crossed over the German lines.

An RFC reconnaissance flight on 25 April had discovered that the Germans were constructing a formidable line of defence behind their own front.

A preliminary bombardment by the British had begun in the middle of June. The first British assault had started on 1 July at 7.30 am on a bright and clear morning. It had taken place along the whole line between Gommecourt and the Somme. At the end of the first day of this, the Battle of the Somme, the British had lost 20,000 dead and another 37,000 wounded. However, by 12 July 1916 the whole of the German first trench system had fallen into British hands. The second German trench system was attacked on 14 July and again on 21 July. The weather became extremely bad and the British offensive was mostly unsuccessful. Starting as a pilot on 7 July this was where Trafford first became involved in the battle.

Trafford's brother George was also involved, on the ground. On 28 July 1916 he wrote again to Father in England. He gave his address as 'The Parados':

'My dear Father, my back is lying against the parados of a trench and my legs make a bridge to the parapet which dips away to the left so that I can see over it very comfortably. My head is out of view from the enemy to the front and right and I can lie here quite comfortably and quite idly till the battery begins firing again. One of my Signallers had just asked the date — to date a message — we make out that it is the 28th and I remember that it was your birthday two days ago. Many happy returns, happier returns I would rather say. This spot which must sound to you so alarming is in reality pretty safe — because it is quite near the Hun and he prefers to send his shells a little further from himself; the real danger is coming through the barrage; it was very hot this morning; one has to exercise a little commonsense and circumvention — that's what it amounts to — and with ordinary luck one ought not to get hit. This place is proving a great nuisance; we have miles of wire out which is constantly getting cut. I have been here every other day for a week or so — we are short of one officer and another is too unwell for this sort of job. Anyway it's a happy enough life altogether in the summer as far as one's own part of it is concerned, and as harrowing as you can imagine when one sees the dead and the dying and hears of regiments being cut up by machine guns.

I am not one of the optimists about the war and shall be quite surprised if it ends before Xmas. I suppose we may at any moment hear very good news from Russia — but it's a very long time coming and the German war machine must be far from run down if he can put up the fight he has done.'

George went on to give news of Trafford:

'I had a note from Trafford some days ago. We must be a long way apart; he seems quite happy and much struck by the comforts of life compared with the infantry. The RFC, I make out, do themselves very well and generally have a roof over their heads and brick walls to lodge within. But they must have some very strenuous times. On this first front our mastery of the air is undisputed and very heartening.'

The RFC's policy of the strategic offensive was proving to be successful. The Germans were obliged to concentrate on dispersing the RFC's bombing attacks and invading flights. This left the RFC's artillery spotting reconnaissance and photographic aircraft to work with little hindrance. No German aircraft was able to get behind British lines.

Trafford's first recorded flight as a fully-fledged pilot in action was for No. 7 Squadron on 19 July 1916. The Squadron had ten aircraft and eleven pilots. Lieutenant Leigh-Mallory was sent up alone 'in very hazy weather' in B.E. 2d 5750 for eighty minutes. A 'B.E.' was a Bleriot Experimental in which the Observer sat in front, the pilot behind. Trafford's task, on this first flight was 'Corps Reconnaissance': his report on the flight states 'Successful. Two bombs dropped'.

Trafford flew again the same evening — from 7.07 pm unti 8.03 pm — this time accompanied by 2nd Lieutenant Elliott as his Observer. Their task this time was Wireless Telephone Practice. Their report states 'unsuccessful'. He flew again the next evening, but after 100 minutes this flight ended in a 'Forced Landing Near St Pol'.

Trafford flew on most days providing the weather was adequate. There were many different tasks. On 23 July he flew for an hour to perform Artillery Observation. But his report states, in direct fashion: 'Unsuccessful owing to Wireless Failure. Brass socket on safety plug loose. Operator should not have put out "K" at Aerodrome.'

On 28 July he carried out Artillery Observation with the 13th HAG from 3.20 until 5.55 pm. This he reported as 'Unsuccessful. Shoot interfered with by Hostile Aircraft. Two 20lb bombs dropped. One bomb fell in the wood.'

The British attack continued through August and September. On the afternoon of 2 August, Trafford's task was Photography, but he reported the flight as 'Unsuccessful. No photos taken.' On 4 August there was Photography Practice. Eventually, on 5 August, he reported happily 'Photography Successful. 15 Photos Taken. 15 Plates Exposed.'

On 6 August he flew four times: first a half-hour flight, ('OK') then two half-hour Liaison Course flights; finally an hour of 'Flock Flying'. Next day it was 'Group Flying' in the morning for twenty minutes, and 'Bombing' after lunch but 'Started late owing to engine trouble, could not get height, and returned'. Trafford's last flight with No. 7 Squadron was on 12 August, when for three hours in the evening he flew on 'Patrol. Special, Ordered by letter. No Hostile Aircraft seen.'

The next day, Trafford was transferred to No. 5 Squadron, who were working with XIV Corps on the Ypres Salient. He was kept busy there — flying 48 missions in the next 49 days. Analysis shows that 14 of these missions were Bombing, 13 were Engine Tests, 8 were Artillery Observation, 3 were Photography, 3 were Liaison Practice, and the rest were other tasks such as weather tests and bringing in replacement planes.

The squadron's aircraft were 90 horsepower B.E. 2 c's which could carry two 112lb bombs. Some of these flights were particularly challenging:

23 August: Urgent Special Photos from 4000 to 5000 feet ("Successful").

29 August: Reconnaissance ("Had to return owing to petrol tank being shot through. No movement observed. Two 20lb bombs dropped. One hit target, other fell short.")

3 September: Bombing ("Successful"). The squadron commander reported that on that day they had delivered ten 112lb bombs on Mouscron, of which eight were observed to have burst.

15 September: Counter Battery Bombing ("One hostile battery (3 guns) located firing (bomb) sent down. Train seen leaving Level Crossing for LANGEMARCK, (bomb) sent down on way home.")

Tactics did not remain static. That same day, on the ground, the British introduced a new and frightening weapon: the Tank. And in the air, on 17 September, the German Air Service also changed its tactics. Single combat was forbidden. Instead the Germans organised themselves into pursuit squadrons called Jagdstaffeln. These proved to be very efficient fighting forces. One was led by the legendary Manfred von Richthofen.

On 20 September Trafford was given a new task, 'Wireless telephone', which proved significant for his future. His report stated: 'Successful. Clear speech received from a distance of 15 miles.' Then, on 22

September, it was Liaison Practice with 2nd Army Signalling School: 'Successful. Report forwarded VIII Corps, 38th Division.' But on 23 September there was a difficulty: A Brigade Bombing raid did not go according to plan. Scheduled for 10.40 am to 12.25 pm Trafford was flying as Brigade Reserve Leader, and reported to his own Squadron Commander: 'Unsuccessful. Gave signal to return to Aerodrome as no machines from other squadrons were following.' The other two planes in this mission from his squadron reported: 'Returned when leader fired green light.'

Meanwhile, from the army on the ground, George wrote to their father on 2 October 1916:

'I haven't heard from Trafford just lately — I hope he is as cheerful as when he last wrote to me. The RFC has been doing notable work down here and the Hun balloons hardly dare to go up.'

On 8 October Trafford wrote one of his rare letters home:

'My dear Mother

I have not had any letters for days so there may be one on the way from you. We moved about a week ago. My new address is 5th Squadron, 15th Wing, RFC, BEF. Since we came here the weather has been appalling; today it is raining and will rain, I think, the whole day.

We are not nearly as comfortable as we used to be; our rooms are awfully poky and we have Flight Messes as opposed to the Squadron Mess we used to have.

This is a very interesting part of the line. Unfortunately I cannot tell you anything about it.

Concerning winter clothes. I don't know yet quite what I want. I think that I had better wait till I come on home, which I hope to do in about a month's time. Do you realise that I have already been out here 3 months? It doesn't seem like it. How is all going at home?

I have been pretty busy since I came here. I have done a certain amount of flying, but besides that there has been a lot to do making the Mess and our room liveable in.

I have just completed 100 hours flying out here. Much best love to you both.

Yr loving son Trafford.'

On 1 November 1916 George wrote again:

'My dear Mother.

Your parcel arrived some days ago and very seasonably, for we have had it really cold and I was delighted and kept warm by the waistcoat; you've chosen splendidly; it's a most comforting garment and very comely too. Many thanks also for the two medicinal items of the parcel; I have used the furniture polish or whatever it may be and it seems very good; but I doubt of any opportunities here to use the salts. The crystallised ginger was excellent and the gingerbread still continues to be so.

Our chief occupation here lately has been to fight the rain and mud; I feel that I know already what the winter will be like and it's not a pleasant thought. Evidently little can be done under these conditions; and that will perhaps be the worst of it — that we shall have little to do. Inactivity will matter much less to officers than to men; we're more comfortable than they are — there's no getting away from that — and personally I'm in no great danger of being bored so long as I can read and write. Still it will be a somewhat depressing experience. My present dugout is fairly comfortable; true, in the deluge two days ago it sprang no less than four leaks, and the walls and floor are still pretty damp: but some works I have carried out since then will I hope prevent the worst of calamities. And then I have recently acquired an oil stove and however much it may stink and begrime my pillow I know it for a cosy friend and it will learn clean habits. At this moment I'm sitting at my table which is covered by a very pretty green and red tablecloth and carries a quite typical strew of books and papers — or rather it is apt to do so; at present my neat little piles are irreproachable. The bed occupies quite one third of the floor space; but I have managed to fit in my canvas arm-chair and a stool near my bedside takes more books, and, when I am in bed, an oil lamp. High above the head of my bed is a shelf for the hair-brush, toothbrush etc. Washing takes place outside and is apt to be a chilly occupation; the great difficulty is to keep one's feet out of the mud, and there's too much standing on one leg while one washes then dries the other.

The war seems too depressing to talk of just now; the bad weather out of season has spoilt our chances on this front; and the enemy's effort against Roumania is a surprising marvel which augurs no good for the future. No news of leave yet; I can hardly hope to get back long before Xmas — perhaps not till after that. Forgot to say thank-you for the slipperettes — they are very comfy with gumboots.

My love to you both, yr. loving son, George.'

On 2 November Trafford was promoted to be a Temporary Captain and appointed as a Flight Commander. He was allowed to go home on leave — and there was another reason for this. Mary and Ralph visited him and Doris at Norwood. Mary recorded in her diary: 'T. very well, and Doris too.' On 21 December 1916 Doris gave birth to their first child, a boy whom they named Thomas Leigh Leigh-Mallory.

When Trafford returned to the continent, he became worried about the casualties in his flight. He wrote about it in a letter to his brother George. George commented on Trafford's feelings in a letter to his mother which is also wonderfully evocative of the mud and the trenches. It was written in pencil on 11 January 1917:

'My dear Mother,

Thank you for your letter — I was sorry to hear of Michael Carew

Hunt's death — though it seemed certain that he would not recover from what you last told me. I have been very busy since I came back — a change of job.

The adjutant is away on a month's leave (lucky dog!) and consequently another officer was wanted at headquarters — at the Group that is — not to do the adjutant's work; the orderly is doing that and I have taken his place. The utility of me at the moment is chiefly that I know the country pretty well and can tell the colonel what can be seen from where; and then I have to look after the camp here and see that we aren't too uncomfortable. I've been occupied during the last few days on getting an O.P.* built. Last night I went up to look after the final operations; a hole had previously been dug and I wanted to make it 4 ft deep and put the roof on. When we came to dig we found firstly a layer of slush and then a substance with the consistency of toffee; it was impossible to throw it out so I got hold of a bucket (a very rare convenience) and we drew mud out of our hole as one draws water out of a well; but after a time the toffee stuck to the bucket as well as the spares and the men working in the hole stuck to the toffee and the toffee stuck to them. I never saw anything so pitiable. We had to abandon our digging and just stick the roof on and make a floor to cover the mud. Luckily it was too funny to be entirely fed up and the men were mostly quite cheery.

Your parcel turned up rather late — about a week after I got back here.

Many thanks for its numerous contents — most of all the plum pudding which was excellent. The metal puzzle remains unsolved — which is the best proof of its success. I have disposed of the pouches and the men were well pleased with them — also the draughts for the recreation room. The scarf seems a very nice one and kept me warm last night.

Has Ruth told you her news? She seems pretty certain that another baby is on the way. I'm very pleased and she is quite delighted — it'll be a great thing to have a companion to Clare.

I had a letter from Trafford a few days ago and have been trying to get in touch with him — so far unsuccessfully. He has evidently been much upset by the casualties in his flight but I hope as he thinks probably, he could be sent home soon for work at the base. I hope I shall manage to see him somehow before long.

It was nice seeing you in Birkenhead; my leave was wonderfully refreshing altogether. I was delighted to find you and Father so happy — it's a great and good thing to keep one's spirits in these times and it's more difficult at home than out here in spite of all the dreariness of this devastated country. As a matter of fact things are livening up a good bit now. Last night when we were working there

---

* Observation Post.

was a bombardment going on on our left with almost the intensity
we became accustomed to in the summer, though it didn't last very
long. The line is a curious sight at night — the flares going up at
regular intervals, as it seems, and then all round these guns going
off; last night the flashes from our side must have been about three
per second and one could see many of the bursts quite plainly too.
Then the Hun started, and his bursts were even more plainly
visible in our lines. I was rather glad our Corps hadn't begun the
fray for we had no cover just where we were.

It's snowing this morning — the atmosphere is too dense to see
more than a few hundred yards so there's nothing for the batteries:
but there'll be plenty to do in clearing the snow away if this goes
on.

Yr. loving son. George.'

Please tell Father that I'm hoping he won't forget his promise
with regard to Cheshire cheese and think the colonel would
appreciate it.'

In mid-November 1916 there were rain and snow storms. The
battlefields became a sea of mud. Further assaults by either side were
impossible. By the end of 1916 the Germans had succeeded in
preserving their continuous front. The British attacks had taken the
pressure off the French. The Allies had recaptured nearly all the ground
which they had lost earlier in the year. But there was no sign of an end
to the war.

On 7 December 1916 Lloyd George succeeded Asquith as Prime
Minister in London. At once he instituted his famous War Cabinet.
Lord Curzon was President of the Joint War Air Committee.

Near the end of 1916 a conference was held at Chantilly between the
Commanders-in-Chief of the British and the French armies to discuss
plans for the coming spring. It was decided that the Germans must not
be allowed to take the initiative as they had at Verdun in the early part
of 1916.

Pressure would be maintained during the winter. February 1917 was
chosen for the next big Allied effort. But before the Allies' ideas could
be carried out, the Germans forestalled them with a methodical retreat
to a new and formidable defensive system of trenches which became
known as the Hindenberg Line. Allied air reconnaissance had photographed the Line's preparation but it had been regarded as a reserve
position.

A further setback for the Allies was the Russian Revolution on 12
March 1917. It reduced the pressure on Germany on the Eastern Front
and led to the defection of Russia from the Allies. The Germans found
themselves able to transfer fresh Divisions across from the Russian front.

There was a general British advance from 17 March 1917. Private
Farquahr, a member of Trafford's squadron, told the author that:

'The conditions in the early spring of 1917 were terrible. You could
throw a raw egg at a brick wall and it would fall back. It was frozen

hard. We had to boil the petrol up in No. 8 Squadron before putting it in. We knew we were not supposed to do it. But none of it was as bad as with the infantry in 1915. That was impossible.'

On 1 April 1917 Trafford's brother George wrote a letter to their mother in England which provides interesting background about the Allied advance:

'My dear Mother, I am writing in bed and I have a roof over me — both unusual circumstances! For the first time it isn't easy to get letters written nowadays, nor posted afterwards.

Last night I was up till 3 am; tomorrow I shall almost certainly be up all night; and the days are very busy. As for the billet, we're in great luck at this moment; almost every house in the vacated country is completely wrecked — burnt out by the Hun; but this village escaped. For the next few weeks anyway — probably for all the summer we shall either sleep in the open, or if our position is sufficiently concealed, in low tents. It's rather cold for that sort of game at present — the only variety displayed by the weather is in the number of sleet showers per diem. But we're glad to be on the move. The deadly routine of life is knocked out — it is much more a life of adventure and interest — constant reconnaissance work and new country to be explored as the infantry moves on. It's not wildly interesting country; rather bleak and cold; hardly a sign of spring to cheer us yet: but it is a joy to live in unstrafed country again. I have taken several opportunities of exploring woods and copses for signs of life and gardens too. So far I have only seen snowdrops several times; anemones, about ½ doz. yesterday; and today in a garden yellow crocuses, cheerful little beggars! Not much to boast of perhaps, but a great pleasure to me. I suppose with you spring is equally backward. I reckon it will be another three weeks before we have a primrose in bloom here.

I'm glad to be with the battery now, though I was no less glad of my experiences behind the lines earlier. I was afraid we should be left behind, but once the communications over the river were established that was not the case — while the two steps above us are on the other hand completely out of action and we are handed over to the division.

I call this an unstrafed country and so it is comparatively speaking — the mess of battle hasn't ruined it. Nevertheless the Hun has played some nasty tricks — actual tricks of course in many places and one has to be very wary — but particularly destruction of buildings, poisoning of wells and the wanton cutting down of fruit trees which is pitiful to see. The most noticeable relief is never or practically never to see a trench — but I suppose we may come up against that again before long. Many thanks for two good letters from you — I'm very sorry you seem to keep so unwell. But you seem to have a good plan for getting change. I wish Ruth could join you but I'm afraid she'll think it too far with the impedimenta and in these days of restrictions. I'm very glad Mary is going to Westbrook — it will do her good to be there — at least it ought to. I haven't yet received any parcel from you — it is very disappointing — but I dare say it will turn up yet and thank you very much for your efforts. It's important to stick exactly to the address 40 Siege Bty, R.G.A. B.E.F. I don't know that R.G.A. matters, but *Siege* is vital, and it doesn't do to put anything in like the Group or the Corps. If I leave the battery I shall always have my mail sent on if it is properly addressed.

I hope Father is keeping fit for Easter. Will he be taking a holiday after that?

Well I expect I had better be going to sleep as I have a strenuous day before me tomorrow. I rather like this plan of writing in bed — it is so quiet — a great contrast to our present mess with six of us living in the smallest conceivable space and the administrative and fighting work of the battery going on here.

Much love to you both.

Your loving son, George.'

A British attack in front of Arras was planned for 9 April 1917. For three weeks beforehand, army cooperation planes were engaged on helping the artillery to systematically destroy enemy barbed wire. For the final five days there was an intensive air offensive — with the object of driving enemy airmen away so that cooperation planes could work unhindered. These five days were very costly: 75 British aircraft were destroyed and 105 pilots and observers were casualties; 19 killed, 13 wounded and 73 missing. Another 56 machines were wrecked through flying accidents.

The assault by the British infantry in the Battle of Arras began at 0530 hours on Easter Sunday, 9 April 1917. The weather was poor so that the first full day's flying was not until 13 April. On the 13th, the Richthofen formation alone claimed 13 British machines.

The British assault was intended to divert German strength away from the French front. A week later, on 16 April 1917, the major French offensive under General Nivelle opened on the Aisne. It was a colossal failure and fell far short of the planned shattering blow to the Germans. The result was that the British carried the brunt of the fighting on the Western Front for the remainder of 1917.

When the Battle of Arras took place, the air situation was not favourable to the British. The German single-seater Halberstadt and Albatross planes were proving themselves superior to almost every British machine except the Sopwith Pup, the Sopwith Triplane and the new Bristol Fighter, which were as good as the German planes. April 1917 was named 'Bloody April' by the RFC. It lost 131 aircraft and 316 airmen, one third of its whole strength in France in one single month.

It was on the very last day of 'Bloody April' that the German Air Service introduced new tactics. Four Jagdstaffeln were combined into one Jagdgeschwader, led by Manfred von Richthofen. When this huge formation first appeared it was promptly nicknamed 'Richthofen's Circus'. The Germans officially called it Jagdgeschwader I. Richthofen himself flew in an all-red plane, so becoming known as 'the Red Baron'.

Trafford, however, was not destined to encounter Jagdgeschwader I, at least not during this spell of operations, because on 22 April he was posted back to the Home Establishment in England. However, the family presence in France was not to be depleted, because soon after Trafford came home, Mary's husband Ralph went back to France. A few days after Trafford's return, he and his father motored down to his sister Mary's house for lunch and tea, just in time to say goodbye to Ralph.

Trafford was promoted again — to the rank of Squadron Commander and Temporary Major. He was given command of No. 15 Reserve Squadron on 10 May 1917.

Meanwhile the Allies were making preparations on a gigantic scale in Flanders. At 3 am on 7 June an artillery barrage opened and the Allied infantry advanced. The battle continued for eight days until the 14th by when the whole Messines Ridge had been taken. The offensive restarted on 31 July when nine Divisions of the Fifth Army assaulted seven and a half miles in front of Ypres. It rained for four whole days, making the whole area into a quagmire. Low clouds and poor visibility interfered with air activity. August 1917 was the wettest for years. A British attack on the 16th was only partially successful. The deadlock grew deeper as the Germans introduced a new form of defence in this area — concrete blockhouses instead of trenches, which were quickly nicknamed 'Pill-Boxes'.

The daylight invasion by Gothas in June and July 1917 publicly emphasised the unsatisfactory British organisation of the air. General Smuts was appointed by Lloyd George to make a report on all matters pertaining to the air. He recommended the amalgamation of the different naval and military air services, and the formation of an Air Ministry. The necessary Bill was passed through Parliament in November 1917. Major-General Sir Hugh Trenchard was appointed to be Chief of the Air Staff: the Royal Air Force was born on 1 April 1918.

Chapter 5
War's End

Trafford was appointed to command No. 8 Squadron on 27 November — at the age of twenty-six. Ralph wrote to Mary on 7 December: 'I've heard that Trafford's Squadron — No. 8 — is or was a good one.'

In early November Passchendale Ridge had been captured by the British. On 20 November 340 British tanks attacked Cambrai without the usual preliminary bombardment.

Trafford's brother-in-law, Ralph, then an Acting Major in charge of number 333 Siege Battery, wrote to his wife Mary on 29 November:

'This country was once in possession of the Hun — it's wicked to see the wanton destruction he caused before he went back. Practically every single tree is cut down, all orchards levelled and every single house blown up as if by internal explosion. In France practically all roads have avenues of trees along both sides. Every one of these is cut down and lies alongside the road. It's the most thorough destruction possible and makes one hate the Hun more than ever. It must have been awfully pretty country once . . . and it's still jolly nice to be here after the hideous waste we've always been in before.'

But on 30 November the Germans counter-attacked. The British were pushed back to the Flesquieres Ridge on 7 December. There were no further attacks in 1917. Ralph wrote the following series of letters to Mary that winter, containing news of Trafford:

19 December

'I had heard that Trafford's Squadron was somewhere up north. I wish he could come and work with us sometime. But I hope it will be he that moves and not us! I don't want to move again just yet . . .'

11 January

'Trafford walked in this afternoon! It was most awfully nice seeing him but we couldn't have as good a talk as we might have as our Group Commander came in to see me shortly after Trafford arrived and they all stayed for tea. However Trafford is going to send his car over for me one day soon and I'll go over there for a night . . . He was looking awfully well and evidently is liking his job very much. He's no end of a swell of course — more so than a mere Battery Commander! He's evidently got a jolly good Squadron and is very proud of it.'

13 January

'Trafford said he was hoping to get home on leave before very long.

I think they manage it pretty regularly every three months. But he hasn't done two months yet . . .'

28 January

'Yesterday afternoon Trafford sent his car over for me — or rather he came in it to fetch me back with him. We got over there for tea. Trafford has an awfully nice hut, and he gave me a bed in it with him and it was all very snug and comfortable. He's quite a swell of course and as a Squadron has about 50 officers in it, it's a fine command. This morning I watched the machines starting off and landing etc., while Trafford did his work. Then after lunch he took me up for a trip! We had a gorgeous flight for 40 minutes and I enjoyed every second of it . . . Trafford was so good and careful I never had a moment's anxiety, and we went up to about 4000 feet and had a grand view of the country . . .'

During the first three months of 1918, German air activity had increased in a crescendo. Following their revolution Russia had made a separate peace with Germany. This freed more German resources for the struggle in western Europe.

On 21 March, after an intense five-hour bombardment the Germans attacked on a 54-mile front. Trafford's No. 8 Squadron was at Bertangles. Trafford himself was on leave in England — but he returned on the 25th, in plenty of time to take charge of his squadron for the battle which followed.

From 21 to 28 March, the Germans pushed their infantry forward in a huge offensive which was intended to finish the war in their favour. Despite stiff Allied resistance, the Germans advanced inexorably until they were finally held in the north of France on 29 April.

On 24 April there was a German assault on the Somme front — when for the first time tank encountered tank. However, during all this time the Allies retained a superiority in the air. British planes were up during every moment of daylight — bombing and machine-gunning. The German Air Service suffered a serious loss when Manfred von Richthofen was shot down on 21 April. He had eighty 'victories' to his credit: his death had a bad effect on the morale of the German Air Service.

The huge German attack finally forced the Allies into closer cooperation. There was a conference of Allied chiefs at Doullens on 26 March and it was agreed to unite their commands on the Western Front under Marshal Foch.

Ralph described the German attack in his letters.

15 March

'The lovely weather still goes on. We're still keeping pretty busy, ready to give the old Hun socks any time he asks for it! No chance of leave yet awhile . . . They won't let us go until the old Hun has shown his hand a bit more, I should think. I shouldn't be surprised if we moved any time now, there seems to be a lot of movement going on, so I've gradually had everything that is not wanted packed up ready for a move. Though really I've no reason for expecting one . . .'

Next day he wrote that they were planning to lay out a garden and to buy a piano for the Mess!

18 March

'A wet day at last. And the old Hun seems to have thrown away any chance he had and funked it, for which I hardly blame him. Our garden is looking sweet!'

21 March

'A very noisy morning, as you'll probably have seen in the papers before you get this. As usual we don't know a bit what's been happening, but suppose the old Hun has had the cheek to try his luck and is duly getting it on the neck. So we're pretty busy, and no time to write more.'

23 March

'We got some sleep early this morning for the first time for what seemed like several days, but was really only 48 hours. Naturally I can't tell you much of what's been going on, but we gathered from a newspaper that the Hun attacked on a 50 mile front. No doubt you'll have read all about it long before I see it, so you may have been worried. But we got out somehow and got most of our kit away too, which was good work. We'll probably be moving about a good bit and often one can't find anywhere to post, but you know I'll get a line through whenever I can. The old Hun may have got a bit of ground, but he's paid for it pretty heavily from all accounts.'

24 March

'We're still in this comfortable spot and may be here for some days yet . . . From all I can gather, the Hun is staking everything on this attack and is making a colossal effort, but so far we've held him very well, though of course we have had to give up some ground. But he means to break clean through and I think his programme is already much upset. Our last position is now in Hunland! But he didn't get any of my kit. And remember the cheerful fact that our "old things" [his code word for the Guns] are so valuable that we are well looked after and get away in time. We are having the easiest time we've had for ages, just waiting for orders, until the situation is clearer. I'm afraid the Post Office is leaving, though! The lovely weather still goes on . . .'

28 March

'We're just moving from here to — where do you think? Back to the old neighbourhood we were in all last summer! Probably well out of this battle, which, though sickening in some ways is very nice in others.'

29 March

'We left the town we were at yesterday afternoon and travelled steadily in our cattle truck till 3 am when we stopped for a bit and then came slowly on. This is North of anywhere I've been before.'

30 March

'At last we're settling down again to a normal existence, and have really been very lucky. Though we're back in this unspeakable mud, we've found a certain number of excellent dug-outs already made by a Battery that has just moved out. The latest news seems quite good and in fact the situation seems to improve each day. With luck the old Hun will be sorry he ever started the Push and it's just the way to end the War as he must be using up his Divisions at an appalling rate.'

5 April

'Very glad to hear that they got a p.c. from Trafford — and I hope they've heard again that he is all right. I expect he'll have lost most of his kit — as the Hun came on faster in his part than anywhere else . . . The RFC — or RAF as it is now — did jolly well, didn't they.'

One of the Observers in No. 8 Squadron, Haslam, who later got to know Trafford well, described to the author what Trafford was like as their commander:

'I wouldn't say that he was at all popular in the squadron. Only one or two actively disliked him. The few who liked him were the few who realised what he was actually doing. His manner was a bit standoffish. He was a bit separated from the great majority in the squadron. His first question always was, when we were shot down: "Is the aircraft alright?" Freddie West would reply "Yes thank you Sir, we're both alright." '

In retrospect, Haslam commented that: 'The higher Leigh-Mallory got, the better he fitted the job. Leigh-Mallory was a bit standoffish in a way — but I remember one of the Flights celebrating a decoration: he joined in and was thoroughly in the party.'

One of the private soldiers in the Squadron, H. T. Farquhar, told the author:

'When he first arrived he was a proper little Charlie Chaplin with turned out toes and breeches like butterflies. He always had a stick and an attache case. He spoke in clipped sentences, never saying a word too much . . . He came on all right . . . He could tear anyone off a strip. He was a bit of a martinet in the mess, we used to hear. He was more of an isolationist: I don't think he was a mixer. He was not well known, but he was a hardworking bloke . . . the hours he put in, going round all the flights . . . One incident: we had a Recording Officer — he had trained to be a solicitor. One night I was on the box: it was belting with rain. The DR came up with a message, undid his coat, and I saw he was a Staff Sergeant. I phoned the RO: he said "Leave it on my desk till the morning." So I rang up the CO, Leigh-Mallory. He said to me: "I'll see it." So I fetched it over to him. It turned out it was to do with the attack that morning with the Brigade Commanders to be on the airdrome at 5 am! As it turned out it was foggy.'

Farquhar said that there were a number of characters in No. 8 Squadron. There were 'The Three Ones': Corporal Wilson, who had one lung; Corporal Curly Howard, the medical orderly who had one eye; and Charlie Barton, almost bald 'who had one hair'. Another character was Bill Harper. He was the blacksmith in the squadron who became Trafford's batman. Afterwards he became a goalkeeper for the Arsenal Football Club.

One officer in No. 8 Squadron was Lieutenant Ferdinand West who joined it in France as a trainee pilot, aged twenty-two, having been in the trenches in 1915 and 1916. One day in November 1917 at Grantham as a trainee pilot, West was flying a de Havilland 6 Trainer.

'For some reason or other,' said West, 'DH's were considered machines in which you could not loop the loop. I was feeling frisky. I did a loop, and got into trouble with a Captain in my flight who reported me to my commanding officer, Major Leigh-Mallory, for disobeying general instructions. Although Leigh-Mallory did not say so, it was my impression at the time that he was pleased at what I had done. Immediately after Christmas, when Leigh-Mallory knew I had passed my flying tests, he said "I'll try to get you to the Squadron I'm going to command" which confirmed my impression.'

Number 8 Squadron's work was principally with the army. They photographed the enemy's lines and they helped the British guns by watching where their shells dropped and communicating back using morse code — for example 'you are 300 yards 3 o'clock'.

Number 8 Squadron, under Trafford, carried out the first-ever air-to-tank liaison. The requirement arose because the early tanks had a narrow, restricted vision and were therefore easy targets for the enemy. No. 8 Squadron's job was to spot the enemy guns and to warn tank commanders where they were. Plane-to-tank communication was the main problem. They started by using a morse buzzer and batteries but they found the buzzer's range was insufficient. The tank-drivers suggested using different coloured flags. But the flags became very oily in the tanks: 'It was damned hard to tell what colour they were so we had to fly very low,' said West.

At last, on 31 July, Trafford had success to report:

'Tests with 5th Tank Brigade. Successful. One Observer directed a tank for over two minutes by means of wireless telegraphy. The position of several anti-tank guns which were opposing was signalled by the Observer, who also dealt with them by bombing. All signals from Aeroplane to Tank were acknowledged by red groundflares. Machine was flying at 500 feet.'

Three days later, the good progress was continuing:

'Practised directing two tanks on aerodrome by means of Wireless Telegraphy. All signals were received from heights of 500 to 1500 feet. They were very clear and correct. Signals were acknowledged from tank with red flares.'

and

'Signals received correctly from distance up to 4000 yards and average height of 1500 feet. 30 messages sent.'

An activity carried out that day by Captain West was: 'Practised dropping flares with accuracy on target representing anti-tank guns.' Progress was rapid. Only the next day, Trafford was able to report:

'Messages received readably from 9000 yards at 1700 feet though faint. Tank engines not running. Messages strong from 5000 feet.'

But the German assault continued. For Britain April 1918 was one of the blackest months of the war, and on the night of 19 May forty-one German planes set out to bomb London. Only thirteen reached their destination but they dropped eleven tons of bombs, killing forty-nine people and injuring 177 others. This was the greatest — but also the last — raid on London.

Trafford was confirmed in his rank on 1 April as a 'Major, Aeroplanes'. As CO of the Corps Army Cooperation Squadron he would have had to devote a great deal of time to liaison with Corps HQ. He would have needed to be continually aware of the problems facing the Corps along its whole front, and be ready to give advice on the extent to which his specialist Squadron could contribute to their solution. He would have needed too to be alert to any technical developments that might be adaptable to his specialist Squadron's role and what changes in tactics and associated training these might call for. Also, because of the broad front which he had to cover, his squadron was deployed to a number of different locations, all of which he needed to visit frequently. So he was unable to fly operationally as much as he had in his Flight Commander days. But he flew planes himself whenever it was necessary. On 23 April he flew on 'special reconnaissance of GHQ line, 3.15 to 4.25'.

On another occasion recalled by Farquhar:

'West took a plane up and pranged it. Next day Leigh-Mallory took it up. He did three or four circuits and made one of the best landings we'd ever seen. It was the first time we saw him take a kite up.'

On 17 May, Trafford recommended both West and Haslam for the Military Cross. His recommendation was accepted and he was very pleased:

'I'm very delighted you got it. It gave me much pleasure recommending it. There will be a big attack sooner or later. I want you chaps in your flight to keep it up as much as you can.'

On 27 May twenty-eight German divisions supported by tanks, attacked the French on a 35-mile front north-west of Rheims. They advanced until held at the River Marne on 6 June. On 9 June a fresh German assault began. After repeated attacks during the following week, the Germans crossed the River Marne. They continued to advance slowly south- westwards although at a high price. However, American troops were now pouring into France at fifty thousand per week to reinforce the Allies. The tide finally turned against the Germans on 18 July when the combined Allied armies struck back.

In late July Trafford introduced a change in fighting tactics in his squadron which caused controversy among his flyers. He ordered that Observers must carry and use a pair of Lewis guns. It had been shown that the chances of downing an enemy plane were not very good using a single gun when flying at high speed, unless the enemy obligingly flew straight and level. Trafford considered that by doubling the fire power, both the bullet density and the cone of fire would be increased, improving considerably the chances of scoring a lethal hit. But some of the Observers were dismayed. They wanted to keep to the single gun because it was very hard to shoot straight with two guns which were mounted together on a single pivot and moved sideways but did not fire in phase together. In view of the objections Trafford went up in a plane and tried it for himself. He was satisfied that he was right, so that was that.

On 7 August Trafford told his flight commanders there was going to be a huge attack against the Germans. That same day the chief of the RAF, Major General Sir John Salmond, visited No. 8 Squadron. Trafford invited him to go to the marquees which each flight commander had. He brought Salmond into the marquee where West was in the process of instructing his pilots. West recalled to the author that he saw Trafford come in but did not recognise Salmond with him. When West finished Salmond spoke:

'I am very greatly impressed with the enthusiasm. This is the most important factor from my point of view.'

He went on that the Fourth Army C-in-C particularly wanted to know the location of Germany's reserves.

'That's your task. I have asked the Army Cooperation Squadron to solve this task.'

Next day, 8 August, became known to the Germans as the Black Day of the war.

It was the commanding of the Army Cooperation Squadron that laid the ground for Trafford's subsequent RAF career — but the task which Salmond had set them led to the end of West's flying career three days later. What happened was reported by West to Trafford the day after it happened in typically modest fashion:

'11 Day of Month.

Sir, was brought down after uneven flight yesterday at 11.45 am. My leg was blown off but managed to do a good landing. One Hun followed me down to twenty-five feet. Haslam wounded in ankle. I lost my left leg. Was operated. Luck to everybody. Capt. West.'

What had happened was this: West and his usual Observer, Lieutenant Alec Haslam, were on Tank Patrol, working closely with the IVth Tank Brigade. They were flying their Armstrong-Whitworth near Rosieres when they noticed a great deal of movement near Roye which was the objective of the British tanks. West brought his plane down to a low altitude.

The official report continues that West

'was attacked by seven German aircraft. When caught in a gap between two clouds, Captain West was hit in the left leg by three explosive bullets, almost severing his leg which fell among the controls, thus rendering the machine almost unmanageable. Captain West lifted his leg away from the controls, and in spite of heavy fire from the hostile machines, succeeded in landing his machine. Meanwhile his Observer although wounded through both ankles, brought heavy fire to bear on one of the hostile machines, which was considered by the infantry to have crashed. Captain West after landing fainted, but upon recovering insisted on handing in his very valuable report.'

Haslam, the wounded Observer, described the incident to the author sixty years later:

'The German flight leader got under our tail from a long way away and he opened fire on us much before I expected. His first burst got us both in the legs. West was hit just below the knee between two bones. Our rear gun had only 97 rounds before you had to change drums. The German had more and that possibly determined his tactics. He came up close. But I hit him in the radiator and he went down straightaway.'

West won the Victoria Cross, one of nine awarded to the Royal Flying Corps during the war. Sixty years later, Air Commodore Freddie West VC explained to the author how he had succeeded in flying their plane back and landing it safely under such a huge physical handicap:

'I was very young and strong and healthy and had a bit of luck. They amputated my left leg in a chapel in the field. They thought I'd go under.'

It was a very dangerous time for all RFC flyers. Sydney Smith, an Observer who had stood in for Alec Haslam when he was on leave, told the author:

'We each expected to last six weeks . . . in that time we turned over the whole strength of the squadron.'

Photography was the most dangerous activity. The planes flew in a straight line at only 1500 feet altitude, so they were sitting targets for the German machine-gunners. One day Smith's gun jammed after firing only fifty rounds. The Germans 'put 400 into us but I was never actually touched by a bullet'. When they landed, Trafford saw Smith's torn uniform and commented to him: 'That nearly spoiled your matrimonial prospects.'

The land and air battle continued. By 5 October, the Allies had captured the whole of the Hindenberg Line, and they took Cambrai on 8 October.

On 3 November George wrote home with news of Trafford:

'I was delighted to see T. He was in tremendous form, happy and gay and full of life. He gives me the impression of success, not merely from the fact that he affects magnificence, rushing about in a splendid Crossley car and giving orders with the curt assurance of an Alexander the Great, or Lord Northcliffe or Rockefeller, but he so evidently enjoys every detail of successful action and has such a wonderful singlemindedness of forward-looking conviction.'

Trafford was mentioned in a Despatch from Field Marshal Haig dated 8 November, 'for gallant and distinguished services in the Field'. He subsequently received a certificate recording this which was signed by the then Secretary of State for War, Winston Churchill.

Trafford's precise final report for No. 8 Squadron in the last three months of the war — from 8 August to 11 November — demonstrates the intensity of the fighting. His squadron's strength was 19 Pilots, 20 Observers and 17 B.F. planes:

Total flying time	:	2134 hours 16 mins
Bombs dropped	:	715 × 2lb 6 × 40lb (phosphorus)
M.G. rounds fired	:	74,880
Persons Casualties	:	9 killed, 24 wounded, 5 missing, 8 injured
Machines Casualties	:	Failed to return 5 Returned to AD for repair 55 Struck off strength, unsalvable 4 Recommended to be returned to AD but repaired in the squadron 2

Peace came with the Armistice at 11 o'clock on 11 November. The Germans had hoped to hold out until the winter weather to make further Allied operations impossible.

George wrote to his father on 15 November:

'How delighted you must be as I am that Trafford has come through the war so splendidly. I spent a night with him early this week and we celebrated peace together at Cambrai; he was bubbling over with joy and activity.

He has evidently done extremely good work and lately has shown himself a person of enterprise and resource. I very much hope he may be decorated as he well deserves; but such distinctions are partly a matter of chance — the chance of being attached to an ordinary channel of recommendation and Trafford in having worked very much apart from his immediate superior officer the Wing Commander misses the best natural chance of recommendation.'

Trafford was next attached to No. 12 Wing in France between 20 November and 6 December. But he was still able to attend No. 8 Squadron's celebratory dinner on 27 November. Trafford retained the charming and poignant menu — which was:

Tomato Soup au Numero Huit	Peas de Big Ack
Fish au Bristol	Trifle au Spare Parts
Cauliflower au Graten	Egg Savoury de Lewis
Roast Duck de Bermicourt	Fruit (si possible)
Roast Fowl de Bellevue	Coffee de Paix
Potatoes a la Scrounge	Zero Hour 7.30

More good news followed for Trafford. On 1 December Doris produced their second child, a girl whom they named Jacqueline.

On 8 December, George wrote to his wife in England:

'I'm now with Trafford, having stayed a night with him on my way back to the battery from leave in Paris.'

Despite George's misgivings, Trafford was awarded the DSO.

His father wrote delightedly on 8 January to congratulate him:

'Everyone is delighted about it. It is the greatest distinction our family has won for many generations and we are very proud of you.

George also wrote to him:

'My dear Trafford,

I have come back for good, the Lord be praised. I wonder if there is any chance of seeing you before you return to France . . . And will you take back those boots with you? . . . How did your lectures go off? And how do you like Winston Churchill's appointment?

Love to you both.

Your loving brother George.

P.S. Ruth says you have been decorated with DSO. It is true? Is it just the required thing and I'm sure no one deserves it better, so I've little doubt it it true, and I congratulate you with the best will I've ever put to that sentiment. It's just splendid, G.M.'

A few days later another letter reached Trafford. This one came from Captain Freddie West VC. He was recovering from his wounds in Rome where his Italian mother lived; it had been posted from the Grand Hotel in Rome:

'Dear Major,

My heartiest congratulations for your well deserved decoration — I had not seen an English paper for weeks and funny enough yesterday I picked up in this hotel and old "Times" and between the names of the officers who were awarded the DSO I had the pleasant surprise to see yours — I had to undergo another operation but now I am OK and hope to be back quite soon — I do not know what I am going to do in the future, all depends what kind of job the Air Ministry is going to offer me — I do hope they are going to keep me in my present rank, as I am not looking forward to go back to Lieutenant.

Well Major, my heartiest congrats once more, and please give my kindest regards to your Wife.

Yours sincerely,

F. W. F. West.'

Haslam also wrote to Trafford:

'Heartiest congratulations on your DSO . . . You will let me say that I think it was a great pity and very bad luck that you never really had the ideas and plans of last summer (for Tank work) put into full operation . . . If you can and will give me any assistance or advice towards getting into flying as a pilot I would be very glad of it.'

Trafford's wife, Doris, accompanied West to Buckingham Palace to receive his Victoria Cross since he had no family of his own in England. Freddie West became godfather to Trafford's daughter. His life story is recounted in a book called *Winged Diplomat* by P. R. Reid.

When the war ended, Trafford had to think again about a career. He considered going back into the law. But he discovered that he had lost four years. Those people — and there were some — who had not enlisted in the armed forces had moved up the legal career ladder in civilian life. Trafford would have needed to retrain. He had eaten the right number of dinners in the Inner Temple but had not yet been called to the Bar. He made a decision — to try to stay in the Air Force and see what the future would bring, but without relinquishing his options with the law.

The war had not dealt unkindly with Trafford. He had, in common with most of his generation, lost the 'fun' days of his early manhood, but he had come through it relatively unscathed and his close relatives had also been spared. He had been set back in his chosen career, but he had laid the foundations of another. His command of the Army Cooperating Squadron had given him a unique specialisation, which would perhaps always set him a little apart from his peers. But when the need for that specialisation arose, as it surely would, Trafford would be there, 'waiting in the wings'. His command experience also seems to have made him appear pompous and remote from those under him. Pomposity perhaps would have come naturally to him, because he had been brought up in the atmosphere of the Church of England and had aspired to the law. Both these professions have an element of pomp and ceremony. Remoteness is harder to understand, as he seems to have been a good mixer, with a friendly disposition. However it is not uncommon for commanders to find it necessary to repress the friendly side of their nature for fear that it may be exploited as weakness. It was General de Gaulle who wrote in *The Edge of the Sword* that the path of the leader was a lonely one.

At war's end there were 28,000 officers and 264,000 airmen in the RAF. Almost all would have to be demobilised, there being no prospect of further hostilities. Anyone who hoped to stay in the Royal Air Force with a permanent commission would have to make an application and hope.

Chapter 6
Everest and Geneva

Trafford remained on the continent with the army of occupation. His wife Doris and their two children travelled out there to be with him at last.

After the Armistice on 11 November 1918 he was appointed to the Armistice Squadron at Sart-le-Spar which was in charge of the aerodrome where the planes landed for the Armistice Conference. The airfield was grass and full of poppies waving in the wind. The squadron was also responsible for the airmail service.

Haslam described life with L-M and the Armistice squadron:
'Leigh-Mallory was out there single at first. His wife Doris soon came. We saw little of him. We used to go into Saar after lunch, eat cakes at the magnificent confectioners' shops and then go to the swimming pool. Some of us were invited to a meal with the Leigh-Mallorys. Leigh-Mallory acquired the nickname "Good God Doris" because he always seemed to address her like that whenever she dropped a brick.'

When the conference was over, L-M was moved back to Bellevue aerodrome. A report, dated 24 March 1919, states that he had nineteen pilots under his command there — of whom three were on leave in England, one was on a course, and one was under arrest.

At this time, other RAF officers whose names were to become famous in the Second World War were at a similar stage in their own careers: Dowding was a Brigadier-General; but Portal, Park, and Sholto Douglas were all Majors — like L-M.

Peace-time flying again became prominent in the public eye. During the night of 14/15 June 1919, two RAF officers made the first-ever non-stop trans-Atlantic crossing. Their names were Captain John Alcock and Lieutenant Arthur Whitten Brown. They flew a Vickers Vimy from Newfoundland to Ireland in sixteen hours twelve minutes.

By the end of the war Britain had become the world's leading air power. Each of the victorious nations looked around to see where the most likely next threat to them might come from. The British decided to concentrate their own defences opposite France. The French licked their wounds and resolved that the Germans should never again be in a position to invade France as they had done in 1870 and 1914. In the USA, President Woodrow Wilson directed American military leaders to plan upon Britain as the most likely to become their next enemy.

Winston Churchill was at the Air Ministry throughout 1919 and 1920. It was his responsibility to preside over the rundown of the RAF.

Trafford's name was included in the first list of about 200 permanent commissions for the peacetime Royal Air Force, which was published on 1 August 1919. At the same time it was announced that officers would have their own set of titles distinct from the other Services. As the RAF had been formed from both the Royal Naval Air Service and the Royal Flying Corps, these titles were a mixture of Naval and Army ranks. With these new titles to learn, *The Times* newspaper printed an error which caused amusement in the RAF: some Observers were listed as Squadron Leaders and some Squadron Leaders appeared as mere Flying Officers. Even today there is some confusion about RAF ranks in the public domain. For those who may not be familiar with them, they are tabulated at the end of this chapter. A thorough understanding of them will make it much easier to follow Trafford's progress.

Although there had been more than enough applicants of wartime vintage to fill all the RAF posts for years to come, Trenchard foresaw the need to ensure a steady stream of young regular officers bent on a full career in the RAF. In 1920 he opened the Royal Air Force College at Cranwell.

Trafford's commission was in the rank of Squadron Leader, and on 19 September he was posted to South East Area as an Inspector of Recruiting; this must have been a frustrating experience after his previous appointments. Sadly, his No. 8 Squadron was disbanded. Haslam, a former member of No. 8 Squadron and an admirer of Trafford was, by the beginning of 1921, at Andover. It was Trafford's great good fortune that Haslam was tasked with planning an establishment for the School of Army Cooperation at Old Sarum near Salisbury in Wiltshire. He told the author that, because the Geddes Axe was cutting the RAF,

'We doubled every job we needed except the Wing Commander. When it came through, our establishment plan had remained uncut! The establishment had been doubled and now required two Squadron Leaders. I suggested Leigh-Mallory — and he was posted to Old Sarum as the No. 2 Squadron Leader. I think he had been sidetracked as Inspector of Recruiting. There was a lot of competition at the time and I think it was quite a turning point for him.'

So in February 1921 Trafford moved to the School of Army Cooperation at Old Sarum. He remained there for two and a half years, during which, in the last quarter of 1922, he attended a three-month instruction course at the Army Senior Officers School at Woking.

Trafford met Haslam again on a Southern Command exercise, the finale of which was described by the latter to the author:

'Leigh-Mallory and I were the two air force chaps on it. On the second day at the end, there was the usual pow-pow at Bulford. "Uncle Harper", who was commanding, called for a summary from his chief of staff, and right at the end remembered, "Oh yes, and there's the Air Force." He turned to Leigh-Mallory and asked him to give his summary.

L-M got to his feet and made a brilliant and very concise summary. He showed that he had understood the whole thing from the army point of view. Several officers said to me afterwards "First time I've understood the whole thing." ' '

Meanwhile, Trafford's brother, George, was teaching at Charterhouse public school. During the holidays he was chosen to take part in the first-ever European expedition to Mount Everest. He performed so well that next year he was selected again. This time he took part in an assault on the summit of Everest. On this climb he broke all previous records by leading a party without oxygen to a height of 26,800 feet, and descending afterwards back to camp by candlelight.

George's elder sister, Mary, recounted to the author that George, who always had a quick temper, was asked during a subsequent lecture tour in New York why he had wanted to climb Mount Everest. She explained that his immortal reply 'Because it is there' was because he was irritated by the silliness of the question. George tried to analyse his real motive for mountaineering in a note, now preserved in the Pepys library at Magdalene College:

'The desire to climb mountains is commonly held among laymen to be an incomprehensible psychological freak. One explanation nevertheless is commonly given — that we climb to win admiration. No mountaineer will accept that . . . It is incomplete of course, but it is probably true to say of most mountaineers among several reasons that they climb to win admiration. "Fame is the spur" . . . I do not suggest that no one would climb mountains unless he hoped to be esteemed for his performance but only that mountaineering like the greater part of man's activities is not as a rule wholly independent of praise . . .'

In October 1922 there was a General Election in Britain. Lloyd George was defeated and the Conservative Party under Bonar Law won a comfortable majority. Bonar Law made moves to abolish the RAF. But he was overruled in favour of a proper study by a sub-committee chaired by Lord Salisbury. This sub-committee took the opposite view and recommended the strengthening of the RAF so as to provide Britain with adequate air defence against the most powerful potential enemy within range of London and the industrial Midlands — which was thought to be France even though relations were friendly at that moment.

Meanwhile in Germany in 1923 there was an unsuccessful 'putsch' involving an unknown Austrian, Adolf Schicklgruber.

That same year Trafford finally gave up any thoughts of a law career and withdrew from his membership of the Inner Temple. Having a wife and two young children, he could not hope to earn enough money starting at the bottom of the legal profession. This decision was the easier to make, because his RAF career was developing well. From May 1923 until April 1925, Trafford worked at the Air Ministry. For eighteen months he was involved in air training duties, and afterwards joined the Directorate of Organisation and Staff Duties.

Although his career was progressing satisfactorily, on the domestic front there was a problem with one of the children. Trafford and Doris's elder child Tom, now aged eight, had to have a mastoid operation: this affected his brain. He became an enormous responsibility and a financial drain on the family which continued throughout their lives. They tried many cures but unsuccessfully. One prospect which seemed to offer hope was faith-healing and spiritualism: this brought some relief — which so interested Trafford that it became a hobby for him and, in the words of his daughter, he was 'quite well into it'.

Brother George left Charterhouse school because he had gained an appointment to the Lectures Committee at Cambridge University. However he was persuaded, reluctantly, to set off one last time with the Third Expedition to Mount Everest in 1924. He was the only member who had also been on both previous expeditions. In early 1924, a few months before setting off for his third climb of Mount Everest, George wrote to his sister Mary, mentioning Trafford:

'T looks forward without a doubt to success and promotion in the future, and is quite sure he is at the heart of Imperial Defence at present; I dare say he does his job very well.'

George sailed with the expedition by boat to India. He posted a card to Trafford from Port Said on 17 March. It said:

'How are you getting on? Hope you have got rid of the flu and flourish — send me a line sometime to Ev. Ex. c/o British Trade Aset Jatung Tibet. Greetings to Doris. G.M.'

This turned out to be their last communication. The next news which Trafford heard about George was of his presumed death at or near the top of Mount Everest. The news came in a telegram to his father from the Alpine Club on 20 June 1924.

On 8 June, George had set out for the summit of Everest, carrying oxygen, accompanied by Andrew Irvine, a tough Oxford rowing blue aged twenty-two. The pair were sighted just after midday by a colleague on the expedition, Odell: he estimated they were then 800 feet below the summit and climbing 'with considerable alacrity' but also that they were about two hours behind their schedule.

The two climbers were never seen again. Other members of the expedition believed that they could have reached the summit around 4 pm but then, too exhausted, had either suffered an accident or had fallen asleep. It is uncertain whether they were carrying a camera; if they were, and if their bodies are ever discovered in the future the camera's film may show whether George was — or was not — the first to reach the summit of Mount Everest. Trafford and Doris attended Memorial Services for George both at Magdalene College, Cambridge on 25 June, and in Birkenhead. Then, on 27 July, Trafford wrote a long letter from the family's holiday in Worthing to his sister Mary who was in Ceylon with her army husband Ralph:

'My dearest Mary
Thank you awfully for the letter you sent me. I have been thinking

of you often during the last few weeks, for I know how deeply you will be feeling George's death and how wretched it must feel being so far from England at such a time.

It seems highly probable from all the later accounts that there is a very great chance that they did actually succeed in reaching the top and that on the return journey they became benighted. If this is so one can but feel that George had a most peaceful and pleasant end, dying in his sleep, his last view of life being quite the loveliest he ever witnessed. Such an end would somehow appeal to George and in view of the cheerfulness of his last letter I am sure he was happy. Anyhow he leaves a fine record behind him of self sacrificing courage, which will set a high standard for future generations of his relations to live up to.

It seems an extraordinary thing to me that all this should happen just when George had got the one job for which he seemed absolutely cut out.

Personally I find it difficult fully to realise the loss of someone whom I have seen so little of during the last ten or twelve years. I have so many pleasant memories of the jolly things we did together and of how generous and kind George always was to me, yet I find it very difficult to realise that we shall never have any jolly times together again, and never see each other again. I am sure you must share some of the same feelings.

I frankly do not know what Mother and Father are feeling. Father is so centred in his work at Birkenhead that I find it increasingly difficult to penetrate his reserve. He has recently spent a week here, and at the end of the week I found we had never had a heart to heart talk of any kind; what little conversation we had was mainly about the weather and food. Avie tells me he was exactly the same when he stayed with them early in June. I am very fond of the old man and I am sure he is very fond of me and yet I always find intercourse with him increasingly difficult. This being the case I really honestly do not know what Father is thinking or feeling or how this blow has struck him.

Mother you must admit is a difficult personality to diagnose. She is a clever woman, of that I have no doubt whatever; she does and says extraordinary things, but who can tell what is really going on inside? The only time I have seen her was when Doris and I went up for the memorial service. Then she was too full of arrangements for the Service and the Bishop coming etc to think of anything very much else. However she has recently been on a 10 days visit to Avie so I expect she will give you some fairly recent news.

I feel somehow that we have lost touch a great deal these last few years which I am afraid is to a great extent my fault. I am such a perfect devil about writing letters. I hardly ever write a letter to anyone, friend or relation, however I have resolved that in the future I must write to you more often so that we can keep in close touch with one another.

We are having a lovely holiday here. I return to my labours next Tuesday but will go back and to from here every day till the beginning of September when we will return to London. We have been awfully lucky with the weather up to the present. We have been bathing every day; Tom can swim a few strokes unaided now; both of them are awfully brave about going in which is a great thing.

We are also getting some very nice tennis. Golf we find rather expensive as they charge 5/- a day green fee which is really absurd.

Please congratulate Ralph most heartily from me on his promotion. I was so pleased to hear about it.

I am so glad we had that awfully jolly gathering in London before you left. I shall always cherish very happy memories of the last time we all four met together.

Much love to you all. Love from Doris.

Your loving brother. Trafford.'

In January 1925 Trafford was promoted to Wing Commander. He received — and preserved — a telegram from Folkestone 'Heartiest Congratulations West' and a short letter from the Chief of the Air Staff. Now aged thirty-two Trafford was marked out as having a promising future. He was sent to the RAF Staff College for a year starting in April.

Trafford, Doris and their two children spent Christmas 1925 with his parents at the Birkenhead vicarage. But on 12 January Trafford sent a postcard from Florence in Italy to Doris at their home at 'No. 1 Bungalow, RAF Andover'. A second postcard followed from Venice, saying that they would be returning from the holiday on the 19th. It is not clear who was on the trip or why Doris could not go too, but it was most likely to have been a Staff College Course visit.

After finishing at the RAF Staff College in April 1926, Trafford was posted to 12 Group to do staff work for the following year.

On 2 May 1926 the family gathered at Mobberley village church for the dedication by the Bishop of Chester of a memorial window to George. Their mother wrote an account to Mary in Ceylon — voicing her anxiety that the letter might not arrive because of the General Strike in support of the coal miners which took place from 3 to 12 May.

'We seem to be in for a very bad time and I don't think anyone really thought a Gl. Strike would be allowed. Trafford quite thought it would be averted and came here on Friday evening as arranged. Then on Saturday when negotiations broke down he became anxious and would have liked to go back straight away, only the Emergency Order was not issued until very late, so it ended in his staying (for the Service and) until 1 o'clock on Sunday and then going straight off to the train at Alderley Edge by which means he would get back to his office by 7 pm. I was *so* glad he did get to the Service. He and Father started from here at 8.15 and picked up the Bishop and they arrived punctually at 10.10 at the Church . . .

It was said on the wireless yesterday that Mr Baldwin said that all his work for 3 years had now been undone and that we are face to face with the most serious crisis the country has known for three hundred years . . .

It may come to Revolution, but one can hardly think so. I feel that nationalisation of mines and railways etc will be the outcome — but under <u>what</u> government — that's the question.'

On 16 June 1926, Trafford's father wrote from his vicarage to Mary in Ceylon:

'My dearest Mary,

It seems ages since we had a proper chat. I am alone at present as mater is paying a round of visits in the south — with Aunt Annie till tomorrow and then on to Trafford. I stayed with him and Doris about a month ago and found them very comfortably housed and with a good sized garden. It is really a charming home. I was fortunate enough to see the first tailless aeroplane in flight — it is like a gigantic moth — but when it comes down it descends perfectly straight — no running along the ground. They say it will entirely change air travel and people with private aeroplanes will be able to land at your front door. When they ascend they only run a very few yards, about 12, and then right up.

We are busy about the restoration of the Organ at St Johns . . .

My best love to you all, ever dearest Mary.

Yr very loving father

H. L. Leigh-Mallory.'

In April 1927 Trafford was transferred back to Salisbury. He was appointed to be Officer Commanding of the School of Army Cooperation. Their home was now Ford House in Ford village. They remained there for three years, during which Trafford began to receive some public recognition. He and Doris attended an evening concert at Buckingham Palace on 21 June 1927. Required clothing for the ladies was 'Court Dress *with* feathers and trains'. On 18 May the following year, Trafford attended a luncheon with King George V and Queen Mary.

On 21 May 1927 there was a flying sensation. Ever since 1919, a prize of $25,000 had been offered by a hotel owner in New York for the first successful non-stop solo flight across the Atlantic Ocean in a heavier-than-air machine. A young American, Captain Charles Lindbergh aged twenty-five, finally achieved this by flying from New York to Paris in 33 hours and 39 minutes in a Ryan monoplane which he had named 'Spirit of St Louis'. One hundred thousand people awaited his arrival at 10.30 at night. He had flown nearly 3600 miles but had not finished his sandwiches and still had enough petrol to fly halfway across Europe. His modesty and courtesy subsequently made him a legend.

It was about this time that Trafford and Doris met the Dodgson family at a tennis club near Salisbury. Philip and Eveline Dodgson had established a nursery glasshouse business near Fordingbridge in Hampshire. They had three young children. The families became extremely close friends. They decided to buy holiday equipment together: the two husbands both wanted a boat, the two wives wanted a caravan. The men won this argument: their first boat was called 'Dorothea' and it was kept in Poole harbour.

It was sold in 1928, because next year the Dodgsons bought another boat by themselves. Trafford never had sufficient surplus money at any time.

Trafford was a very healthy person. Up till this time he only once had to go into hospital, or military 'sick quarters': this was in September 1929 when he complained of pain in his back, limbs, forehead and at the back of his eyes. He stayed in bed for four days.

In December 1929 the Air Council expressed its 'appreciation of the work being done by Wing Commander Leigh-Mallory while in command of the School of Army Cooperation', and on 1 January 1930 Trafford was posted to the Army Staff College, Camberley, to be an instructor where his speciality 'was very much Army Cooperation' according to his daughter. This was a predictable step in a rising career: for the three years until 1929 another instructor there had been Lt Col Bernard Montgomery — with whom Trafford would work closely later.

Trafford occasionally played in the Staff College tennis team, called 'The Cadets'. One player, later Lt Gen Sir Jack Woodall, remembers 'Leigh-Mallory as a most likeable chap, a most experienced airman, ambitious and absolutely dedicated'. Another player, later Lt Gen Sir Harold Redman, remembers Leigh-Mallory having 'great personal charm. He was always friendly and approachable; very alert and understanding; quick to get to the root of a problem, and anxious to help in any way that he could.'

Trafford was able to fly up to visit his parents in Birkenhead. An undated note survives in Trafford's handwriting, on printed notepaper headed 12 Bungalow, Staff College, Camberley. Presumably it was written out for a radio operator during a flight:

'I have flown up with the idea of spending a couple of nights with you. I intend to land at Sealand (between Birkenhead and Chester) aerodrome in about 5 minutes. If you cannot send the car over for me, will you please phone to the Duty Pilot and give him a message. I shall see him on landing. T.'

At Camberley Trafford and his family felt the force of snobbery that the Army felt for the Air Force. His daughter said: 'People looked down on us when we arrived at Staff College. My father had "made it" with no money, a major disadvantage.' Trafford however was determined to give a good impression of the Air Force. Like every instructor he was allowed a horse: he called his Rufus, and later he bought a jumper called Mary which he rode on drag hunts.

Croquet at the Manor House, Mobberley in 1865. The small boy is Trafford's father, the youngest of a large family.

Trafford (on the rocking horse) with his sisters Avie and Mary.

Annie Leigh-Mallory, L-M's mother.

At his prep school, St Leonards, Summer Term 1904. Trafford is third from the right in the front row. (*RAF Museum, Hendon*)

L-M on a donkey at a family picnic at Chester in 1911.

A family group at The Rectory, Birkenhead. *Back row left to right*: Canon Herbert Leigh-Mallory (father), Trafford, George. *Centre row*: mother, uncle Wilfred, sister Avie and friends Olive and Brian Blood.

Trafford (*right*) about to go climbing in North Wales with his brother George. George took part in the first and second expeditions to Mount Everest and he was persuaded, reluctantly, to set off one final time for the third expedition in 1924. He was to disappear without trace.

At the outbreak of war in 1914 L-M enlisted in the Lancashire Fusiliers as a private soldier. A week later he was promoted to Second Lieutenant. Note the badges of rank on the cuffs: these were later moved to the shoulders so that they could be less easily spotted by the enemy in battle. (*RAF Museum, Hendon*)

Just married! Trafford and Doris Sawyer were married at All Saints Church, Upper Norwood on Wednesday 18 August 1915. (*RAF Museum, Hendon*)

In 1915 L-M applied to join the newly formed Royal Flying Corps. He was accepted and is seen here in his first aeroplane, a Farnham biplane used for training.

L-M (*left*) in his early RFC days.

Trafford (*seated, centre*) in the winter of 1917 in front of an impromptu RFC hangar. (*RAF Museum, Hendon*)

Armstrong Whitworth FK8 — 'Big Ack' — which equipped Number 8 Squadron 1918. This was the squadron which L-M commanded from November 1917. (*Chaz Bowyer*)

Captain F.M.F. West, VC, MC, Number 8 Squadron RAF, 1918. Freddie West served in L-M's squadron and was recommended by him for the Victoria Cross. He became a close friend of L-M and was godfather to his daughter. (*Chaz Bowyer*)

L-M (*centre*) with the warrant officers of his Number 8 Squadron in early 1918. (*RAF Museum, Hendon*)

At his final banquet at the college before leaving, Trafford received the traditional Owl statuette, and a charming three-verse poem accompanied it. His daughter remembers it in part:

> . . . a little man
> who wears a coat of blue
> and teaches aeronautics
> to blokes like me and you.

The third verse ran:

> So put him in his coat of blue
> He's sure to do his best.
> Just put him in the picture
> L-M will do the rest.

In 1930, Trafford lectured at the Royal United Service Institution on the question of air cooperation with mechanised forces, on which he was now a leading authority.

Meanwhile, on 3 October 1930 the revived concept of hydrogen-filled Air Ships received a fatal blow. The biggest Air Ship in the world, the R101, on an experimental flight to India, hit the ground near Beauvais in France at 2.50 am in darkness and rain. It was totally destroyed by fire and forty-seven out of fifty-four people on board were killed.

The Times for 9 April 1931 reported that the Gordon Shepherd Memorial Prizes for the year 1930 had been awarded by the Air Council, and that Trafford had won the second prize, value twenty pounds. Prizes were offered for essays 'on reconnaissance and kindred subjects'.

On 28 July 1931 Trafford was posted to the Air Ministry as Deputy Director of Staff Duties. In January 1932 he was promoted to Group Captain. He remained at the Air Ministry, but moved to the Directorate of Operations and Intelligence.

On 2 February 1932 the Disarmament Conference assembled at Geneva under the auspices of the League of Nations. Sixty-one sovereign states participated under the Presidency of Britain's Foreign Secretary, Arthur Henderson. Trafford was sent to Geneva to join the British delegation as Air Adviser to the British representative on one of the committees. This first experience of international negotiation was to stand him in good stead in the future. Apart from his annual leave which he spent with his family in England, he lived permanently in Geneva during the conference, separated from his loved ones.

Beside the work at the conference, there was a busy social round. Among others Trafford met the Aga Khan and became a friend of the Begum. He also met regularly each week for lunch with Brian Robertson, the Military Adviser, and Philip Noel-Baker with whom he formed a life-long friendship. Specially selected as they must have been to attend this conference, these three men fulfilled their promise. Philip Noel-Baker went on to become a famous Member of Parliament and winner of the Nobel Peace Prize; Robertson moved to South Africa, but rejoined the British Army when war broke out, and rose to become a Field Marshal; and Trafford also went on to do great things. Indeed, to quote a letter from Philip Noel-Baker to the author 'Trafford was one of the great Commanders and in my view also a great man'.

In retrospect, the greatest chance of success for the Disarmament Conference was near the beginning on 22 April 1932, which was the last occasion when five major world leaders were present. Tardieu, the French Prime Minister, afterwards became anxious about the coming election in France, left and did not return; Grandi of Italy left at the same time, giving no clear reason. The other three — Ramsay MacDonald, Bruning the German Chancellor and Stanton, the American Secretary of State — remained but there was never a more favourable opportunity to reach an agreement.

On 30 January 1933 Hitler became Chancellor of Germany, his National Socialists having become the largest party in the Reichstag in the elections of July 1932. The 'purge' of 30 June — when General Von Schleicher, previously head of the German government for two months, was murdered with his wife by the SS — started the march of events away from peace.

On 27 March 1933 Japan walked out of the League of Nations because it refused to recognise the puppet state of Manchukuo. On 14 October 1933, Germany withdrew from both the Disarmament Conference and the League of Nations on two grounds: that there must be real and substantial disarmament by the heavily-armed powers, meaning in particular France, and that there must be equal rights for different nations. Tardieu on his last stay at Geneva on 21 April 1932 had repeated once again that 'France would never agree to further reductions of her own armaments or to an increase in the armaments of any nation.' France was then the strongest military nation in the world. Tardieu's policy was simply to hold Germany to the terms imposed at the Treaty of Versailles and to keep France strong.

Noel-Baker told the author that he, Leigh-Mallory and Robertson were equally appalled by the result of the conference — and that all three of them asked to be moved. As soon as the conference was over, Trafford returned to the Air Ministry in London to become Deputy Director of Staff Duties.

Relative Ranks — Royal Navy, Army and Royal Air Force

Royal Navy	Army	Royal Air Force
Admiral of the Fleet	Field Marshal	Marshal of the Royal Air Force
Admiral	General	Air Chief Marshal
Vice Admiral	Lieutenant General	Air Marshal
Rear Admiral	Major General	Air Vice-Marshal
Commodore	Brigadier	Air Commodore
Captain	Colonel	Group Captain
Commander	Lieutenant Colonel	Wing Commander
Lieutenant Commander	Major	Squadron Leader
Lieutenant	Captain	Flight Lieutenant
	First Lieutenant	Flying Officer
Sub-Lieutenant	Second Lieutenant	Pilot Officer

Chapter 7
Iraq, Twelve Group, and War Again

Trafford scarcely had time to take up his duties as Deputy Director of Staff Duties. At the turn of the year he was sent on a twelve-month course at the Imperial Defence College (IDC), the most senior of all the services' staff colleges. This course included Army manoeuvres. Trafford's handling of the fighters under his command was such that no 'enemy' reconnaissance aircraft could get anywhere near to the troops to which he was attached: the umpire had to ground his air force because otherwise the exercise would have had to come to an early end. The fact that Trafford had been selected to attend the IDC meant that he was expected to go much further in the RAF. Before he could reach Air Rank, however, he needed to have experience in command at Group Captain level. Consequently, immediately after completing the IDC course, on 19 December 1934 he became the first regular commander of No. 2 Flying Training School at Digby in Lincolnshire. The school had been re-opened in October as part of the RAF expansion scheme in the light of the German military resurgence. The training aircraft were the Avro Tutor, the Hawker Hart and the Hawker Fury. L-M started a rebuilding programme during which seven old aircraft hangars were removed and were replaced by two new ones.

Trafford and his family occupied the Commanding Officer's residence — Digby Lodge — during his time there. He and Doris both wrote their Wills there and at Whitsun they went for a cruise to the Channel Isles with the Dodgsons, which ended at Weymouth.

While Trafford was undergoing his annual medical check-up at Digby, his only complaint was a slight restriction of movement in his right shoulder, which was the result of an old injury: this was treated by an osteopath and did not affect his A1 medical category, which meant that he was judged fit for flying duties anywhere in the world.

One year in command at Digby was enough to convince the 'powers that were' that Trafford was fit for promotion. To enable him to reach the highest ranks, however, he needed some overseas service. His wartime service in France was too far in the past, and his time at Geneva did not count, as he had been too remote from the RAF during that assignment. Accordingly, just three weeks before Christmas 1935, he was posted to RAF Headquarters at Hinaidi, Iraq, as the Senior Air Staff Officer (SASO) to the Air Officer Commanding (AOC), Air Vice-Marshal Mitchell. This was an Air Commodore appointment.

Britain had taken on a policing responsibility in the Middle East after 1918 because of local political turmoil but also the oil discoveries. The RAF's work there was to prepare an Iraqi Defence plan against possible attacks from any of Turkey, Iran, Saudi Arabia, or even by France through Syria. There was also work on development of the civil air route from Britain to the East, the reinforcement of British forces in Aden and of the Royal Navy in the Persian Gulf, the training of Iraqi personnel, and other matters including search and recovery of civil aircraft that were missing.

Trafford arrived in Iraq three weeks before Christmas 1935. He immediately caught a stomach-bug — which put him into hospital for four days 'with a griping tummy pain' between Christmas and the New Year. But at least he received his formal promotion to Air Commodore. As soon as he was recovered he got to know his staff, called on the local dignitaries, and familiarised himself with his immediate environment. Then from 24 February to 3 March he was taken on a familiarisation tour of the Persian Gulf and of the South Arabian coast. His task was to get to know local British political agents and local notabilities. With a small party he set off by air and visited on successive days Muharraq, Abu Dhabi, Muscat and Salalah. On the 27th he slept in the Sultan's Palace at Salalah, a solid white building set back from the sandy shore of the Arabian Sea, among coconut palms: the airfield and the fertile plain of Dhofar lay just inland, with the jebel rising skywards beyond. It was in this same palace that, some thirty-five years later the Sultan, Sultaan bin Taimur was to be deposed in a gun battle by his own Army, in favour of his son, Sultan Qabus. On leaving Salalah, Trafford returned to Hinaidi via Muharraq, where he stopped to visit the Bahrein oil fields.

Trafford lived in the AOC's Staff Mess in Baghdad which was located by the river and next to the AOC's house, because he was unable to take his family to Iraq. So, once again they were faced with separation — this time for two years — with only one visit home on leave in all that time. But he did manage to take his own car with him — a Wolseley 10. It was considered a great joke by his colleagues but it lasted well because he used it only in the town and used his official car outside. He also had the use of a non-Arab French horse — called George — which he took over from the previous Air Commodore. The horse was too big and too fast to be raced.

Despite the separation, the period in Iraq was enjoyable and interesting for Trafford. He made a flight to India as part of the demonstration that British forces in India could be reinforced by air, and continued on to visit Singapore. Back at Baghdad, there were many ways to pass the time. For leisure, before drinking 'gimlets' (gin and lime) while watching the sunset there was shooting, archaeology, trips into the desert, and hunting with the Royal Exodus Hunt who prided themselves on their pack of English foxhounds. His two preferences were tennis and sailing. He sailed a circular 'Guffa' which was covered with pitch inside and out. His usual boat crew was the wife of another Briton stationed there, named Alison, with whom he became good friends. He became the godfather of her daughter Diana when she was christened at Sutton Coldfield on 28 June 1937.

On the night of 28 October 1936 there was a *coup d'état* by the Iraqi armed forces against the existing Prime Minister with the apparent connivance of the young king. During the night the Iraqi Air Force suddenly left Hinaidi: the British did not know why and believed it was 'some tribal trouble'.

Afterwards the RAF made contingency plans. L-M became responsible for the strengthening of the defences of the various RAF bases, the installation of blockhouses and of unclimbable perimeter fences.

In February 1937, AVM Courtney succeeded AVM Mitchell as AOC. By 25 March Courtney had completed his courtesy calls and was sufficiently familiar with his new Command for Trafford to leave the HQ. He, Trafford, paid a visit to the RAF base at Dhibban, where he tried out the machine guns in the blockhouses, made changes to give them an adequate field of fire, and had the fences floodlit at night. He also ensured adequate recreation facilities for local personnel — a bus service for swimming in Lake Habbaniyah, and the construction of tennis and squash courts. In June he made several visits to the British Embassy in Baghdad to discuss plans for the evacuation of British refugees in case of emergency.

In June AVM Courtney departed from Iraq and L-M took over as AOC, in which capacity he remained until being recalled to England, to become the AOC of No. 12 Group, Fighter Command, with his HQ at Hucknall, with effect from 14 December 1937. Although 12 Group had been opened on 19 May, L-M was its first AOC, the Group having been formed out of stations and units separated from No. 11 Group, whose HQ were at Uxbridge. On assuming command of No. 12 Group, L-M set up home with Doris at Woodborough Hall, Hucknall, Nottinghamshire.

The L-M family holiday in 1938 was at Land's End with the Dodgsons. This year the males of the two families made a weekend sailing trip to Alderney in the Channel Islands. They started from Lymington River 'with a wonderful soldier's wind': the weather forecast said the wind would reverse later, which they hoped would bring them easily back to England. However on the way out a sudden storm split their mainsail and caused them to reef twenty-seven feet of sail. At one point they wandered 'so close to a large ship that they could see the rivets on its side', according to young Guy Dodgson. His father dislocated his collarbone and had to have his arm in a sling. Bill Murphy, an army officer aged about thirty who had his eye on L-M's attractive daughter Jacqueline, was 'as sick as a cat' (as he told the author).

Murphy said that 'the heroes were Trafford Leigh-Mallory and young Guy'. When they finally limped their boat into Cherbourg harbour on the Sunday, they were welcomed by a French undertaker because their flag was flying at half-mast. They had no passports. The soldier of the crew — Bill Murphy — needed to be back in England by Monday morning for a military demonstration on Salisbury Plain. The British consul at Le Havre refused to help him until his office opened on Monday morning — so eventually Murphy in desperation ran up the crew's gangway of a ferry waving an empty envelope in his hand and hid in a coil of ropes until the ferry sailed.

When the ferry reached England he was arrested, but on the dockside wrenched himself free, and ran like a hare through the dock gates. Outside the gates Evelyn Dodgson was waiting for him with a car and they made a clean getaway, the mystery of his identity and escape never being cleared up. Meanwhile Philip Dodgson and Trafford obtained new sails for the boat in Cherbourg and returned safely, but late, to England.

L-M spent a great deal of time visiting the air stations under his command. One of his staff was Squadron Leader Kenneth Cross who was Auxiliary Liaison Officer. One of L-M's responsibilities was to turn about ten volunteer weekend-only squadrons into units capable of fighting.

Cross and L-M regularly visited these auxiliary stations, weekend after weekend. They stayed at very many different pubs in places as far apart as Cheshire, Yorkshire and Scotland. Cross recalled that 'L-M's energy was abundant and inexhaustible, and he was very good company.'

L-M set about organising his No. 12 Group to a peak of efficiency. Cross said he

> 'reckoned he was an extremely good operational organiser. He had never been a fighter pilot himself but the organisation of Fighter Command fascinated him. It required a great deal of leadership and hard work.'

On one occasion, when touring the airfields under his command in Lincolnshire, L-M was invited to go to supper at the home of Field Marshal Montgomery-Massingberd who had recently retired as Chief of the Imperial General Staff. Montgomery-Massingberd lived at Gunby Hall in Lincolnshire, a beautiful Georgian mansion near Skegness.

L-M telephoned the Field Marshal to fix a day and understood that it would be an informal meal between the two of them. However, on the day itself when L-M's driver stopped his car in front of Gunby Hall, L-M saw a lady looking out of an upstairs window: she was wearing an elegant blue evening gown and he felt embarrassed because he was in his working RAF uniform.

So, when the Field Marshal met him at the front door, L-M apologised that he only had his working uniform and had not appreciated that the dinner was to be a formal affair. Montgomery-Massingberd replied that it was only going to be supper between the two of them so L-M need not worry. L-M answered that he had seen a lady in a blue evening gown at an upstairs window, but the old soldier denied that any such person was in the house.

After the meal L-M was shown round the house and was astonished to see the lady in the blue gown with lace over her shoulders — but in an oil portrait at the foot of the main staircase! The portrait was of Mrs Emily Langton Massingberd, the mother-in-law of the Field Marshal. She had died aged forty-nine in 1897, according to newspapers 'after an operation following a long illness'. She lies buried in the graveyard of the Gunby chapel apart from other family members with a cross stating simply that she 'passed over'. She was a vigorous early campaigner for women's rights, temperance and against vivisection. She founded the Pioneer Club for Women in London's Regent Street which was much criticised at the time. Whether she was a restless spirit, whether Trafford's interest in spiritualism made him able to see her, or whether it was all a fantasy must remain pure guesswork.

The Massingberd family say that during the Second World War Gunby Hall was threatened with demolition to make way for a new airfield — but that L-M put in a plea which helped to save the house. It now belongs to the National Trust.

On another evening during his touring round air stations L-M was invited to supper at the Cambridge home of his niece Clare Millikan, who was the daughter of his late brother George. She had recently married the son of an American Nobel Prize-winning physicist. She remembers Trafford as 'full of bounce and vigour', and that he particularly enjoyed eating her strawberry meringue, a super-sweet concoction which she had recently learned how to make.

He did not mention details of his current work. But she enjoyed listening to his account of one incident in Iraq when quick-thinking had been necessary to put down some kind of rebellion. He told her it had been a matter of bluff: he had had far less force at his command than most people would have risked but had been able to show the confidence — always one of his strong points — to pull it off.

Another of Trafford's nieces, Barbara, the daughter of his sister Mary, was invited to stay a weekend at Woodborough Hall with her army fiancé Owen Newton Dunn. On the Sunday morning L-M and Owen played golf. Owen says he found L-M friendly but aloof and received no help as to whether he should address him as 'Air Marshal' or 'Uncle'. The topic for discussion was the recent discovery of a piece of gold or silver in a nearby lake.

Doris looked after L-M well, but knew when to pull his leg. After one church parade, their daughter recalls that when Doris thought that L-M was guilty of pontificating, she interrupted him with: 'It is getting chilly: I think you should put on a woolly vest'.

On 30 September 1938 L-M issued an instruction to his commanding officers headed 'European Crisis: in the event of war being declared in the immediate future'.

Following the Munich crisis in September 1938 L-M's daughter, Jacqueline, decided to join the Women's Auxiliary Air Force.

On 1 November Trafford was promoted to the rank of Air Vice-Marshal. Aged forty-six he was among the younger of the twenty-two AVMs then serving, their average age being forty-eight years.

On 21 March 1939 L-M wrote Dowding a detailed five-page letter, which began:

'In view of the present emergency, I wish to bring to your notice what I consider to be my main requirements to enable 12(F) Group to make full use of the equipment at present available.'

Dowding's SASO was Air Commodore Keith Park. He wrote the acknowledgement to L-M and dealt with the details. There was no sign of the later tension between the two men, but a subsequent letter between L-M's two sisters says:

'I remember Doris telling me years before the war that Park was a shining light in the Air Force and would be jealous of Trafford if ever he got promotion above Park. I have an account of what Mountbatten thought of Trafford after being in his Control Room for a whole day!'

Not everybody took war preparations as seriously as L-M. On the same day that L-M wrote his letter to Dowding, 21 March, No. 12 Group was to hold its monthly air exercise. But it was cancelled. The May exercise — planned to be two and a half hours of bomber raids to test the Group's defences — was postponed 'as it was not possible to obtain the necessary cooperation from bomber aircraft'.

On 1 June the monthly exercise was cancelled unilaterally by the bombers less than three hours before it was due to start because of an unfavourable weather forecast: two thousand Observers had already turned out and weather conditions subsequently proved to be excellent. L-M protested vigorously. Park wrote a note to Dowding supporting L-M who, he said, had been 'naturally very angry'. Dowding supported him in a letter to ACM Ludlow-Hewitt at Bomber Command — who eventually replied on 17 July that the cancellation had not been justified.

An example of L-M's firmness of purpose occurred during the air exercises of summer 1939. He insisted that his Auxiliary Squadrons must go over to their war stations: some objected, saying they were volunteers and it was their only holidays, but L-M got his way.

L-M was greatly liked by his staff, but he did not get on so well with his station commanders at that time. Until war broke out they were appointed by the Air Ministry and he was not allowed to pick them himself. Cross said that L-M 'never went for popularity but he always stuck up for his staff. He was madly ambitious but he never trimmed for the sake of ambition.'

On 7 July 1939 L-M made a speech at an Aviation Dinner at the Grand Hotel in Birmingham which was held to celebrate the opening of a new airport nearby at Elmdon. He replied to the toast, 'The Royal

Navy and the Royal Air Force'. Deliberately adopting an optimistic tone he spoke about the Munich crisis of September 1938, at which time Britain had been grossly deficient of aircraft. Now they realised the enormous debt which was owed to industrialised areas like Birmingham. Notable strides had been made. As an old war pilot, he could say that today they had in the young men who had come forward even better pilots than they had got ten years ago. He thought the defence system would gravely shake the morale of any attacking air force, so much so that after the first attempt, the full volume of the attack would in a very short time die down to a small trickle. During the past eighteen months, the three services had forged a shield of defence which was immensely strong, and its very strength would mean that it would never have to be put into operation.

In August 1939 the Home Defence Exercise was the longest ever held by 12 Group. It began at 2000 hours on Tuesday the 8th and continued until 1900 hours on Friday the 11th. Enemy bombers, mostly in formations of three during the day phases, raided Group airfields at heights between 20,000 feet and twenty feet at speeds between 150 and 250 mph, making use of cloud cover and throttling down to achieve silence. Twenty-seven attacks were made on sector aerodromes, twenty-five by day and nine low-flying.

During the exercise L-M also had to find time to receive fifty-five visitors to his Hucknall headquarters, including Dowding and his SASO, Keith Park. Yet on the first night L-M insisted that his Operations Room personnel must practise a ten-minute evacuation into trenches outside.

L-M wrote a report of the exercise for Dowding with a long list of detailed recommendations for changes including inadequacies in black-outs, gas clothing, too few cooks, room lighting, and training of searchlight operators: he suggested changes in the standing Fighter Command Battle Orders. He commented that

'. . . the low flying raid was exploited with great success and in nearly every case Sector Stations were taken completely by surprise. The employment of the low flying raid gives comparative immunity to the Bombers and is difficult to detect and attack.'

Dowding replied to L-M on 31 August, congratulating him on the speed with which he had got out his report on the Exercise and on the amount of detail.

On 1 September, Germany attacked Poland. On Sunday morning, 3 September, the Prime Minister, Neville Chamberlain, broadcast to the nation. He said that the British ultimatum to Germany had expired without a reply having been received, and consequently Britain was at war. Within a few minutes of war being declared, 'the wail of the banshee' was heard. It was a false alarm, like so many others at the start of the war, being triggered by two French officers who had chosen to fly to London without giving any advance warning.

On 26 September, L-M wrote to Dowding from Hucknall:

'In view of the small number of Squadrons in any one sector, and taking into consideration the fact that the Germans may deliver large scale raids on such important places as Birmingham, Derby and Sheffield, it is highly desirable that it should be possible to concentrate aircraft from as many other sectors as possible on to the front of the threatened target.'

Dowding's SASO, Keith Park, misunderstood this, believing that it meant concentrating many aircraft onto a few aerodromes. He drafted a reply for Dowding which said that he found it 'very difficult to understand'. Dowding added at the end to L-M: 'I am not criticising you. I admire the energy and foresight which you are bringing to your task.'

L-M immediately replied to Dowding:

'What I have in mind is a German mass attack of say 300 to 400 aircraft being delivered against one of the important objectives in the Midlands. In any one sector I have only 24 aircraft for day operations, and consequently if such an attack develops, I must be able to bring in aircraft from adjoining sectors to counter it . . . This scheme provides purely for air re-inforcement, and it is not intended that any aircraft should land at an aerodrome other than their own . . . I can assure you that in any operations of this nature I shall always be watching the situation to the south of me most carefully, as I realise the re-inforcement of London may, in certain circumstances, become my primary task.'

Perhaps Park was becoming jealous of L-M's success. He commented grudgingly in a private note to Dowding that it was 'rather strange that we have never been told of the plan or the result of trials'. Dowding ignored this remark and drafted his own reply to L-M dated 9 October:

'I had misunderstood your former letter, and if one Sector Commander does not try to handle more than 4 Squadrons the plan ought to work all right.'

On 13 October there was good family news for L-M, a respite from his preparations for war. His son Tom was announcing his engagement to Miss Jeanette Kacirek.

Chapter 8
Big Wings

Despite the declaration of war against Germany, there was a period of little military activity — which became known as 'The Phoney War'. L-M continued to work on building up the strength and efficiency of his Fighter Group. He piloted his plane himself on visits to stations which were under his command.

The Times of 30 March 1940 reported L-M taking the salute at Fighter Command's 'first modern operational station somewhere in England'. He had walked between the lines and stopped occasionally to speak to some of the older personnel who wore the ribbons of the First World War on their tunics. Soon after, he was reported in the papers again — this time making a speech when he opened a Cadets' Drill Hall at Nottingham. He said:

'I do not doubt that when the winter is passed, Hitler will attack with all he has got, and we shall have to deal with very large numbers of aircraft. I should be very stupid if I indicated that the Germans could not penetrate this country, because they will. But we have the machines and pilots to inflict such casualties that they will not keep it up.'

The 'Phoney War' ended when the Germans invaded Norway on 9 April 1940. On 10 May Winston Churchill became Prime Minister in place of Neville Chamberlain who remained in the Cabinet. During the single month of May, Hitler's 'Blitzkrieg' lead to the defeat and occupation of France, Belgium and Holland — which Germany had failed to achieve between 1914 and 1918.

Great Britain was left to stand alone. The British Expeditionary Force began fighting in France on 10 May — but had to be evacuated from Dunkirk between 26 and 31 May. Theo McEvoy, later L-M's assistant, thought that it was during the Dunkirk operation that L-M first realised that fighters must be used in larger formations to resist German strength. After the evacuation of Dunkirk, the British government concentrated on countering a German invasion of Britain. The Battle of Britain began. Churchill said on 18 June:

'Let us therefore brace ourselves to our duties, and so bear ourselves that, if the British Empire and its Commonwealth last for a thousand years, men will still say: This was their finest hour.'

L-M now was given authority to appoint new station commanders of his own choice. One, Harry Broadhurst, came to Wittering from fighting in France where (he said to the author) he 'saw a whole nation running away'. L-M chose another commander who had two artificial legs, after first listening to his explanation for having broken a Spitfire. His name was Douglas Bader; he started working for L-M in command of 222 Squadron under Mermagen. Soon afterwards, L-M summoned Bader to headquarters at Hucknall again: but instead of a reprimand for damaging another Spitfire, L-M gave him command of the Canadian 242 Squadron whose morale was low after returning from France.

L-M found a ready ally in Douglas Bader. Bader was a charismatic man whose great weakness, according to his friend Cross, was that: 'he knew better than anyone else. He had never worked in an Operations Room and frequently complained that his squadron was sent up too late. Bader had some of the virtues lacked by L-M, extroversion and charisma, but he lacked any experience of battle responsibility.'

L-M had an ability to pick good subordinates. Broadhurst told him that his WAAF driver 'was a real tom-boy who hunted with the Quorn each Friday'. L-M agreed with Broadhurst that she would make a good officer: he forwarded a recommendation which was turned down. L-M was appalled; he telephoned the Air Council, and got the decision reversed. Subsequently she rose to become head of the WAAF.

Wednesday 10 July is generally taken to have been the opening date of the Battle of Britain. At the start of the Battle the Luftwaffe had around two thousand fighters and bombers: the RAF's defensive strength was around seven hundred fighters. The first encounter with German planes was made by Spitfires from No. 6 Squadron based at Coltishall in L-M's 12 Group. For the following month the Luftwaffe tested Britain's coastal defences and attacked ships.

11 July was a good day for L-M: he was made a Companion of the Order of the Bath — for having been 'Mentioned in Despatches' by Dowding on 7 March. It was also his forty-eighth birthday: a thankyou letter survives for a present from his son's fiancé Jeanette:

'Very many thanks for your birthday handshake and for the telegram of congratulations you sent me. Air Marshal Gossage tells me he saw you at Roehampton and much admired your agility in the water. I am glad you found the I.C.I. place to your liking. Tom seems very happy there. Mummy is gradually getting better but it is a very slow job getting rid of pleurisy apparently. Jacqueline seems to have been working very hard on her course. She finished 9th out of 37 which is jolly good I think. She is now getting a detachment of her own at Reading — some 60 women I understand. Please remember mé to your Mother and Father. I hope your mother has news of her mother in France.'

As a good leader, L-M knew how to involve himself with his team. One evening Bader's 242 Squadron held a champagne party for their pilots. L-M came over and entered into the spirit of things by doing a Highland Fling on a mess table. There is no doubt that he enjoyed being with his pilots, and, more significantly, listening to them. He also led by example: he was known to work until 3 am on occasion, rising again at

6.30. He once spent twenty-seven hours in the Operations Room, and then had time to go out to speak to pilots returning from flights, taking them sometimes into the Mess for a drink.

The Battle of Britain had three phases. The first phase involved massed German bombers escorted by fighters making attacks on British shipping, coastal targets and fighter airfields. Night attacks grew as time progressed. Then, at the start of August there was a lull in the fighting while the Luftwaffe regrouped itself for an all-out assault on Britain.

The second phase of the Battle began on 19 August, which happened to be Doris and Trafford's silver wedding anniversary. But there was heavy fighting that day, so, although an announcement had been placed in the newspapers, there was no time for a proper celebration.

Bad weather between 19 and 23 August reduced the pressure of the German attack temporarily. Churchill paid tribute to the Royal Air Force in a speech to the House of Commons on 20 August — in immortal words:

'Never in the field of human conflict was so much owed by so many to so few.'

The Germans now attacked inland airfields, aircraft factories and industrial targets. Night attacks increased. On the 24th they attacked RAF airfields: during that afternoon all of 11 Group's squadrons were engaged in the air. Keith Park requested help from L-M's 12 Group.

The fighting was intense, day after day. No. 11 Group took the main brunt of German attacks, and L-M had to restrain his squadrons who wanted to get into the battle.

Cross recalled a particular occasion when he thought 12 Group missed a golden opportunity. L-M had always insisted that the commander's chair in the Operations Room at Hucknall was to be occupied, twenty-four hours per day. But on this particular occasion it was occupied by the Educational Controller of the Group. L-M himself was away visiting the air station at Wittering. A wave of German bombers, unescorted by fighters, could be seen approaching on the radar screen at Wittering. L-M instantly flew back to his Operations Room. Before he got back, 12 Group's fighters had been scrambled to patrol over cities such as Sheffield — but instead it proved to be a German raid on airfields. By the time L-M was back at Hucknall the German raid was over and an opportunity had been missed.

The last two days of August saw the start of the most intensive fighting of the whole battle. On 5 September No. 19 Squadron at Duxford lost its commanding officer, Squadron Leader P. C. Pinkham.

On Saturday 7 September Dowding held a significant conference at HQ Fighter Command. Those present included Park and Sholto Douglas from the Air Ministry but not L-M. Dowding said he had called the meeting to decide the steps to be taken to 'go downhill'. Douglas queried whether Dowding was not being too pessimistic. Dowding replied that 'it must be realised that we *are* going downhill'. Park said that he strongly agreed. Dowding told Douglas: 'I want you to take

away from this meeting the feeling that the situation is extremely grave.'
Both Dowding and Park were expecting to lose the battle!

Fortunately that day, the Luftwaffe changed its tactics. Believing that
they were not knocking out the RAF's airfields, the Germans
transferred their efforts to the bombing of London in order to demoral-
ise the population. On the first day the Luftwaffe sent three hundred
bombers accompanied by six hundred fighters in two waves. Daily
bombing attacks followed with about equal air casualties on both sides.

A huge German attack on 15 September was intended to be the
prelude to the invasion of Britain on the 17th. The Germans believed
that the RAF was down to its last fifty Spitfires: fortunately this
information was wrong, and the Germans' dismay was reinforced when
they met a Big Wing from 12 Group sent up by L-M.

The Luftwaffe lost sixty fighters, the RAF lost twenty. It proved to be
the turning point of the battle. Hitler postponed his invasion plans
without fixing a new date for the invasion of Britain.

There has been major controversy about L-M's 'Big Wings'. The
difficulty in the battle was that, as British aircraft numbers were
depleted due to losses, Keith Park's 11 Group, which took the brunt of
the attacks, found that it could not hold the attacks by itself. Park
agreed to ask L-M for help where necessary. L-M responded to
suggestions by Bader and others of the concept of the 'Wing' with planes
taking a little longer to attack because they waited to build up a larger
formation first. The 'Wing' was very successful whenever it engaged in
battle but came under criticism for sometimes arriving later than
individual planes or squadrons would have arrived. There were two
major factors inherent in the Big Wing, both psychological. First, it was
a significant morale booster for the RAF pilots, who no longer felt
themselves to be fighting against heavy odds; secondly, the Germans
had believed that the Royal Air Force was very weak — until they
encountered renewed and larger defending Wings. This contributed considerably to Hitler's decision not to continue attacking Britain in the air.

By mid-September L-M had sent up Big Wings on five occasions. The
results already appeared very promising, so he sent a rapid but thorough
report to Dowding on 17 September, with a copy and covering letter to
AVM Evill:

'Dear Strath,
I herewith forward a report on recent operations of my Wing,
which I thought might interest you. I am convinced myself that it is
the correct way to tackle these large German formations and
would like to point out that the successful Wing operations require
a good deal of experience on the part of the squadrons operating
together, and I anticipate that Wing operations will tend to
improve as time goes on. Bearing this in mind I think the results up
to the present have been distinctly encouraging.
Yours ever,
Trafford'

His report was:

1. Experience has shown, that with the mass attacks on London and the south of England, the enemy has used not only larger formations of bombers but very considerably larger formations of protecting fighters. In view of this, when 12 Group have been asked to protect North Weald and Hornchurch Aerodromes, it was considered wholly inadequate to send up single Squadrons for this purpose and therefore a Wing has been employed. Up to the present five such operations have taken place. Definite roles have been allotted to the Squadrons on each occasion, with the general idea of having Spitfire Squadrons above the Hurricane Squadrons so that the former could attack enemy fighters and prevent their coming down to protect their bombers, whilst the remainder of the Wing break up and destroy the enemy bombers. The details of the Squadrons employed showing casualties to the enemy and to our own fighters, are given in Appendix "A".

2. FIRST WING PATROL

   The Wing, consisting of three Squadrons with 34 aircraft, left Duxford at 1645 hours on 7th September to patrol North Weald. When at 15,000 feet they noticed AA fire to the east and saw about 100 enemy aircraft flying north at 20,000 feet. The bombers — Do. 215s and He. 111s beneath them — were in tight box formation with Me. 110s circling around them and Me. 109s 5000 feet above them. The three Squadrons were at a disadvantage through the loss of any element of surprise and also through the necessity of having to climb up to the enemy. There was the added disadvantage in that when attacking the bombers, the fighters were coming down on them from the sun. It was, however, essential to attack quickly and in the process the Squadrons got spread out and a general battle followed, in which aircraft picked out individual targets. Our pilots had to defend themselves from the enemy fighters with the result that they destroyed considerably more fighters than bombers in this action.

3. SECOND WING PATROL

   The Wing, consisting of three Squadrons with 33 aircraft, left Duxford at 1700 hours on 9th September to patrol North Weald and Hornchurch. When they were at 20,000 feet they saw two large rectangular formations of enemy aircraft, which each consisted of at least 60-70 Do. 215s with a very large number of escorting fighters. The upper formation, which appeared to consist of Messerschmitts and He. 113 fighters, was 500 feet above the lower one, which also had fighters in the formation. In all there must have been between 150-200 E/A. The enemy, which were at 22,000 feet, were flying north about 15 miles to the southwest of the Wing. The Spitfire Squadron

(19) climbed to 23,000 feet to attack the fighters whilst the Hurricanes climbed to attack the bombers. The number of escorting fighters was large enough to enable some of them to dive on our fighters as they attacked the bombers, whose formation had then been broken up. In the result, therefore, more enemy fighters were destroyed than bombers although the proportion of bombers destroyed was increased when compared with the first action. Bombs were dropped by the enemy during this engagement, which took place over the southwest suburbs of London, but the enemy were driven off to the southeast. The leader of the Wing considered that at least 20 further bombers could have been shot down if additional fighters had been available to renew the attack after the bomber formation had been broken up.

4.   THIRD WING PATROL

The Wing, consisting of three Squadrons with 36 aircraft, left Duxford just before 1600 hours on 11th September and patrolled North Weald at 23,000 feet. AA fire in the direction of Gravesend drew their attention to at least 150 E/A flying north at 20,000 feet. The enemy were coming north in waves of tight formations of Do. 215s, He. 111s and Ju. 88s, with protecting fighters, the Me. 110s immediately behind the bombers and a large number of Me. 109s behind them at 24,000 feet. It had been arranged that the two Spitfire Squadrons in the lead (a composite Squadron composed of 19 and 266, and 611 Squadron) were to attack the fighter escort whilst the other Squadron (74) attacked the bombers. As 74 Squadron went into the formation of Ju. 88s they were attacked by enemy fighters (He. 113s) diving on them, but continued their attack on the main formation. AA fire which had drawn our fighters' attention to the enemy was troublesome during the engagement, and hampered the plan of attack. In spite of this 74 Squadron stuck to their task and inflicted considerable losses on the enemy bombers, while the other two Squadrons joined in the general melee and engaged both fighters and bombers.

5.   TACTICAL CONCLUSIONS ON THE FIRST THREE PATROLS

(I) During the first three Wing formations, the following two main difficulties were experienced:

a) The fighters who were attacking the bombers got unduly interfered with by enemy fighters. This would appear due to the fact that there were not sufficient fighters both to neutralise the enemy fighters and to attack the enemy bombers successfully.

b) It was also found that after the Wing attack had been delivered, there were enemy bombers who had become detached and were easy targets, but who could not be attacked because there were no fighters left with sufficient ammunition.

(II) As a result, the following conclusions were arrived at:

    a) For an operation of this type to be really successful, three objects have to be achieved —

        (i) to neutralise the enemy fighters while the attack on the bombers is being made;

        (ii) to break up the bomber formation;

        (iii) to shoot down the bombers after (ii) has been achieved.

    b) From the size of enemy formations we have met up to the present, it was considered that at least two Spitfire Squadrons are required to neutralise the enemy fighters.

    c) In addition to the two Squadrons required to neutralise the fighters, at least three Squadrons are required to break up the enemy bomber formations and carry out the main attack on them.

    d) It was hoped that when the bomber formations had been disintegrated one of the two Squadrons neutralising the fighters might be able to detach itself and shoot down isolated bombers.

6. FOURTH WING PATROL

In view of the conclusions reached, the Wing consisted of five Squadrons with 56 aircraft, and took off from Duxford before noon on the 15th September. The three Hurricane Squadrons patrolled at 25,000 feet with the two Spitfire Squadrons about 2000 feet above them. They saw about 30 enemy bombers (Dorniers) south of the Estuary flying northwest with a large number of Me. 109s protecting them. The leader saw Spitfires and Hurricanes, belonging to No. 11 Group, engage the enemy and waited to avoid any risk of collision. As the Hurricane Squadrons went in to attack the bombers, Me. 109s dived towards them out of the sun, but, as the Spitfires turned to attack them, the enemy fighters broke away and climbed towards the southeast, making no further effort to protect their own bombers, who were actually endeavouring to escape towards the west and the south. They did not all, however, manage to save their skins in their precipitous flight, as the Spitfires were able to destroy a number of them before they got away. In the meantime the Hurricanes were able to destroy all the Dorniers that they could see and one of the Squadrons saw a further small formation of Dorniers, which had no doubt broken away from the main formation in the first attack, and promptly destroyed the lot. One of the Spitfire Squadrons, seeing that the enemy fighters were getting out of range, also came down and took part in the destruction of the enemy bombers. In this engagement, the pre-arranged idea worked perfectly, for there were sufficient numbers of Spitfires to attack the enemy fighters and prevent them from exercising their primary function of protecting their own bombers, which were destroyed by the three Hurricane Squadrons at their leisure. The enemy were outnumbered in the action and appeared in the circumstances to be quite helpless.

7. FIFTH WING PATROL

The same five Squadrons which had taken part in the Fourth Patrol, though with the slightly reduced number of 49 aircraft, took off again in the afternoon at about 1430 hours. They climbed up through a gap in the clouds, which was 8/10th at 5000 feet, the three Hurricane Squadrons in line astern with the two Spitfire Squadrons to the right and slightly above them. They saw AA fire and then a large number of enemy aircraft at 20,000 feet. The leader of the Wing found that he was at a tactical disadvantage as he had not had time to reach his patrol height, with the result that this formation was attacked by Me. 109s, as they were trying to get in position. Because of this, the leader of the Wing told the Spitfires to attack the bombers, and the Hurricanes to break up and engage the fighters. The results of the engagement were satisfactory so far as they went, but under the circumstances it was impossible to break up the bomber formation and so achieve the same tactical superiority as in the Fourth Patrol.

Dowding forwarded L-M's report to the Under Secretary of State at the Air Ministry with these approving comments of his own:

'It will be seen from these figures that the losses inflicted on the enemy were not increased in relation to the number of our fighters engaged on the later patrols when a larger number of Squadrons took part. Nevertheless, the losses incurred by the Wing were reduced and I am, in any case, of the opinion that the AOC 12 Group is working on the right lines in organising his operations in strength.'

Dowding noted in his own file: 'I am sure that L-Mallory is thinking on the right lines' but added a note of caution on the figures that 'claims are generally exuberant'.

On 19 September, Hitler ordered his invasion fleet and troops to be moved away from Britain — although air battles over Britain were to continue for several more weeks.

The Luftwaffe changed their tactics. They attacked British airfields and they sent fighters and bombers together in order to tempt the RAF into combat. However, the Luftwaffe could not sustain its rate of losses. Attacks continued throughout October but with a higher proportion of night raiding.

Why was there a difference in success for the RAF fighters in the Battle of Britain after their failure against the Germans in France earlier in the year? The difference, in the opinion of Cross, was two-fold: first, radar (then called RDF or Radio Direction Finding) allowed the British to track and report aircraft over the sea; secondly the knitting together of the Operations Rooms: the latter required an immense amount of chivvying and encouragement. According to Cross, 'L-M was better at it than anybody else. It was the organisation on the ground that won it for us.'

During the battles, L-M sat 'in the chair' in his Group's Operations Room and conducted the battle himself. Having carried out the most pre-war practices, Cross considers that L-M had become the best Group commander. By contrast Park at 11 Group walked up and down his Operations Room, giving advice to other people who were sitting in the chairs and having to take the responsibility.

On 1 October Park issued his own memorandum to his own commanding officers to put his arguments against Wings, despite the favourable attitudes of his superiors. Park's memo reads as follows:

1. There is a feeling among pilots in some Squadrons that the only way to defeat the enemy raiders against this country is to employ our fighter Squadrons in Wings of three Squadrons. The object of this Note is to explain why such formations have been used off and on during the past five months, yet have not been made the standard method of grouping our fighter Squadrons in home defence fighting.

2. During the operations by No. 11 Group over France and Belgium, Squadrons were originally employed singly. When the enemy opposition strengthened, Squadrons were employed in pairs. Moreover, when Squadrons could only raise three Sections each, they were employed in Wings of three Squadrons. The conditions were that our Squadrons were being operated on a pre-arranged programme and could be allotted to their tasks some hours in advance and were normally collected and despatched from forward aerodromes on the coast. This gave ample time for Squadrons to be arranged into pairs or Wings, under conditions which do not obtain in the defence of this country, when the enemy can and has made four heavy attacks in one day, giving only the minimum warning on each occasion.

3. In spite of the favourable conditions during the operations over France for the employment of Wings of three Squadrons, the best results during the whole of this operation were obtained by Squadrons working in pairs. Whenever possible, two pairs of Squadrons patrolled the same restricted area; two at high altitude to engage enemy fighter patrols, and two about 5000 to 8000 feet lower to engage the enemy bombers, which, in those days, did not normally employ close escorts as they were operating over their own territory.

4. Experience in home defence during the last two months' intensive operations has shown that there are many occasions

in which the use of Wings of three Squadrons is quite unsuitable, because of cloud conditions and lack of time, due to short warning of the approaching attack.

5. Experience over many weeks has shown that when there are two or more layers of clouds, the Squadrons of a Wing have great difficulty in assembling above the clouds at a rendezvous, also in maintaining touch after passing through clouds when on patrol. Instead of devoting their time to searching for the enemy, Squadrons have frequently had to devote much of their attention to maintaining contact with other Squadrons of a Wing of three. Unless the sky is relatively clear of clouds, pairs of Squadrons have been more effective in intercepting the enemy.

6. Quite apart from cloud interference, the lack of time due to short warning of the approach of raids frequently renders it inadvisable to detail Wings of three Squadrons. Experience has shown that it takes much longer to despatch, assemble and climb to operating height, a Wing of three Squadrons than one or even two pairs of Squadrons. Frequently Wings of three Squadrons have been attacked by enemy fighters whilst still climbing or forming up over their Sector aerodromes. It has been found better to have even one strong Squadron of our fighters over the enemy than a Wing of three climbing up below them, in which attitude they are peculiarly vulnerable to attacks from above.

7. In clear weather when the enemy attack develops in two or three waves, there is often time for the Squadrons of Sectors on the flank of the attack, e.g., Debden, Northolt and Tangmere, to be despatched as Wings of three Squadrons to meet the third incoming wave or to sweep across and mop up the retreating enemy bombers and close escort. There is rarely time for London Sectors to get Wing formations up to the desired height before the enemy reaches important bombing targets, e.g., factories, docks, Sector aerodromes.

8. Until we have VHF in all Squadrons, it is not practicable for three Squadrons in a Wing to work on a common R/T frequency; at least, that is the considered opinion of the majority of Squadron and Sector Commanders. Pairs of Squadrons can and do work successfully on a common frequency whenever the State of Preparedness in a Sector permits. Here again some Squadron Commanders prefer to be on a separate R/T frequency in order to have better inter-communication within their Squadrons.

CONCLUSION:

9. As a result of five months intensive air fighting in No. 11 Group, it is clear that Wings of three Squadrons are not the most suitable formations under many conditions of TIME and

WEATHER. On the whole, Squadrons working in pairs have obtained better results in home defence, specially as our practice since July has been to detail two or more pairs of Squadrons to intercept raids in massed formation. However, when conditions are favourable, Squadrons will continue to be despatched in Wings of three, but the only person who can decide whether Wings or pairs of Squadrons should be despatched is the Group Controller. He has the complete picture of the enemy's movements on a wide front from Lowestoft to Bournemouth, and must quickly decide whether the time and cloud conditions are suitable for pairs of Wing formations. Squadrons must therefore continue to study and develop fighting tactics in Wings of three Squadrons, which will probably become more common in the Spring of 1941.

    10. Two copies of this Note are to be distributed to each fighter
        Squadron, and one copy is to be read by each Sector
        Controller.

On 5 October Park wrote to Dowding with a series of complaints, some smallscale, about the help he was getting from 12 Group. Dowding replied, disposing immediately of one complaint about insufficient training of a particular pilot, and rejecting Park's claim of strain on ground personnel. He asked L-M to comment on Park's complaints about 12 Group.

The same day at headquarters Evill wrote a note to Dowding:

    'There is a fundamental difference of attitude between the two
    Groups, which arises from the difference of the conditions under
    which they are fighting . . . It seems to me that 11 Group's
    requests are entirely reasonable except that they tend to ignore the
    value of utilizing the large formation when time permits. I have the
    impression that 11 Group's Squadrons have been to some extent
    affected by constant fighting against superior numbers . . . It must
    be good for our Fighter Squadrons as a whole, and unhealthy for
    the Germans, for us to push in a 3 strong Wing on occasions and
    reverse the position. I feel that Park should give more recognition
    to this fact and should endeavour to so organise things that he can
    deliberately use the strength of 12 Group's Wing at an effective
    moment in dealing with a mass raid.'

L-M wrote a careful and detailed reply to Dowding on 9 October. He said that the particular requests from 11 Group for help had been made too late. It would be much better if 11 Group could ask for help when the German strength 'was boiling up over the French coast' and not waiting until it reached Kent. He added that when he had sent single squadrons at the height asked for by 11 Group 'they were invariably too low and therefore at a grave tactical disadvantage'. He ended with an assurance to Dowding that 'I am only too anxious to co-operate with 11 Group in any way possible.'

He added a covering note to Dowding saying that:

'I have two main objects in view in conducting Wing operations.

  (a) To meet the GERMANS on favourable terms, and so inflict heavy casualties on them whilst incurring few casualties ourselves, and

  (b) To raise the morale of our fighter Squadrons, as I believe that this has been seriously prejudiced by the very heavy casualties which have been caused to Squadrons, owing to the frequency with which a small number of our own fighters have had to tackle overwhelmingly superior numbers of GERMAN aircraft.

I hope and believe that the Wing operations have, in a measure, achieved both these objects.

Yours sincerely,

T. Leigh-Mallory.'

But on 10 October Park wrote again to Dowding. He enclosed 'a brief report' of the attack on London on 7 October. He wrote that 'recent attacks which take place at such short notice and are over so quickly . . . make it quite out of the question to bring a Wing of three to five squadrons from 12 Group into the engagement':

'These large Wings from Duxford have been most helpful on several occasions in the past when the enemy used large formations of long range bombers, who circled about over North-West France, picking up their fighter escorts, thus giving ample warning.'

★   ★   ★

There was a few hours of relief for L-M on 12 October. His son Tom married Miss Jeanette Kacirek. L-M and all the family were able to attend.

★   ★   ★

On 17 October there was a famous meeting at the Air Ministry in King Charles Street, London. It has since become legendary as a turning point, both in individual careers and in RAF fighter tactics. It was called to examine L-M's Big Wing tactics and his claim that these were the most effective way to hit the enemy hardest.

The then-current Chief of the Air Staff, Marshal of the Royal Air Force, Cyril Newall, was absent because of illness and in any case only had one week to serve. His successor, Air Marshal Sir Charles Portal, was present but the meeting was chaired by Air Vice-Marshal Sir Sholto Douglas. Others present included Dowding (AOC Fighter Command), Brand (AOC 10 Group), Park (AOC 11 Group), L-M (AOC 12 Group), and Air Commodore Slessor (Director of Plans). McEvoy was present as a member of Douglas' staff. L-M brought along Douglas Bader — although he was by far the most junior officer present — because he could provide firsthand knowledge, having himself led Wing formations into battle.

Park criticised the use of Wings because in a crisis 11 Group did not have time to wait for them to be assembled: it was vital to get straight into battle. L-M defended Wings against Park's criticisms. He said that experience already showed that they paid handsome dividends when it was possible to organise them. Bader was invited to speak by Douglas and gave a good account.

The conclusions, as recorded in the Minutes, were that

'the employment of a mass of fighters had great advantages, though it was not necessarily the complete solution to the problem of inter-ception . . .' and that 'it would be arranged for 12 Group "wings" to participate freely in suitable operations over the 11 Group area.'

Magnanimously, L-M wrote immediately the next day to Park. Park replied on the 20th: 'I much appreciate your offer to send down the Duxford Wing to get some experience in the present type of fighting.' Park went on to ask L-M for the Wing to be placed on a standing patrol during a definite period of the day. L-M turned this suggestion down, believing it better to be available at all times to get into the battle providing 12 Group was given proper warning.

On 24 October Dowding issued revised orders:

'as a result of recent discussions . . . 11 Group must always give 12 Group the maximum possible notice of a possible intention to call for assistance . . . 11 Group must remember 12 Group's require-ments with regard to warning, and even if it is doubtful whether assistance will be required, warning should be given to enable 12 Group to bring units to readiness and standby.'

However Park wrote again to Evill at headquarters on the 26th, complaining that L-M's Wing on the 25th had not engaged the enemy: L-M had telephoned Park at noon offering the Wing in view of much enemy activity in the Dover Strait; but the Wing had eventually returned home due to radio contact difficulties and to having seen two of Park's own squadrons above them.

Again the next day, Park wrote complaining to Evill: he said that the squadrons which had been sent to 11 Group from 12 Group — particularly the famous 302 (Polish) Squadron — were achieving below average results because they did not know the essential fighter tactics and how to fend for themselves. Expressing the opinion that: 'I think that the 12 Group mania for "Balbos" has done a grave disservice. . . ', he further complained that the Duxford 'Balbo' had twice failed to see incoming German raids although one pair of his own squadrons had promptly intercepted the raiders:

'I suspect that the components of the "Balbo" were so pre-occupied in maintaining their mass formation that they did not even sight large raids of German fighters.'

Meanwhile, L-M's elder sister Mary wrote to her daughter Barbara on 23 October giving news of various relatives in the war:

'I heard from your uncle Trafford. He had to go to London on Friday and was going to sleep at his Club but found it bombed — so he went out as far as Chorley Wood to sleep on his way home and came in for a raid there. He also heard in London that the Ealing warehouse where all their furniture is has been burnt out and none of their things saved. So at the moment he is feeling the war is a bit hard!'

This fire and the destruction of so many of L-M's personal records made his biographer's task immensely more difficult.

On 29 October Park wrote yet again to complain to Dowding. That day help had been requested by 11 Group from the Duxford Wing at 10.30: it had taken off at 10.47 and having gained height had left Duxford at 11.07 — but it had arrived too late to catch the Germans. Park described the delay between take-off and departure as 'twenty-five minutes', a curious exaggeration. It turned out that 11 Group had only sent up two of its own squadrons before calling for 12 Group's help.

Dowding replied on 5 November:

'I think the answer is that 12 Group should not be called on for assistance unless and until 11 Group gets into difficulties owing to the number of its own squadrons which it has had to use. It is absurd to call on 12 Group when only two of 11 Group's Squadrons have been dispatched.'

The losses on each side, between 10 July and the end of October were:

Luftwaffe losses   :   Fighters and Bombers   1733;   Crew   3089
RAF losses   :   Fighters   915;   Crew   503

During November the Luftwaffe continued their attacks but on a much reduced scale.

On 13 November Dowding again had to issue instructions that maximum warnings must be given by 11 Group preceded by the preliminary warning. When the Germans were active, 12 Group would hold two squadrons at fifteen minutes' notice. Better facilities for communications were to be put into place.

The argument between L-M and Park was terminated on 17 November. Portal wrote to tell Sholto Douglas that he would take over from Dowding as C-in-C of Fighter Command from the 25th. Dowding was being retired. Some said that this was the result of a conspiracy between Sholto Douglas and L-M, but there were more telling reasons. First, Dowding was already overdue for retirement. He had been kept on because he was the only man at C-in-C level with sufficiently intimate knowledge of the system, which he himself had set up, to conduct the Battle. Second, he was tired after the strain of the Battle and his apparent readiness to admit defeat, expressed at the conference on 7 September, could have been interpreted as a lack of will to win. Third, he had failed to resolve the running and divisive argument between

L-M and Park, which was having its effect at squadron level. Finally, Dowding was first and foremost an air defence man. The time for offensive action was not far off. Portal may also have decided that new battles with different tactics required new brooms.

L-M wrote from 12 Group on 7 December to his new C-in-C, Douglas, starting with the assumption that the principle of Wings had at last been accepted by the headquarters of Fighter Command, and Douglas wrote in his file at HQ Fighter Command on 17 December:

'I am very much in sympathy with the AOC 12 Group's proposals. I am convinced we must try and get larger formations of fighters against the enemy mass formations . . . We must give the AOC 12 Group's proposals every possible support.'

On 18 December L-M was appointed to replace Park in charge of 11 Group. Park was transferred to No. 23 Training Group: later in 1941 he became AOC Egypt, and in 1942 AOC Malta. In February 1945 he became Air C-in-C, South East Asia Command — in succession to L-M who was appointed to that post before him.

Park is thought by some to have been roughly treated but he was certainly tired and prone to illness after carrying the brunt of Germany's air attacks for so long. A change and a rest may have been best for him and therefore for the country he was serving.

Cockings, the chauffeur who knew them all, had his own assessment: 'Dowding never delegated and used to go on errands himself. Park was liable to explode'

Chapter 9
Eleven Group and Dieppe

The role of 11 Group, which was previously defensive, could now be changed under L-M's command. It was now possible to begin attacking the Germans on the continent. For starters, two Spitfires made an attack at low level on Le Touquet airfield on 20 December 1940. One day later, the first night intruder operation was carried out by Blenheims over enemy bases.

L-M took his best staff with him to Eleven Group — including Bader, Broadhurst and Victor Beamish. The latter's task was to travel round the air stations and report back to L-M on the state of morale, who should be promoted, and who should be decorated?

Broadhurst said to the author about L-M that:

'People thought that L-M was pompous. But I think that he was shy and therefore he used people like Victor and me. He overcame it by having a group of people whom he really believed in — of whom I became one. Bader had a lot of influence over him. But one of the nice things about L-M was that he did listen to our opinions.'

Sweeps of massed British fighters started going across the Channel. When accompanied by bombers they were called 'Circuses'. These attacks continued for most of 1941. They were easily picked up by German radar but their combined strength offset the lack of surprise to some extent.

One inevitable consequence of the change from defence over Britain to attack over the continent, was that more pilots started to be lost. Previously they had 'ditched' into English fields: now the fields into which they fell belonged to the enemy.

In those early days of the offensive, the learning curve was steep and painful. L-M was subject to criticism for the mounting losses. But as we have seen L-M was receptive to ideas from the men who were doing the job and those trusted few whom he had gathered round him on his staff. Broadhurst's comment on those times is particularly relevant:

'In my opinion we learned a hell of a lot — how to get these raids in, by deceiving radar and by counter-offensive techniques. Later when I was posted to the Middle East, I found they were still in the First World War business — they'd learned none of the deception techniques such as sending in high-level fighters and sneaking the bombers in underneath.'

Portal was asked by the Prime Minister, Churchill, in a note on 9 February about the Fighter Sweep on 5 February 'when we lost eight fighters for two enemy destroyed and one probably lost'. Portal replied that there had been 'a serious breakdown between the Fighter and Bomber Commands. The Bombers were late and the various waves of fighters were thrown out of gear in consequence.'

Churchill replied that 'It would seem desirable when an Operation of this kind is to be undertaken, that the Officer Commanding by far the larger number of aircraft to be used, irrespective of whether they are Fighters or Bombers, should have unified Command.' Portal responded to Churchill on the 18th, informing him that 'We always employ many more fighters than bombers.' And so L-M was given responsibility for the bombers.

As well as his worries about fighting Germany, L-M had to worry about the finances both of his parents and of his son. He wrote about the latter to his new daughter-in-law on 26 February:

'Very many thanks for your letter. It has been on my mind for the last few days but this is the first moment I have had an opportunity to write.

I am very glad to find that you have such a balanced outlook on the financial side of your life. I was quite sure you would have and I made it a condition of sending the £10 that Tom should tell you as I felt you ought to be able to discuss these matters together. I also strongly advised Tom to hand over the control of the money to you.

It is very good of you to offer to send me your own ten pounds, but I am glad to say there is no need. However I do rather object to having my spare money invariably swept away by other people's extravagance.

I feel quite confident that you and Tom now have enough to live on quite reasonably. No one expects a fellow in Tom's position to entertain people and stand them a lot of drinks. In fact a man gains far more respect by looking after his own affairs properly. I very much hope that Tom will hand over the control of the money to you on his own initiative. If another crisis comes along I shall insist on it.

Tom is much happier and settled now he is married and I never had any doubts about your making him an excellent wife.'

By April there was a lull in the Luftwaffe's raids on Britain. L-M called a meeting at his Uxbridge headquarters. He told his commanders:

'We have stopped licking our wounds. We are going over to the offensive. Last year our fighting was desperate but now we are entitled to be a little more cocky.'

But on the continent of Europe, the war was not yet being won. Greece was conquered by the Germans in three weeks. German parachutists captured Crete from 30,000 British and Commonwealth troops.

On 17 April L-M sent the first flying 'Circus' — of around one hundred Spitfires to accompany twelve Blenheim bombers — across the Channel in order to bomb Cherbourg. L-M's prime concerns were now offensives over the continent together with anti-invasion planning.

The offensives did not always go well. In 'Circus Thirteen' on 18 June nine pilots were lost. L-M made an immediate report and told Douglas that he had the feeling that he would be 'on the mat'.

Douglas conveyed this comment to Portal — who wrote back:

'. . . the only thing which disturbs me is that he (L-M) seems to think he is open to criticism for having sustained the loss of nine pilots in the operation. Nothing was further from my mind when I asked to see an account of the operation than the thought of criticising its planning, execution or result . . . I hope you will let him know my feelings.'

German success on the continent continued. In June they invaded Russia. Sholto Douglas chaired a conference at Fighter Command headquarters on 19 June — with the purpose of deciding how to help Russia by preventing Germany from transferring forces from West to East.

L-M believed that Blenheims (which could carry about a ton of bombs) were insufficient. He persuaded Bomber Command to release some of their four-engined Stirlings which carried about six tons of bombs each. These were sent across the Channel supported by up to two hundred Spitfires — the formations attracting the name of Beehives. L-M's tactics were successful: Goebbels was obliged to bring back Luftwaffe fighter squadrons from the Russian front in order to deal with L-M's 'Beehives'.

On 21 June a Beehive flew to St Omer. A Big Wing from Tangmere led by Bader was sent in ahead of it to 'de-louse'. But on 9 August Bader failed to return from another large formation over France. Eventually news came that he had been shot down near St Omer. He had landed safely by parachute but one of his artificial legs had been damaged. Negotiations with the Luftwaffe were opened, and concluded successfully — and a spare leg was parachuted from a Blenheim from 15,000 feet, to reach Bader eventually in his prison camp. L-M's daughter Jacqueline vividly recalls her father's great pleasure when he heard that the spare leg had reached Bader safely.

During the early part of the year, a high-level American group including Colonel Spaatz had visited England, and had called at some of the air stations under L-M's command. At the end of November L-M sent Broadhurst on a return liaison visit to the USA. There he met Spaatz and others, lectured to their fighter squadrons and tried out their new planes.

During the night when Broadhurst flew back across the Atlantic, the Japanese made a surprise bombing attack on the American naval base at

Pearl Harbor in Hawaii and virtually destroyed the American Pacific Fleet. Contrary to the expectation of Japan, this helped a wavering America to make up its mind to enter the war on the British side.

Broadhurst also brought back a gift for L-M from the USA:

'I knew that L-M always liked Edgworth tobacco, and I found him a huge tin of it which I brought back. When he asked me to make my report I also gave him the tin. The following week I was gazetted with a Bar to my DSO, and L-M sent me the news. I wrote back to him that I had never realised how easy it was to win a Bar to the DSO.'

Throughout 1941, Fighter Command continued to sustain a high rate of casualties. Douglas wrote about them to Portal on 10 December:

'. . . desperate shortage of experienced pilots and potential leaders. I am convinced, as is also L-M, that this is the main reason for the somewhat heavy casualties we have been suffering lately when we have undertaken large scale offensive operations.'

In December, Churchill suggested to Portal that night fighter wings be issued with day fighting machines in order to introduce dual purpose squadrons. Portal investigated and wrote back on 27 February. He reported that the objections to this idea had proved to be insuperable because day and night operations involved entirely different forms of training — and added:

'Experience showed that most successful day fighter pilots were under 25. Successful night fighters were usually nearer 30. Commanders of nightfighter squadrons, some of whom achieved the best individual results, were almost always even older — over 30.'

The war against Germany and Japan continued to go badly. On 25 December 1941 Hong Kong fell to the Japanese. In early February 1942 Singapore fell too, despite being defended by 70,000 troops. In North Africa on 26 May Rommel launched his offensive — despite a two to one inferiority against the British. He captured Tobruk on 29 June: 32,000 British troops surrendered and the remaining British forces retreated back to Cairo.

By the summer of 1942, the British armies had failed to win a single battle against either the Germans or Japanese since the start of the war!

In the Air Ministry changes in command were planned. It was envisaged that L-M would be sent to the Middle East to replace Drummond, who would be brought home to a Fighter Group as relief for whichever AOC relieved L-M.

The British attacks slowly grew in confidence. On 14 February Churchill authorised the resumption of full-scale bombing of Germany itself. Portal wrote to Churchill on 5 March to recommend that daylight 'Circus' operations over France be renewed — with the object of inducing German fighters to accept combat.

Churchill replied:

'You are terribly short of Fighter Aircraft and no one can tell how heavy the calls may be in the future. However, it pays us to lose plane for plane, and if you consider Circus losses will come within that standard it would be worthwhile. I know that you cannot give an absolute guarantee.'

L-M continued to try to gain a decisive advantage in the air over the continent. Portal suggested to Douglas that it might be worth trying to catch German fighters when they were short of petrol landing after one of the sweeps. L-M replied to Douglas about this on 22 April:

'I did try out the type of operation suggested in your letter — in fact I tried it out in two ways. Firstly I put in fighters pretty low down, climbing up across the sea and crossing the coast at about 5000 feet, then sweeping rapidly inland in advance of the main raid coming in. This was before the Germans developed their RDF, and I hoped to get the Germans just after they had left the ground. We combed as far as St. Omer pretty thoroughly in this manner, but never made contact with the Germans gaining height.

When conditions look favourable I will again try pushing a fresh wing across to see if we can sweep up any Germans who are intending to land, but his RDF system has improved so much in the last few months that it is very difficult to get a formation into France without it being detected and reported with great accuracy.'

To emphasise the RAF's difficulties, Douglas wrote to Portal on 21 May and enclosed a table to show that nearly two thousand fighter pilots had been sent to the Middle East and Malta in just over one year, which was nearly one hundred per cent of the Fighter Command operational strength in pilots . . . and 'we get very few pilots indeed back in exchange'.

L-M, seeking new resources, told Broadhurst, who knew the Americans personally, to go to Spaatz and ask him to train his bombers by bombing Germans instead of training them purely in Britain. Broadhurst reported back to L-M that the suggestion seemed to be acceptable. They went together to High Wycombe to the American headquarters in the Girls' School. There they found bottles of whisky and packs of cards on the American commanders' desks. Invited to play poker, L-M was reluctant but an American offered to 'watch over his hand'. The session ended with Broadhurst down twenty pounds but L-M twenty-five pounds 'to the good' and having cemented American willingness to start bombing Germans. L-M's daughter explained that their family used to play poker at home and that L-M was a very fine bridge player.

Despite setbacks the British, reinforced by the Americans, began to think about how to recapture the continent of Europe. This was discussed at a meeting in early March between the Combined Chiefs of Staff and President Roosevelt.

The idea of a simultaneous land and sea operation was put forward. One month later a rapid study seemed to indicate that a practical possibility would be to seize and hold a bridgehead. In March Lord Louis Mountbatten was appointed 'Chief of Combined Operations', and was simultaneously given high rank in all three services. The War Cabinet's Defence Committee decided to make a landing on the continent during 1942 — codenamed 'Sledgehammer' — with the object of inducing an air battle with the Luftwaffe and thus helping Russia. They appointed three force commanders: Vice-Admiral Sir Bertram Ramsay for the navies, Lieutenant General E. C. A. Schreiber for the armies. It was Portal's opinion that the most important aspect of air contribution for the eventual invasion of the continent would be the attainment of air superiority over the beachheads. It was therefore decided that the air commander should be a fighter commander. Their choice fell on L-M.

On 22 May L-M attended the Force Commanders' conference at GHQ Home Forces at 30, Queen Anne's Gate in London. Throughout the next six months there were frequent meetings. On 25 June the minutes record that

'the commanders amended the draft comments on the Prime Minister's memorandum on Operation Round-Up and submitted them to the Chiefs of Staff.'

Meanwhile on 25 June at an evening ceremony at the Polish headquarters in London, L-M was decorated with the 'Polish Order of the Polonia Restituta' in recognition of his service in the organisation and development of the Polish Air Force in Britain. He became a Knight Commander of the Order. He received it from the President of Poland, Mr Raczkiewicz, in the presence of General Sikorski, the Polish Prime Minister and C-in-C.

On 4 July Douglas wrote to Portal to suggest that L-M be given the acting rank of Air Marshal:

'As AOC No. 11 Group he has a most responsible job, and he has, I suppose, under his command the biggest conglomeration of squadrons in the whole of the RAF. As you know, for the "Rutter" operation he is controlling no less than sixty Fighter, Bomber and Army Co-operation Squadrons. Even in normal times he has some forty Squadrons under his command.

L-M is now the senior serving Air Vice-Marshal. Some eight or nine officers junior to him hold the acting rank of Air Marshal. He is, in my opinion, as capable as any of the officers junior to him, and in most cases I should say that he is more capable. It seems bad luck that, with his exceptional ability, and holding the very important job that he does, he should in a sense be passed over by some of his juniors.'

Portal replied on 5 July: 'I think that is justified and I am taking it up immediately.'

On 21 July Portal sent a memorandum from the Air Ministry at Great

George Street to the War Cabinet. He advised a reorganisation of the
Royal Air Force:

'It seems logical therefore to base proposals for the reorganisation
of the RAF on the organisation of the German Air Force — who
are not only exceptional organisers, but whose problem since
September 1939 has been similar to that now facing us i.e. land
invasion of their neighbours supported by air power. Useful
lessons can also be drawn from experience in North Africa, where
during battle periods the entire air forces in the Middle East are
devoted to Army support.'

Operation SLEDGEHAMMER — better known as the Raid on Dieppe
— was originally planned for early July. It finally took place on 19
August. The purpose was to carry out a reconnaissance in strength in
order to learn more about how to breach German defences. There had
been an earlier rehearsal — at which the paratroopers landed too far
away, giving L-M a mistrust of using them in future. Harris was
reluctant to supply the bombers which were asked for. The Navy would
not provide adequate ships. On the night before the actual raid,
Mountbatten, the overall commander, stayed at the Leigh-Mallory
house.

Dieppe, according to Broadhurst, was the only occasion when he
disagreed with L-M:

'Usually I was "Broady" but now I became "Broadhurst". I didn't
agree with the plans which were all Wings. On the morning itself I
borrowed a plane from Hornchurch and went off by myself to see
what was happening. You've got to be lucky in this world: I flew up
to a reasonable height; at 18,000 feet I saw half a dozen German
190s with bombs which were diving down on our ships and then
scuttling back to France. I turned round, landed and rang the
Group Controller and told him to detach a squadron, put it at
20,000 feet well above Dieppe. Of course the Germans walked into
it and were shot down. When I got back I was "Broady" again.'

During the Dieppe raid Fighter Command operated 50 Squadrons in
close cover and 6 in close support. They made 2399 sorties. Eighty-
seven aircraft were destroyed, another 43 probably destroyed, and 147
damaged. After the raid it was reported that 'Air cooperation was
faultless'. Losses were heavy — but proportionately they were not
heavier than those sustained over the previous few months in general
offensive operations.

L-M was disappointed that he never received one word of congratula-
tion for the air force's achievement at Dieppe — although they had done
everything they were asked to do. But there were excellent longer term
consequences of his achievement.

On 26 September Portal in his office mapped out the next changes in
air commands which he wanted to make. Tedder, now C-in-C Middle
East, would come back to London to be Vice-Chief of the Air Staff;

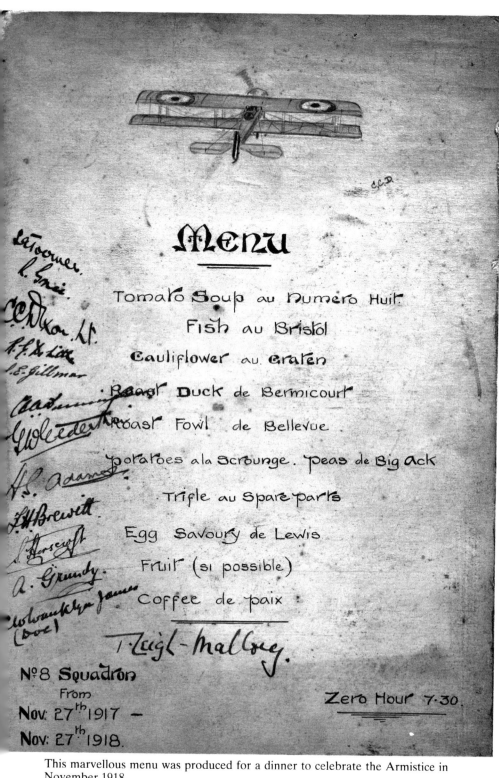

Menu

Tomato Soup au Numero Huit.

Fish au Bristol

Cauliflower au. Graten

Roast Duck de Bermicourt

Roast Fowl de Bellevue

Potatoes ala Scrounge. Peas de Big Ack

Trifle au Spare parts

Egg Savoury de Lewis

Fruit (si possible)

Coffee de paix

T. Leigh-Mallory.

Nº 8 Squadron

From

Nov. 27th 1917 —

Nov. 27th 1918.

Zero Hour 7.30.

This marvellous menu was produced for a dinner to celebrate the Armistice in November 1918.

L-M (*centre, front row*) on the continent after the end of World War I with representatives of other nationalities and services. (*RAF Museum, Hendon*)

Three generations photographed at Worthing in 1923. L-M with his father, Canon Herbert Leigh-Mallory, and son Tom.

Doris, Jacqueline, Tom and Trafford sailing in the Solent in 1938.
(*RAF Museum, Hendon*)

The Leigh-Mallorys with their great friends Evelyn and Philip Dodgson.

Shortly before the outbreak of war in 1939 L-M was given command of Number 12 Fighter Group. The AOC of Number 11 Group was Keith Park (*above*) with whom L-M was to have a long running disagreement about tactics. (*Chaz Bowyer*)

The legendary Douglas Bader who commanded 242 Squadron under L-M in the Battle of Britain. (*Chaz Bowyer*)

Air Chief Marshal Sir Hugh (later Lord) Dowding; AOC-in-C, RAF Fighter Command during 1939–40. (*Chaz Bowyer*)

Sholto Douglas with HRH The Duchess of Gloucester (WAAF Commandant), shortly after his appointment as C-in-C, RAF Fighter Command. (*Chaz Bowyer*)

In April 1942 King George VI visited stations of RAF Fighter Command and he is seen here with L-M who was now Air Marshal Sir Trafford Leigh-Mallory, C-in-C Fighter Command. (*RAF Museum, Hendon*)

Leigh-Mallory with General De Gaulle when he visited Fighter Command in March 1942. (*RAF Museum, Hendon*))

This illustration appeared in *Illustrated Magazine* in December 1942. It shows L-M discussing forthcoming operations with three members of his staff. They are Group Captain Pike, the Senior Administrative Officer (*left*), Group Captain H. Broadhurst, the Deputy Senior Air Staff Officer, and Air Commodore G. Harcourt Smith, Senior Air Staff Officer.

Sholto Douglas would leave Fighter Command and take over from Tedder; Leigh-Mallory would take over as C-in-C of Fighter Command on 15 November — or, if Douglas refused to move, L-M would take over in the Middle East. Portal's plans worked out and L-M was appointed as Air Officer Commanding-in-Chief of Fighter Command with effect from 28 November 1942.

Douglas wrote to Portal on 12 October that he had discussed L-M's successor at Eleven Group with him. L-M preferred Saundby to Saunders for 11 Group, and preferred Basil Embry to Pike for Night Operations at Fighter Command headquarters. On the 20th Portal wrote to Douglas:

'L-M has still not told me whether he has any objection to Saunders as his successor. We still think here that this would be the best choice and if you can help to persuade Leigh-Mallory to accept him I shall be very much obliged. I am sure he will not regret it.'

L-M moved to Fighter Command Headquarters at Bentley Priory in November. It was in a Georgian mansion with a historical tradition. Sir Walter Scott was supposed to have written a part of *Marmion* in the summerhouse beside the lake below the house. During the war camouflage was placed over its white stucco front and clocktower.

On 1 December L-M received his promotion to the rank of Air Marshal (Temporary) — and went to see the King at Buckingham Palace on 16 December.

Illustrated magazine made L-M the subject of a two-page feature in their edition of 5 December. It described him as:

'calm and unhurried in manner, he is nevertheless possessed of an incredible amount of energy and endurance. Those who work with him know that if he is at his desk till two in the morning (which often happens) he may well be back by 7 am. He drives himself harder than any of his men. His days off last year can be counted on the fingers of one hand, and his idea of a day's "rest" is several strenuous sets of lawn tennis followed by a round of golf on a hilly course.'

On appointment to Fighter Command, L-M set out to visit all his air stations. He was accompanied by his Personal Assistant, Flight Lieutenant Michael. They were driven in a Buick car by his chauffeur, Sergeant Cockings. Cockings appreciated L-M's consideration for him. He told the author that on one occasion, after seven days continually on the road, they made one particular stop for petrol at Tangmere, near Chichester. Seeing how tired Cockings was, L-M said that he would drive. Michael sat in front and L-M told him to give Cockings a cigarette and to let him lie down in the back. But L-M was tired too. He took the car over a bridge at seventy miles per hour and they all hit the car's roof. When, after that, L-M took the wrong way round a roundabout, he stopped the car and said: 'You had better drive, Cockings.'

'So I got no sleep,' commented Cockings, 'but he was a very considerate man.'

Cockings said that not all commanders behaved so well. 'Sir Sholto Douglas was a very hard taskmaster.' On one occasion he had driven Douglas to stay at L-M's house at Twelve Group. There were no signposts and Cockings took a wrong turning. Douglas reprimanded him and added 'No excuses'.

'Douglas was always behind you pushing whereas Leigh-Mallory was never in a rush.'

Chapter 10
Fighter Command
and the AEAF

It was not long before L-M set about making changes to Fighter Command. The tone was set by his statement on 19 December:

> '. . . it appears unlikely that the enemy would deliver large-scale night attacks on this country for some time to come. Owing to the acute shortage of manpower and the need for men in other branches of the services as well as in the factories, a low limit could safely be fixed on which night time defences would operate.'

L-M was awarded a knighthood in the New Year Honours for January 1943. He had again been mentioned in Despatches, and became a Knight Commander of the Order of the Bath.

His workload continued intensively and the range of his responsibilities was very wide. Planning for the invasion of Europe was the number one priority in L-M's forward thinking. The place and date had not yet been decided, but it was characteristic of L-M that he began, early in 1943, to train some of his Spitfire squadrons to operate from aircraft carriers. There were sessions at Fighter Command Headquarters with the Planning Staff of Norfolk House.

On 6 February L-M attended a meeting to discuss lessons learned from an exercise codenamed 'Cuckoo II'. The minutes end with his comment that 'Few RAF officers know how an exercise should be run and umpired. Need for training in exercise duties.' On the 17th L-M met the American General Anderson. On 18 and 19 February L-M chaired conferences at his Bentley Priory headquarters to discuss coordination of organisation of Groups and Air Forces in a move to the continent. L-M subsequently wrote to Portal suggesting the formation of a Composite Group which would work as a mobile organisation as air operations moved onto the continent.

The offensive operations were still progressing, but the bomber force had grown from the six Blenheims of 1941 to upwards of 500 B17s of the USAAF. But L-M was frustrated because the short range of his Spitfires prohibited him from escorting the Americans all the way. Increasingly the role of Fighter Command was to escort the B17s on their outward journey, only to leave them in their hour of greatest need — then, having refuelled, to rendezvous with the battle-weary force some hours later, to protect them from the few fighters still harrying them. So the pressure was on to re-equip some of the Spitfire squadrons with the Mustang III, which would have the range to escort the B17s wherever they went.

On 25 February he awarded special silver medallions to sixty American pilots which were given to commemorate the work of the Eagle squadrons in the early days of the war. He said that the Luftwaffe had lost a hundred and seventy aircraft in the intense fighting over Dieppe in August 1942. Previously it had been said that ninety-one German aircraft had been brought down and twice that number probably damaged or destroyed.

There were few moments of light relief. One, during February, was when an all-star cast put on a revue to entertain personnel of Fighter Command: after the show, a photograph appeared in *The Tatler* of L-M standing beside Lilli Palmer.

On 15 March at his commanders' conference L-M suggested that:

> 'in order to demonstrate to the public that we are keen to take our share in contributing to our own service, we should hold a Wings For Victory week in Fighter Command.'

On 23 March, however, the usual commanders' conference was not held — because L-M was absent. On 27 March, he had set off on a nine-day tour of nine air and army headquarters in North-West Africa. His instructions were

> 'to study and to report on the workings there with a view to applying them to north-west Europe, and to examine the detailed organisation and methods of tactical control which apply to forming a composite allied group.'

He was accompanied by Victor Groom. They travelled first to the Allied Force Headquarters at Algiers where the commander was Tedder. From there they moved to General Spaatz's Headquarters for North-West Africa at Constantine. He also met Coningham at HQ North-West Africa Tactical Air Force (TAF) and Montgomery at HQ Eighth Army.

Of Montgomery, L-M reported afterwards that 'the Army Commander 8th Army is strongly opposed to having an RAF organisation permanently at Corps HQ.'

At Souk El Khemis he met up with Kenneth Cross who had worked for him at 12 Group. They sat up till 3 am in his caravan arguing about how to conduct tactical operations in conjunction with the army. L-M envisaged joint decisions. But he was persuaded that because the Army always moved slower it ought to say what it required and the RAF then could say what it could do to help.

After the tour L-M recounted what he said was one of the more embarrassing moments of his life. The lavatories at the Algiers headquarters were situated in an Arab school and there were no doors. As he sat answering the call of nature, an American sentry marched back and forth — and saluted each time he passed L-M!

L-M's conclusions were written up in a clear report dated 12 April. His major conclusion was that 'All air forces must be centralised under one Commander-in-Chief. The headquarters of British and American staffs must be amalgamated'. From experience L-M could already foresee potential trouble, in getting the Americans to fully integrate their forces with the British under a single command. He followed up his report with a letter to Portal on 15 April, proposing the formation of the Expeditionary Air Force with headquarters within Fighter Command.

Special messages of thanks and congratulations were published on 3 April in the British newspapers for every factory which was making aircraft engines and accessories. These messages had been jointly sent by the Commanders-in-Chief of all the operational commands of the Royal Air Force (Harris of Bomber Command, Leigh-Mallory of Fighter Command, and Slessor of Coastal Command).

In November 1942 L-M had offered his best Intruder squadron to be loaned to the Middle East. On 6 April Portal wrote to L-M that 'since then it has done magnificent work in Malta'. There was 'little likelihood of large numbers of enemy against the United Kingdom' and therefore it would be 'wrong to bring it home'. On the 8th L-M replied that he thoroughly agreed with the decision, adding

'I always feel confident that if the War comes my way and I ever do get a real battle, that you will give me all the tools in your power to work with.'

On 27 April, he spoke at the inauguration of the 'Wings For Victory week' at Orpington. Speaking at the lunch afterwards, he said that there had been gradual steady improvements in the defence of the country since the Battle of Britain. The Germans would be much less successful than in 1940 if they launched another large-scale attack on Britain.

On 15 May he starred in a piece of mis-information aimed at the Germans. The front cover of *Illustrated* magazine had the caption 'Fighter Chief's New Front?' L-M was shown studying a large wall map of the continent with his finger pointing to the western end of the Kiel Canal, clearly (to us now) intended to deceive the enemy. Perhaps training those Spitfire squadrons in carrier operations was part of the same deception plan!

On 24 May he spoke at another 'Wings For Victory week' this time at Windsor. He told his audience that the previous week had been particularly successful for the Royal Air Force against the U-Boats, and that signs were not lacking that the morale of the German people was being gradually worn down by the bombing.

Meanwhile, deep thought was continuing about how and when and where to effect the invasion of continental Europe. A memorandum dated 25 May stated that:

'by process of elimination, the assault landings must be effected somewhere between the Cotentin Peninsula and Dieppe. The decision to invade Europe in 1944 will imply at once the abandonment of long-term policies of attrition in favour of the shorter term policy of direct assault.'

During May and June L-M several times discussed the responsibilities and organisation of AEAF staff at Norfolk House with Air Vice-

Marshal Pirie of the Air Ministry. On 31 May L-M wrote to Portal saying that Montgomery 'gave us a first class talk here last Friday'. It was agreed that the existing Fighter Command organisation would be used as the foundation for building up the proposed cross-channel organisation. Details were finally agreed on 11 June between Pirie and L-M at a lunch together in London.

L-M took on his new — extra — responsibility and immediately announced on a strict need-to-know basis that the RAF and USAAF planning teams would be consolidated together. Their task was to prepare a plan which would give freedom of the air between Cherbourg and Dieppe.

On 21 June the Chiefs of Staff recommended that:

'the Joint Staff Mission in Washington should take soundings to discover whether the US Chiefs of Staff would be prepared to enter-tain a proposal that Air Marshal Leigh-Mallory should be appointed Commander-in-Chief AEAF. No such office has been nominated, although his appointment was approved in principle at Casablanca.'

The reader should appreciate, at this point, that the establishment of the post of C-in-C AEAF was very controversial. Its establishment was not wanted by Tedder, not wanted by Harris, not wanted by Spaatz and not wanted by Coningham. Indeed, it must have been the most unwanted post of all time. But the fact that it was so unwanted was the very justification for its being. All the 'not wanters' wanted to go on doing their own thing, in their own way, in their own time. It was vital that all their efforts be pulled together. Whoever was going to do it had to have a knowledge of both fighter and bomber operations, an understanding of ground force requirements and, above all, a firm belief that the invasion was the decisive battle, which must take precedence over interservice and international rivalries. Trafford was probably the only man at his level who fitted the profile. It was obvious that whoever did the job would get very little credit — that would go to the individual Air Force Commanders — but he would be in the hot seat if things went wrong. He would start with few friends and would need to be a good listener, a good advocate, cunning on occasions, and decisive, firm, and resolute. Such a man was L-M.

On 26 June L-M made a speech in Birmingham. He warned the public against complacency. Although things were going very well, the Germans were a tough people and were magnificent fighters.

'For God's sake do not let us get complacent. Do not let us make the mistake of letting up just when we see victory in sight. I regard the final defeat of the Luftwaffe as the prerequisite for victory.'

The same day *The Times* published a photograph of L-M with the King and Portal.

On the 28th, L-M wrote to Portal to say that he would 'be away for three days — Monday, Tuesday and Wednesday — up at Largs, attending a Combined Operations Course with Dickie Mountbatten and an imposing array of Generals and Air Marshals.'

Early in July L-M was formally nominated by the British Chiefs of Staff to act as Senior Air Officer to establish an Allied Air Force command headquarters. This would plan the employment and activities of all Air Forces in the UK in support of Operation OVERLORD. Immediately he called a conference on 8 July at Norfolk House. L-M, in the chair, stated that it was most important that the whole organisation and the headquarters and their staffs should be set up at as early a date as possible.

The basic study for OVERLORD was assembled rapidly. It was completed on 15 July and was submitted to the Chiefs of Staff in London. It was forwarded to Washington and Quebec for approval by the Combined Chiefs of Staff.

Meanwhile work proceeded on a cover plan for OVERLORD — its purpose being to mislead the enemy and thus cause the Germans to disperse their forces or to concentrate them in the wrong place. In July the suggestion was of an assault on a number of large ports including Stavanger, Antwerp, Cherbourg, Brest and St Nazaire. By November the favoured deception was to induce the enemy to believe that the main assault would take place against the Pas de Calais area.

L-M held his third planning conference attended by Mountbatten on 27 July. On 10 August L-M chaired a meeting at Norfolk House which discussed the future policy of employing airborne forces: it was decided that it should be possible to launch an airborne operation at night in conditions of full moon and good visibility. Planning, training and aircraft provision would proceed urgently.

Another deception project, Operation STARKEY, was carried out on 15 August: it was a large-scale amphibious feint against the Pas de Calais with the object of drawing the German air force into battle. It worked successfully except that the Germans failed to enter into combat. However valuable experience was gained for the planning of Overlord.

L-M's intensive working schedule was interrupted, sadly, when his father Herbert died on 13 August at the age of eighty-seven. Trafford and Doris attended the funeral which took place at the old village church of Mobberley.

In August 1943 at the Quebec Conference L-M was appointed officially to be the Commander-in-Chief of the Allied Expeditionary Air Force. The Naval Commander was to be Admiral Sir Charles Little.

L-M's contacts with the Americans increased. On 6 September he was included at a dinner at Claridge's hotel in London in honour of General H. H. Arnold from the United States.

On 9 September the Joint Staff Mission at Washington wrote to the British Chiefs of Staff:

'Leigh-Mallory has stressed to us and again to the Combined Chiefs of Staff the importance attached to the issue to himself of some form of directive to enable him to get on with his necessary planning and preparations.'

This appeal produced results. On the 19th Portal sent a memorandum to the War Cabinet Chiefs of Staff Committee with the draft of a directive for L-M which he had submitted for approval to the Combined Chiefs of Staff.

The news of L-M's appointment became public. On 22 September, L-M's mother wrote to her elder daughter Mary to tell her the news:

'Now about Trafford. To be made C-in-C of "All Allied Air Forces for defence of Britain and Invasion of Europe"! The US not only to co-operate but work under him! And I see the Air Marshal USA has already got his appointment announced — when according to Trafford it was only fixed the day before yesterday. The announcement of HIS appointment I expect will appear tomorrow. It ought to!'

At the end of September, L-M established his provisional AEAF Headquarters at Bentley Priory. There was an underground operations room which had been developed into the most elaborate combat control communications room in the world. A two-storey battle room combination was constructed next to the old Fighter Command Battle Room: it consisted of a main conference room, maps, data boards, and an adjacent glassed-off room for liaison officers with direct telephone connections to other Army and Navy headquarters: below was a battle room with a large-scale horizontal map in the well and with a gallery around the wall for viewers to see the map below. This room was used until the assault phase of OVERLORD was completed.

In the main building at Bentley Priory there were offices for L-M, his American Deputy, the Senior Air Staff Officer (Air Vice-Marshal Wigglesworth) and the AOC Air Defence of Great Britain (ADGB) (Air Marshal Sir Roderic Hill). Other AEAF officers worked in adjacent buildings or huts.

On 30 September L-M took one of his rare leaves, for one week — leaving as his deputies Hill at Fighter Command and the American General Hansell at AEAF Norfolk House. Even though L-M was starting a new job, Portal was considering him for new options. Freeman wrote a private note to Portal on 2 October:

'I don't believe the choice of AMP (Air Member for Personnel) is so difficult. Obviously the best are:
(1) Tedder   (2) Leigh-Mallory
I can see the objections to either of them. They are mainly political or international. But there is not the same objection to Slessor and he could do the job v well and could be replaced by Sholto.'

Immediately on L-M's return from leave, there was a flurry of excitement when incoming German planes dropped, for the first time, strips of black metallised paper in order to try to confuse British radar:

this was a copy of an existing British technique which was codenamed 'Window'.

At the end of October L-M flew to Washington DC. He wrote to Portal on 1 November:

'My dear CAS

I arrived in Washington at lunch time on Sunday, and had my first conversation with General Morgan that afternoon. I thought you would like to have my general impressions for your personal information.

To start at the top, there seems to be a very considerable distrust of the Prime Minister over here, arising out of the feeling that, while he has agreed to the European plan which is represented by "OVERLORD", he is, in fact, making no serious effort to implement that undertaking. I understand that the President and General Marshall feel this very strongly. In fact, General Marshall feels so strongly on the subject that if he does not get a firm undertaking that we are going to throw the maximum possible resources into "OVERLORD" he (General Marshall) will go to the Pacific, and the American forces will go with him.

With regard to the air side of the present discussions, the main stumbling block appears to be the direction of the strategical bombers. I think that General Marshall is afraid that the present Directive will not result in the implementation of the bombing necessary for the fulfillment of the "OVERLORD" plan to start and end when required and to be directed against the right targets. I am sure that he will not agree to the Directive in its present form. It is difficult to say at this juncture how soon it will be necessary to start the bombing offensive in the furtherance of "OVERLORD" apart from the assistance which has been given to that project by "POINTBLANK". It has not been possible yet to carry out a detailed investigation of the kind of targets that will have to be attacked. It is possible that the time may come when some reconciliation between the requirements of "OVERLORD" and the fulfillment of "POINTBLANK" may arise. I am sure that General Marshall as Supreme Allied Commander will insist that he should be the one to decide when this is to begin.

General Marshall apparently objects to my being responsible direct to the British Chiefs of Staff for ADGB. He considers that I should be responsible to one individual alone, and that himself as Supreme Allied Commander. I have not yet had an opportunity of discussing this with him, but I gather he holds rather strong views on the subject and does not wish me to have divided loyalties. I will do my best to put our case to him for the defence of Great Britain being the primary responsibility of the British government, and therefore of the British Chiefs of Staff.

I gather that my Directive is inextricably linked with that of the Supreme Allied Commander and that a decision has to be made, so far as this side of the Atlantic is concerned, by next Friday, because after that General Marshall will be leaving the country for a period and, I understand, will not be coming direct to England.

We have only touched on the fringe of the airborne problem. I am meeting Arnold this morning and will supposedly hear the whole case then. Morgan has enlarged a certain amount on the American point of view, but I have not heard anything up to the present which goes beyond what we already know or which would alter our opinion in any way. However, I shall only offer my observations on the project when I have had plenty of time to study Arnold's proposals.

I understand that Marshall is not contemplating coming to England to take up his appointment as Supreme Allied Commander for some considerable time. In the meantime they are pressing for the appointment of the British Deputy. The runners are (1) Dill, (2) yourself, (3) Brooke. I know you won't play, and heaven forfend that Brooke should be appointed, so we can only pray for Dill. Incidentally, Dill is away this week, but will be back for the Combined Chiefs of Staff Conference on Friday, and I shall see him then.

I think this is all for today, but I will send you periodical news as it comes to hand.

Monday afternoon
I saw Arnold at 11.30 this morning, and parted from him at 2.30 pm. It is very difficult to set down on paper what Arnold said, because I was deluged with a welter of irrelevant statements most of which bore no relation to fact. He had the senior members of his staff in and delivered a tirade on European air operations, the main burden of which was the overwhelming air superiority of the Allies. He maintained that if the air situation was reversed in favour of the Germans we should have been kicked out of England and the Hun would be hammering at the eastern part of the United States. He could not understand how we had failed to blot the German Air Force out completely, and was determined to find some young man of brains and ability who would be able to accomplish the defeat of the GAF.

The only thing I can say for myself is that I managed to keep my temper and explained to General Arnold how air operations are carried out and how the German Air Force fights — or rather avoids fighting whenever our Fighter formations are about. Arnold was under the delusions that we had been carrying out no attacks against German airfields, in fact that we had made very little offensive effort of any kind. He produced the most fantastic figures for the Allied Air Forces, so I told him what we had and indicated that his figures for his own Air Force were hopelessly inaccurate.

I then went and had lunch with Arnold. We were waited on by two negro servants before whom matters of the highest secrecy were freely discussed.

It is quite obvious that General Marshall and General Arnold are after the co-ordination of air operations between the Mediterranean and Northern European Commands, but they do not appear to have made up their minds as to how this should be brought about. They do not trust the slow machinery of the Combined Chiefs of Staff to effect this co-ordination when active operations are in progress in both theatres. I agree with the principle that the operations must be co-ordinated, because both Air Forces are in a position to attack the same target. Moreover, it may be necessary to co-ordinate the attack of targets in the South of Germany with operations taking place further north. I think the Americans realise that to conduct both wars simultaneously would be a very difficult task for one Commander. Perhaps some quicker machinery of co-ordination between the two major Commands could be found. Ideas on this subject are so fluid that I find it difficult to give you any clear indication of the American point of view, but Arnold has made no firm proposal that the Supreme Allied Commander should command the whole of Europe.

General Arnold also delivered a tirade against the short range of the Spitfire, and seemed to think that we had lacked vision in the design of our Fighters and were not alive to the developments of the war. I did my best to overcome this prejudiced outlook.

Yours ever, Trafford Leigh-Mallory.'

On 4 November the US Joint Planners caused a serious problem. They proposed that there should be two Air C-in-Cs under the Supreme Commander, one to command the Tactical Air Force and the other the Strategical Air Force. L-M objected, having always stressed the need for a single command. He asked to see General Marshall personally and saw him for an hour on 5 November, writing afterwards:

'Marshall considered that his Air C-in-C should control all air forces participating in the land battle including such part of the strategical bomber force as should be allocated for that purpose. So adamant was Marshall on this point that I consider he will make the control of Strategical Bombers a primary condition of his acceptance of the appointment as Supreme Allied Commander.'

This was not far from L-M's own view, and the matter was resolved in his favour. He received the formal directive to become Air Commander-in-Chief AEAF in a letter dated 16 November:

'You have been designated by the Combined Chiefs of Staff as "Air Commander-in-Chief, Allied Expeditionary Air Force" to exercise operational command over the British and American Tactical Air Forces, supporting the invasion of North-West Europe from the United Kingdom.'

Portal wrote him a personal note:

'Dear Trafford . . . you have a dual function, namely AOC-in-C of Fighter Command and AOC-in-C designate for "Round Up". . . yours ever, Charles.'

This gave L-M command of the British TAF and operational command of the Ninth US Air Force followed on 15 December*. The name of Fighter Command was changed to 'Air Defence of Great Britain' but responsibility for it remained with L-M. To weld together the British and American teams was not at all easy. The British were more experienced, having been in the war for two years longer, and were on average one rank higher than the Americans: but when D-Day arrived the equipment had come nearly twice as much from the Americans as from the British. Approval of the OVERLORD plan by the Combined Chiefs of Staff came in early December with instructions to proceed with the detailed planning.

On 8 December there was a conference at Headquarters Fighter Command to discuss offensive operations by the AEAF Tactical Bomber Forces. L-M said:

'the study of tactical bomber operations carried out during the past few months showed that attacks on airfields appeared to have done the enemy little harm. There was little advantage to be gained by attacking his airfields at this stage: it would require an intensive effort at a later stage to neutralise them shortly before D-Day. Meanwhile industrial operations would be attacked with the strongest possible force compelling the enemy's fighter defences to react in force, thus offering an opportunity to destroy them.'

On 15 December, L-M was promoted to Air Chief Marshal. The announcement was made from 10 Downing Street on 29 December 'as a result of conversations between Roosevelt and Churchill'.

On 24 December Eisenhower was designated as Supreme Allied Commander against the original expectation that it would be Marshall. On the 29th L-M was confirmed as Allied Air C-in-C, Admiral Sir Bertram Ramsay was to be the Allied Naval C-in-C, with Montgomery to command the Allied armies. Spaatz was appointed to command the US Strategic Air Forces. However seeds of conflict were sown when a Deputy Supreme Commander was announced to serve under Eisenhower: it was to be Tedder, an airman, who would have no line authority but would be senior to L-M.

L-M had three successive American Major Generals as his Deputy C-in-C of AEAF — first W. O. Butler, then H. S. Vandenberg, and finally R. Royce. To work with Americans was a difficult challenge: for L-M the AEAF was an Allied command, but to the Americans Europe was a theatre of war although none of them had any direct war experience. During the following year the difference would be continually felt.

---

* The forces amounted to 148 RAF Squadrons and 165 USAAF Squadrons.

Nevertheless, relationships worked themselves out. Bedell-Smith, who worked with Eisenhower in SHAEF said after the war, in an interview*:

'L-M was difficult at first but we found him after a time to be extremely able and honest and loyal. He stood for what he wanted. Had the interest of the RAF very much at heart. After he got to working with us, we couldn't have asked for more. He was just fine.'

Beneath L-M was Coningham, who was nominally under L-M but was personally loyal to Tedder. The Army disliked Coningham intensely ever since, after Alamein in 1942, he had given a press conference at which he had down-rated Montgomery and the Eighth Army. Consequently Montgomery was unwilling to work with Coningham and dealt with L-M through Broadhurst. Montgomery wrote in his 'Memoirs':

'I had two Air Force opposite numbers: Leigh-Mallory, who was Air C-in-C, and Coningham in command of 2nd Tactical Air Force . . .'

This was not what happened in practice. Montgomery preferred to disregard the formal line of communication which had been laid down and dealt direct with L-M.

There was dissension within the air command too. L-M with his army cooperation background firmly believed that the best way the Air Forces could contribute to victory was to support the army — whereas Harris, backed by Tedder and the Americans, preferred the idea of trying to finish the war by bombing Germany.

Work on detailed planning of the overall Joint Plan began immediately: it included teams from Eisenhower and Montgomery's headquarters. The first meeting of the joint Planning team took place on 20 December at Bentley Priory and was chaired by L-M. A wide variety of topics was discussed, including the need to speed up the takeoffs of bombers and the need for joint exercises between the British and American Air Forces.

On 21 December, L-M visited the air portion of the Overlord Joint Planning Team which was located at St Paul's School in London. He visited each of the joint syndicates: these were planning air force requirements, the availability and flow of new equipment from the USA, the preparatory phase, the softening of German resistance, and the assault phase.

---

* *Decision in Normandy* by Carlo d'Este, p.127.

Chapter 11
Build-up to D-Day

L-M received his promotion to the rank of Air Chief Marshal on 1 January 1944. On 20 January he went to Buckingham Palace for an audience with the King.

The pressure of work continued, but even so L-M found time to write to Portal on 3 January: 'I feel impelled to write officially to the Air Ministry to suggest that a Flying Branch of the WAAF should be formed' — and stating his reasons.

There was a meeting of the Commanders-in-Chief Conference at St Paul's School in London. L-M was present and listened to Montgomery outlining his revised plans. From that day forward L-M kept in close touch with the senior planners at St Paul's School. Two days later L-M was at the HQ of 21 Army Group to hear the Army Commanders' plans.

On Monday 17 January General Eisenhower arrived in London to take up his role as Supreme Commander of the AEAF. His formal instructions were:

'You are hereby designated as Supreme Allied Commander for the liberation of Europe from Germany. You will enter the continent of Europe and undertake operations aimed at the heart of Germany and the destruction of her armed forces. The date for entering the continent is the month of May 1944.'

On the Friday afternoon, Eisenhower called a conference of his immediate commanders at Norfolk House: it was attended by Tedder (Deputy Supreme Commander), Ramsay (for the Naval Forces), Montgomery (for the Land Forces), L-M (for the Air Forces) and two American Generals, Spaatz and Bradley. The subject of the conference was an exposition of the original plan for OVERLORD.

The minutes record that Montgomery started by commenting that he did not consider that OVERLORD was a sound operation of war. He said that he had throughout been considering how he wanted to fight the land battle, and it remained to be seen whether the Navy and the Air Force would be able to meet his requirements. He said that from the point of view of the Army, it was desirable to have the maximum number of months of good campaigning weather. Therefore the operation should if possible begin early in May.

Following this conference, Eisenhower wrote to L-M on 23 January. The target date for the invasion would be 1 May. 'This operation marks the crisis of the European war. We cannot afford to fail.' In this light he had reviewed the plan for OVERLORD with his commanders-in-chief 'and we are fully convinced that it is on a narrow margin'.

Next day L-M met the Air Officers Commanding his Composite groups with his SASO, Air Vice-Marshal H. E. P. Wigglesworth. L-M started holding regular meetings of his own commanders on Wednesdays starting from 26 January. The minutes were taken by his personal assistant, Lady Freeman, the wife of the distinguished airman Sir Wilfrid Freeman.

L-M set up the AEAF Bombing Committee under the chairmanship of Air Commodore E. J. Kingston-McCloughry, which was joined by an able young scientist, Professor Zuckerman. This group's role was to prepare plans for the bombing of airfields, rail connections, and other targets.

L-M received a letter from Lieutenant General Morgan, who was Chief of Staff to Eisenhower. The letter expressed the American's doubts as to the effect that bombing would be likely to have on the ordinary population in France. L-M gave this very careful thought and replied on the 31st to Eisenhower as follows:

'I fully appreciate the seriousness of the effect on public opinion among the French, Belgian, and possibly Dutch civil populations that might be caused by the results of our air attacks preparatory to and during Operation "OVERLORD". Nevertheless, we are committed to an operation of war, and I think you will agree that the margin by which we shall succeed will not be such that we can contemplate foregoing the use of one of our most potent weapons.

Among the targets in France and Belgium which will have to be attacked during the preparatory phase will be railway centres, airfields and maintenance installations, and, at a later stage, enemy reserves in the concentration areas. Most of these targets lie close to or in towns and villages.

I can see no alternative but for you to inform the Combined Chiefs of Staff that the Civil population must be warned that in preparing for and carrying out the invasion we shall be compelled to attack military targets to a considerable depth from the coast, and that some of these targets will undoubtedly lie close to, if not in, villages, towns or cities.

Since we cannot give any precise indication of when and where these attacks will fall, casualties among the civilian inhabitants will be inevitable. Although this will be unfortunate, these casualties will have to be regarded as the contribution of these peoples towards the sacrifices that the Allied nations are making on their behalf.'

A telegram came from Washington DC on 31 January strongly pressing that the invasion date should be later. But the Initial Joint Plan was issued on 1 February and all efforts were directed into detailed planning.

L-M gave instructions that no individuals with a detailed knowledge of the planning of OVERLORD were to fly over enemy occupied territory. Detailed attention was given to the whole range of planning topics including replacement of aircraft, evacuation of casualties, censorship, intelligence, radio counter measures, operating instructions, meteorological services, bomb and shell disposal.

On the 16th February L-M told his team of a 'most interesting report' which he had been studying about the TARAWA operation. This had stressed the need for concentration of air support for invading forces at the final stage just before getting ashore. For the last eight hundred yards or so it was impossible for the Navy to cover the troops with supporting fire, and it was of vital importance for the Air Force to fulfil this role.

Meanwhile, Tedder had become unhappy with his job. He had been appointed Deputy Supreme Commander in order that both the British and Americans should have a joint role in the Supreme Command. But Tedder was not satisfied. He had no direct responsibilities. He was an airman and felt that he should have L-M's responsibilities. Whether some old jealousy of L-M lurked in his mind from their university days where he had been one year older and senior is now impossible to say. But he complained about his role compared to L-M's to Eisenhower.

On 29 February Churchill sent a formal Minute (M.194/4) to Portal:

'1. I understand that General Eisenhower is, as foreseen in my Minute of January 9, dissatisfied with the arrangements for the Air Command in OVERLORD. As its structure is certainly awkward-looking, and, as no plan for the support of OVER-LORD has yet been agreed upon by the various Air authorities, I set down below what I have in mind throughout:

2. General Eisenhower, a military man, is the Supreme Commander of all the OVERLORD forces. Air Chief Marshal Tedder is the aviation lobe of his brain. The directive for ACM Tedder should be: "to use all Air forces permanently or temporarily assigned to OVERLORD in the manner which will best fulfil the plan of the Supreme Commander." Tedder, in his own right and as the Deputy of the Supreme Commander, is the authority responsible for making the Air plan to the satisfaction of General Eisenhower. For the purpose he should have a "handling Staff" suited to his requirements and, further, he should have all the services of the Royal Air Force Headquarters Staff under ACM Leigh-Mallory. In practice, ACM Leigh-Mallory will execute such orders as he receives from ACM Tedder in the name of the Supreme Commander, whether, as regards preparing plans or carrying them out.

3. ACM Tedder, as Deputy of the Supreme Commander, should also be empowered to issue orders to General Spaatz, ACM Harris and ACM Sholto Douglas (Coastal Command) in respect of any employment of their forces for OVER-LORD which has been sanctioned by the Combined Chiefs of Staff.

4. As soon as ACM Tedder's Air plan has been framed and approved by General Eisenhower, it will be submitted to the Combined Chiefs of Staff who will do their best to meet its requirements and will specify what Air forces shall be at the disposal of the Supreme Commander and for what periods.

5. So far as the Royal Air Force is concerned, the British Chiefs of Staff will make their recommendations on the Air plan to the combined COS committee. There can be no question of handing over the British Bomber, Fighter or Coastal Commands as a whole to the Supreme Commander and his Deputy. These Commands have other functions which they discharge under the directions of the CAS. For instance, the Coastal Command must provide for the defence of this island against enemy Air attack; and Bomber Command must bomb Germany, and may have other missions. Agreeably with the plan of the Supreme Commander, we shall assign to OVERLORD such use of these Commands, as we may think fit after consultation and in agreement with the United States Chiefs of Staff. The Combined Chiefs of Staff retain the right to vary the assignments should overriding circumstances render it necessary.

6. However the OVERLORD battle must be the chief care of all concerned, and great risks must be run in every other sphere and theatre in order that nothing should be withheld which could contribute to its success.

When the Air plan has been made by the Supreme Commander and his Deputy, the utmost endeavour will naturally be made by the British and United States Chiefs of Staff jointly and severally, to comply with all requests and meet all needs so far as the general conduct of the War renders this possible.

February 29, 1944

WSC.'

Thus L-M's original plans and responsibilities were undermined. But, characteristically, L-M stuck to his job.

On 4 March he discussed with Eisenhower the bringing in completely of the American Ninth Air Force into OVERLORD. The next day he wrote to Tedder referring to his discussion yesterday with 'The Ike'.

Freeman sent a handwritten note to Portal on 7 March:

'My dear Peter,

If I can help in any way with Tedder and Leigh-Mallory I hope you will let me know.

I can speak as an ex-VCAS who once knew something of your difficulties and perhaps make them understand that theirs is not the only point of view.

Yours Wilfrid.'

L-M wrote to Spaatz on 10 March that Eisenhower had decided that the time had come for the US Ninth Air Force to be directed towards

OVERLORD. L-M added 'hoping to see you next Wednesday at Bovingdon'.

Portal replied to Churchill's memorandum on 10 March:

'Prime Minister.

1. Since receiving your minute M.194/4 of 29th February, I have had several talks with Tedder and Leigh-Mallory and both these officers have been seen by General Eisenhower.

2. The OVERLORD strategic Air plan (Plan A) is now in the hands of Tedder as agent of General Eisenhower. Tedder is dealing with Spaatz and Harris over their parts in the Plan.

3. It is General Eisenhower's intention, with which I agree, that the actual co-ordination of operations in the execution of the above Plan when approved by himself and . . . by me . . . shall be in the hands of Tedder with, of course, such reference to General Eisenhower himself as he may desire.

4. The Tactical Air Plan for the assault period (Plan B) for the use of all the air forces assigned to OVERLORD, including strategic bombers, coastal aircraft and the Fleet Air Arm contingent, will be prepared and co-ordinated in execution by Leigh-Mallory under the supervision of Tedder.'

Churchill returned a copy of Portal's note to him annotated with the words: 'I think this is very satisfactory. WSC. 11.3.44.'

On 10 March Eisenhower issued a directive at his C-in-C's meeting to L-M, Ramsay and Montgomery. The target date for the landing was later.

'The object of operation OVERLORD is to secure a lodgement area on the continent from which further offensive operations can be developed. The target date is 31st May.'

On 13 March L-M met AOC Coastal Command to plan how they would fit into OVERLORD.

Churchill continued to take a close interest. He scribbled a handwritten note to Portal on the 14th:

'CAS

Let me see the plan made by ACM Tedder which you said AM Harris liked so much. How does the ACM Leigh-Mallory's railway plan stand now?

WSC.'

Portal replied on the same day:

'Prime Minister.

Although I understand that Tedder's plan is now complete, at least in outline, I have not yet seen it and I am asking him to let me have it as soon as he can. I will certainly then let you see it. What I told you about Air Chief Marshal Harris liking the plan was simply based on what Tedder and Harris told me.

2. Air Chief Marshal Leigh-Mallory's railway plan is part of the main Tedder plan. This railway plan has been completed but there is still considerable controversy about the basis on which it is

compiled and on the results that might be expected from adopting it. Detailed investigations are now being made and I hope shortly to have a meeting with Tedder, Leigh-Mallory, Spaatz, Harris and the M.E.W. experts to try to reach decisions about it. I will let you know in due course what conclusions we come to.'

Churchill replied:

'Chief of the Air Staff.

You disturbed me rather about Leigh-Mallory's railway plan. I understood that Tedder did not approve of it. However I see that a lot of action is going on in this direction, and I should like to be further informed.'

Portal replied the next day that he was trying to keep an open mind until he had held his meeting, and would of course keep him informed of further progress.

On 29 March Professor Zuckerman wrote to his boss, L-M, to challenge the Air Ministry who had said that the German and French railway systems were not at present seriously affected by the bombing campaign.

On 3 April L-M heard that Supreme Headquarters had accepted his concurrent Air Defence Plans for operations OVERLORD and DIVER and had recommended its approval by the Chiefs of Staff Committee.

Next day he received a memo from Group Captain J. E. McComb, to the effect that the new system of reporting operations had come into effect. Operation Records and Intelligence had moved into the Battle Room on a twenty-four hour basis.

There was a major top-level conference at St Paul's School on 7 April 1944. It was given the name 'Exercise THUNDERCLAP'. Churchill and the King were present at the end of the day for the summing up.

On 15 April L-M attended a meeting at SHAEF concerning air operations in support of OVERLORD, at which the overall plan was issued — under the title 'Operation "NEPTUNE-AEAF" Overall Plan'. It allowed L-M to delegate to Coningham 'operational control of the planning and operations of both the British and American tactical air forces'. This did not work out particularly well, because Montgomery refused in his mind to accept Coningham as an equal — and continued to deal with L-M on heavy bomber support and with AVM Broadhurst on tactical air matters.

Later in April, L-M conducted Eisenhower on a tour round the AEAF airfields.

On 3 May he took part in a meeting at SHAEF about bombing policy which was chaired by Tedder. Next day the meeting was in his own office to allocate pre D-Day bombing targets — including CROSSBOW, railway centres, coastal batteries, airfields, naval targets, radar, enemy headquarters, and fuel dumps.

Bombing targets prior to D-Day became a most important area of study. L-M's conferences allocated bombing targets between Bomber Command and the Ninth Air Force.

During the first half of May Bomber Command devoted 84 per cent of its sorties to OVERLORD targets, the Eighth US Air Force 52.7 per cent, the Second Tactical Air Force (commanded by Coningham) 86.8 per cent, the US Ninth Air Force (commanded by Brereton) 91.6 per cent, and even the Air Defence of Great Britain forces contributed 41.2 per cent of their effort to attacking OVERLORD targets.

But inter-service coordination was not yet perfected. On 8 May SHAEF received a protest that the C-in-C Portsmouth· had, without reference to Air Ministry or to AEAF, authorised all ships not to hesitate to open fire by day or night at aircraft flying below three thousand feet! Asked to comment L-M replied:

'There have been numerous incidents when friendly aircraft have been engaged and destroyed by friendly anti-aircraft fire from ships. In a few cases blame rests partly with the pilots, but in the vast majority of cases, blame is attributed to faulty indentification by the ships' gunners.'

He wrote a strong letter to Admiral Ramsay on 22 June, which included the words:

'You will appreciate that feeling runs high not only in those squadrons which have lost pilots to naval action, but in the Service generally — a feeling which absence of apology from those responsible for firing has not helped to dissipate.'

On 12 May L-M issued a directive about Chemical Warfare, based on one from Eisenhower, that 'gas warfare will not be initiated by the Allied Forces and retaliatory measures will only be undertaken after reports of enemy use of Gas have been substantiated.' L-M's directive went on to say that no indications had been definitely received towards the opening of chemical warfare by German forces, but asked that secret substantiated reports of all incidents should be despatched forthwith to him for onward transmission to Eisenhower:

'Toxic chemicals will not be employed; and no toxic munitions will be taken overseas or into port areas except on specific orders from the Supreme Commander.'

However if the Germans did start using chemical weapons, stocks were ready.

'To meet the high initial effort which may be required at very short notice, sufficient blister and choking gas bombs to permit one re-arm will be held at each airfield.'

Reserve munitions would be held in special depots but would become immediately available in the event of chemical warfare started by the enemy.

A sequence of separate rehearsal exercises, known as 'Fabius', were planned — but became coordinated and turned into a dress rehearsal for OVERLORD.

On Saturday 13 May in L-M's office there was a meeting to decide the machinery for day-to-day operations. L-M was dissatisfied with the existing time lag, some twenty-four hours, which damage reports were taking to reach him. They must reach him the same evening to enable him to arrange the next day's programme. The delay was partly attributed to a shortage of photographic interpreters. Photographic Reconnaissance aircraft were normally over the target one hour after bomb strikes but the photos were not at present available until twenty-four hours later.

L-M also complained that the Battle Room at AEAF HQ was not yet fulfilling a sufficiently useful purpose. His experience was that it did not get quick or full information about planned bombing missions and their results. He was told that the shortcomings were due to the attitude of the American Second TAF who had their own battle room at Uxbridge and did not pass on information to his headquarters.

On Monday 15 May the whole plan for OVERLORD was explained by the force commanders in front of the King, the Prime Minister and General Smuts. L-M afterwards dictated the following account:

'Impressions of the Meeting held at St Paul's School on May 15th 1944 at 1000 hours.

The meeting was attended by all the high ranking officers under the general chairmanship of Eisenhower. Those of the first rank, including the King and the Prime Minister, were given armchairs on which to sit, the rest of the company sat on ordinary school forms, all facing a low stage on which a huge map of the area to be invaded had been spread out. The room was an ordinary lecture or school room partly panelled in pitch pine and an incongruous element was a notice upon the wall saying that the sons of clergymen, candidates for scholarships, should apply to the High Master. The Prime Minister was wearing a black short overcoat, looking something like a frockcoat, and smoking a cigar which he did not lay down when the King arrived. He bowed in his usual jerky fashion retaining the cigar in one hand. Churchill arrived with Smuts, the King a few minutes later.

When all were seated Eisenhower rose and made a little speech, moving in its simplicity.

"Here we are" he said "in effect on the eve of a great battle, to deliver to you the various plans made by the different Force Commanders. I would emphasise but one thing, that I consider it to be the duty of anyone who sees a flaw in the plan not to hesitate to say so. I have no sympathy with anyone, whatever his station, who will not brook criticism. We are here to get the best possible results and you must make a really co-operative effort." (These were not his actual words, but the gist of what he spoke.)

After Eisenhower had sat down the three Commanders address-ed the meeting in turn, beginning with Montgomery. Monty was wearing a very well cut battle-dress with a knife-like edge to the trouser creases. He looked trim and businesslike. He spoke for ten minutes in a tone of quiet emphasis making use of what is evidently a verbal trick of his, to repeat the most important word or phrase in a sentence more than once. Thus for example, he would say "It is intended to move towards Caen, towards Caen," etc. He was occasionally interrupted by the Prime Minister, who asked questions which seemed designed to show his knowledge of strategy and tactics. Monty's most striking observation was to the effect that the plan required a very robust mentality on the part of all called upon to execute it. At one point the Prime Minister intervened, saying a trifle wryly that at Anzio we had put ashore 160,000 men and 25,000 vehicles and had advanced only twelve miles. He thought, therefore, that to take a risk occasionally would certainly do no harm. Montgomery's demeanour was very quiet and deliberate. He was not at all showy and seemed cautious, for he made no attempt to minimise the difficulties of the task. One thing he made clear, and that was his opinion that he had the measure of Rommel. He could be described as confident, but certainly not complacent.

His place was taken by Admiral Ramsay, who was a considerable contrast. He exhibited a kind of cheerful pessimism, making it clear that he was more concerned to stress the difficulties and the dangers than to dwell on the easier side of the operation, which perhaps did not exist in his mind. He spoke dryly with great accuracy and showed a complete grasp of the situation. He also was given ten minutes.

Next came the turn of Leigh-Mallory. Unlike the others he was called upon to speak for forty minutes, and had been very nervous at the prospect, referring to it more than once in the days which preceded the meeting as "Operation Monarch". He went into great detail concerning the preliminary air operations, and those which would be conducted from D-Day onwards. He spoke confidently and made it clear that he was absolutely convinced that we had the measure of the Luftwaffe, and that if they tried conclusions with us it could only end in one way — their destruction. Leigh-Mallory appeared to radiate confidence, and two of Montgomery's staff officers were overheard later expressing the opinion that his speech was the best of the three. This, however, may well have been due to the fact that the superiority of the Allied Air Forces over the Germans is so evident that therefore Leigh-Mallory had the easiest task of the three. On the other hand, it should be made clear that his exposition of his plans left his hearers in no doubt not only of his intention, but also of his ability and determination to fulfil them.

Then came the turn of the subordinate commanders. First General Spaatz, who read his speech and was very nervous. He was followed by Sir Arthur Harris who spoke eloquently on the devastation caused by Bomber Command to Germany. Both seemed to be at pains to blow their own trumpets, or more accurately, the trumpets of their own Commands, and both showed invincible faith in the weapon of the bomber. They were followed by a General who described the difficulties of supply and the immense effort which had been made to overcome them. The impression he made was that of a main service strained to the utmost but at last able to meet almost any demand, reasonable or the reverse. The morning wound up with a speech from the King of a conventional kind, in which he said that with God's help this great operation would be brought to a successful conclusion.

This concluded the proceedings in the morning, and in the afternoon the Task Force Commanders were called upon to give their views. The most remarkable of them was Admiral Vian, who obviously did not mind what he said or did to anyone. He was the real sea-dog type, and his eyes glowed beneath strongly marked eyebrows. He made a great impression. General Quesada of the 9th Fighter Command raised the only laugh of the day, when after outlining the methods he proposed to use, he added dryly, "We will move like that throughout our progress over the continent of Europe."

Smuts then spoke, and seemed in a sombre mood and depressed by the size of the task. He did not speak for very long, and his delivery was halting as though he were thinking out loud. The Prime Minister gave a very characteristic speech ending in a passage of great eloquence. He obviously moved his hearers, some of whom were inclined to be critical of his habit of interfering with the operations they had planned.

The proceedings were wound up by General Eisenhower who said that the presence of Smuts was a good omen for he had been present on a similar occasion many months before, when the Allies had set out for Sicily. Eisenhower spoke quietly, but his peroration was very fine. After saying that in a few moments Hitler would have missed his last chance to wipe out all the leaders of the invasion by a well-placed bomb, he went on to urge that they should all regard themselves as members of the staff college of the future. It should be a college in which there was neither Navy, Army nor Air Force, British nor American, but only fighting men there to instruct and to be instructed in the art of war.'

There was no role in the conference for Tedder.

Next day, it was back to routine. L-M met Admiral Ramsay to agree protection by fighters for shipping in the assault area.

On Saturday 20 May, in L-M's office the role of the Planning Staff was discussed. L-M said that, starting from next Tuesday 23 May, he would be holding conferences every two or three days, and subsequently daily, to determine future operations. These would be attended by Spaatz, Harris, Tedder and others. At these conferences he wanted a complete picture of the current state of enemy dispositions, movements, attacks on bridges, roads, and so on. The planning staff would assist in the choosing of target priorities. Next meetings would be on Monday at

5 pm to determine the role of Eighth Fighter Command in OVERLORD; then at 9 pm in the Battle Room to prepare for the next day's commanders' conference.

Leisure time was almost non-existent. However, that afternoon he was able to take time off to attend his daughter Jacqueline's wedding at Stanmore. She married Lieutenant Tony Doherty of the USAAF. Spaatz and Doolittle were also invited. There was a photograph in the following day's *New York Times*.

In the build-up to D-Day, the AEAF had four major objectives — to obtain air superiority, to delay enemy reserves, to support the actual assault, and to reduce the enemy's beach defences. These objectives were achieved by long-range strategic bombing of German industrial targets, coastal batteries, radar installations, ammunition dumps, and the forty main airfields within a hundred and fifty miles of the assault area. Enemy reserves were diverted by a cover plan. Enemy communications were disrupted by bombing of rail tracks, bridges and centres. In addition there were approximately ten thousand aircraft to be kept serviceable and, after the assault, the construction of landing strips on the continent and the provision of sufficient troop carrier aircraft.

On Monday 22 May L-M met Eisenhower again. He asked for clearance for attacks on trains. Next day, L-M chaired the first conference of the Allied Air Commanders in his AEAF HQ at Norfolk House in St James' Square, London. It was attended by Tedder. There was a second conference on the Friday to discuss the detailed plan for D-Day. A third conference followed on the Monday.

L-M then wrote a formal letter to Eisenhower to put on record his fear of colossal losses in the American paratroop operation which would support the initial invasion. He wrote that he felt obliged to notify the Supreme Commander that he was very unhappy about the prospective American airborne operation. He feared that losses would be very heavy and that a large proportion of the force would be lost. Eisenhower replied that L-M was quite right in communicating his conviction as to the hazards but he insisted that the attack must go on.

Then on Wednesday 31 May, Eisenhower came to the Air Commanders conference at Norfolk House. Eisenhower said that for him military operations were always a matter of human beings and not of mathematical calculations, and that he would like it to be known by the men who were fighting the battle how much the commanders reckoned on what they had done and would do. In the preliminary stage of planning, a good motto was 'Doubts must come up; only enthusiasm must go down'. Now that the plan was completed, and the battle on, doubts in the minds of the commanders must not be allowed to reach those who were fighting the operation, and he instanced the airborne operation as one that had been much criticised. They must feel that the best plans had been laid and that the operation was worthwhile. He would like a message from Leigh-Mallory and one from himself to be passed to aircrew at their final briefing.

On 1 June L-M attended a lunch at the Waldorf Hotel in London for the 'Spitfire Mitchell Fund'. He then made a tour of units on the South Coast at Chailey, Selsey, Hurn and Tangmere, and spent the night at Chichester. Next morning at 10 am L-M attended Eisenhower's meeting at his headquarters at Southwick House, on the downs near Portsmouth; it was surrounded by a city of tents.

L-M described his bombing plans for D-Day and the following days. His intention was to establish a belt of bombed routes through towns and villages thereby preventing or impeding enemy movement. Tedder intervened to object saying that this would cause high civilian casualties as well as destruction of historic monuments — and saying that there was an undertaking to the Prime Minister to bomb nothing after D-Day except batteries and radar targets. L-M denied that there was any such undertaking, and insisted that once the battle was joined, strategic considerations must be paramount. At all costs they must prevent the Allied armies from being pushed back into the sea.

L-M then asked Eisenhower whether he had freedom to proceed with his bombing plan and Eisenhower gave his approval to L-M very emphatically 'as an operational necessity'.

Eisenhower also passed on a message from the Combined Chiefs of Staff that

'German attacks by flying bombs and possibly in the future by rockets at best impede and least may seriously interrupt British war effort. Please ensure that due weight is given to the elimination of this threat.'

After the meeting L-M went off to inspect headquarters ships and Fighter Direction tenders. He returned to his own headquarters at around 5 pm.

L-M chaired the final pre D-Day meeting of his Air Commanders on 3 June in his office at 11 am. They reviewed enemy strengths, movements, and set the following night's air targets. Tedder attempted unsuccessfully to reopen the question of the bombing plan. Spaatz, Doolittle and Harris stayed on for lunch with L-M at Bentley Priory.

At 3 pm Montgomery telephoned L-M to ask if there was any change in the bombing plan. L-M assured him that he was standing by the plan absolutely and would resign rather than abandon it. At 8.45 pm L-M left his office and flew to Portsmouth to confer with Eisenhower in view of poor weather forecasts for D-Day, which was still fixed for 5 June.

Next morning, 4 June, at 4.15 am Eisenhower held a second conference; the cloud cover was forecast to be '10/10' so he postponed the assault for twenty-four hours. L-M took off to visit more of his units and returned to his own headquarters at 2 pm. He flew back to Portsmouth to meet Eisenhower again at 9.30 pm. They met again at 4 am on the 5th — at which it was decided to launch the assault on the 6th, which would be 'D-Day'. At 10.30 am L-M returned to Stanmore; it was now D-Day Minus One, and they were committed . . .

At 4.30 pm on 5 June L-M gave an interview in his office to Air

Commodores Heald and Helmore. There is a description of the
scene:

'The Commander-in-Chief held a short conference at 1630 hours in
order to brief Air Commodore Helmore who was to fly over the
beaches during the initial assault and to describe what he saw for
the benefit of the British Broadcasting Corporation; Air Commodore
Lionel Heald in charge of air information for the Ministry of
Information, and Mr Hilary St George Saunders whose task it
would be to keep this diary. There was also present Wing
Commander King of the Air Historical Branch of the Air Ministry.

The conference took place in the office of the Commander-in-
Chief and his Headquarters in Bentley Priory, Stanmore. The
room was one of the principal drawing rooms of the Mansion
housing the Headquarters. A tall, spacious room, with long French
windows giving on to the grounds outside, reached from a balcony
by means of a flight of steps. The main article of furniture in the
room was a large desk facing a large-scale wall map of France and
Belgium. A long table, with a dozen chairs beside it, was set
between the windows for use at the C-in-C's conferences. Opposite
the windows was a large board showing the number of British and
American Squadrons available. Behind the C-in-C's desk, on the
mantelpiece, were a number of photographs of the Allied
Commanders, and one of General Sperrle commanding the
Luftwaffe. The carpet was of the standard Royal Air Force pattern
of pink and blue, as were most of the chairs. Outside, through the
tall French windows, the rhododendron bushes and trees of the
garden were in full bloom, and beyond them could be seen the
landing strip for the puddle jumpers, light aircraft used for short
journeys. It was a day of low cloud but no rain.'

L-M told his visitors:

'When plans for this operation were undertaken almost eighteen
months ago, our problem was to think out a method of using the
air forces in the best way to help the battle. The first way was by
destroying the German Air Force, and achieving air supremacy.
Air supremacy can only be won by day, by deep penetrations by
day such as the American air forces have undertaken, and so by
forcing the enemy to engage. German fighters no longer engage
over France and Belgium: they have all been moved back to the
defence of the Reich. And no doubt he is holding a considerable
fighter force in reserve for the invasion which he knows is coming.

If the reduction of the GAF was the first thing to be done, what
was the second? We thought of attacking oil refineries or tank
factories in Germany, but in the end I decided that what would
probably pay the best dividend was a systematic bombing of the
railway installations, sheds, servicing facilities and marshalling
yards on the rail systems that connect Germany with Northern
France. This general dislocation of the railway system would make

it possible effectively to cut specific routes when the tactical phase of our attack began.

Railways were our chief targets, but there were also batteries, radar targets, "CROSSBOW"* sites and more recently bridges. Today (D − 1) most of our effort has been against the Pas De Calais area in order to divert the enemy's attention from our actual landing area, but I have ordered in that area the following vital points to be attacked — 1 Corps and 2 Divisional Headquarters, 4 Fighter direction and telephone exchanges, 2 key telephone exchanges.

For the future, after the assault has begun, our task is to delay the enemy reserves, to create for the enemy some of the difficulties that we have to face in our own oversea communications. My plan is to create blocks and choke points which will delay the movement of these reserves. That is a thing from which I personally will never be deflected. I have had all sorts of pressure put upon me, to attack airfields and other targets. Such attacks are useless compared with this supreme necessity of holding off the enemy movement into the assault area. Much effort will be wasted: perhaps only 25 per cent will achieve results, but even that will have been worth it.

Pressure has also been put upon me to use strategic bombers for bombing moving columns on the road. In my opinion this is quite useless. Flying at the height at which a heavy bomber must fly, roads themselves are hardly visible, much less columns moving on those roads: and nothing short of a direct hit on such a column has much effect. Besides the country inland is heavily wooded, and intersected with valleys, country in which it is very hard to spot movement. My idea is to create blocks in town and villages that form nodal points, and to keep them blocked by repeated attacks.'

L-M wrote a personal diary almost every day during the period of the invasion of Europe. He dictated it to Hilary St George Saunders. His first entry was on 5 June:

'In considering the long-term preparations, I bore constantly in mind the happy thought that we had a large preponderance of air strength over that of the enemy. My problem was, therefore, how to apply this to the best advantage in the air preparations for the assault. I have always been convinced that to achieve air supremacy, which is of course indispensable for victory, daylight attacks on the enemy must be carried out. I do not, by this, wish to belittle night attacks which are very important because they disorganise the enemy and put a considerable added strain on his air defences. Not, however, until he is attacked heavily and continuously by day will a final issue be achieved. The point I want to reach is one where the enemy is forced to decide whether to

---

* V1 pilotless aircraft armed with a 1000lb bomb.

fight it out till he wins or is destroyed, or to refuse to take that risk and adopt the course of preserving his strength for some future effort to be made at a time when he judges the situation to be most suitable, or possibly most desperate. My own view for this battle which opens tomorrow has always been that the Hun would regard the second alternative as the proper course of action, and that he would keep back a considerable proportion of his fighter effort for use either immediately the battle was joined or shortly afterwards. In this assumption I have been proved right, for during the last weeks the American daylight heavies have been allowed to proceed to their targets, more or less without interference from the air. To my mind this means but one thing — the GAF are conserving their fighters in order to use them in the battle. In passing, I would emphasise that the constant heavy attacks made upon his coastal airfields have driven the Hun further and further back into Holland, Belgium and France.

Bear in mind, therefore, that it is my intention to take all possible steps to provoke the GAF into delivering battle by day. It will then be defeated and destroyed and I shall have achieved air supremacy. So much for my intentions: now as to preparations. When I took command there was a variety of strategic targets open to attack — factories producing raw material especially tanks, oil refineries and oil installations. Both these were tempting, but I soon made up my mind that the best possible target in the preparatory stages would be the German system of communications in Europe. It seems to me that the only way the Hun can force a stalemate at this stage of the war is by making a supreme effort to kick our armies back into the sea after we have got ashore. I think he may take a very big risk in order to achieve this object. He cannot, however, achieve it if his communications have been wrecked or, at any rate, disrupted. Any large-scale reinforcement of his troops near the invasion area could only be made if the railways behind are in good working order.

My first object, therefore, in the preparatory stages was to make such a mess of the railway system that the movement of reinforcements would be impossible. The railway experts whom I consulted when considering this programme urged the destruction of railway centres; that is to say, those places where servicing and maintenance shops exist and also where signalling systems are concentrated. The destruction of these would, they said, pay a big dividend for the attackers. Moreover, to clobber junctions with a large number of points would be of immediate assistance, for they are not easily replaced when destroyed. Another subsidiary result would be to aggravate the coal situation on the French railways by attacking such a centre as Lens, which provides much of the coal for the enemy's troop and supply trains.

We began these attacks against 82 railway targets in the area of the Seine, the Vosges and Belgium, and we divided the area into a northern and an eastern part. The first attack, which took place on 7 March on Le Mans and was carried out by Bomber Command, was successful and was a good augury. I am quite sure that, speaking at this moment, the potential carrying power of the French and Belgian railways has been very considerably reduced and that there are good prospects of being able to maintain them in a state of paralysis. That situation seems to me to be in hand. Of the 82 targets chosen, 50 have been completely destroyed; in 8 of them one or two installations are still intact; and 17 have been badly damaged but need further attention, which they will get. To accomplish this the AEAF have made 8000 sorties and dropped 5600 tons; the American 8th Army Air Force 3300 sorties and dropped 7000 tons; and Bomber Command, operating at night 4600 sorties dropping 20,000 tons. Besides railway centres, bombs have been directed on to rail and road bridges. Here also, I think a great measure of success has been achieved. Of the 10 rail and 14 road bridges between Rouen and Paris, 8 rail have been completely broken and 10 road, while 1 rail and 2 road bridges are impassable. We have also destroyed the bridge at Conflans over the Oise, the bridges at Heerenthals and Hirson over the Albert Canal, the bridges at Hasselt over the Doner, at Konz over the Moselle, 3 bridges at Liege over the Meuse, one at Tours over the Canal, and one at Valenciennes over the Escaut. In addition, 2 road bridges — one at Saumur over the Loire and the other at Beaumont over the Oise — have been dealt with. To do this the AEAF have flown 5209 sorties dropping 5370 tons and the American 8th Army Air Force 445 sorties dropping 367 tons. I have paid particular attention to the rail communications and centres near Paris which have been heavily attacked and are in a bad way.

I should explain that during this period I have been held up to a certain extent in fulfilling my programme by the necessity of attacking the Crossbow targets — that is the rocket apparatus which the Germans have been establishing along the Western coast of France, with the object, probably, of attacking our invasion bases and shelling London. Out of the 107 such targets only 11 now exist. The story of the attack on the rocket installations is a very good one, and I am well satisfied with the results achieved. The Hun began to build them at the beginning of last winter, relying on the bad climate of the winter months in France to keep them reasonably safe from interference. In this they have been much disappointed, for we have attacked them ruthlessly and with great success. I need not emphasise how difficult such targets are to hit. Attacks on railways and roads may be described as my strategic plan. My tactical plan was to go for coastal batteries and for the enemy radar system. In order to deceive him as much as possible I attacked two batteries outside the area for every one I attacked inside it. They are extremely difficult to bomb, but the results have not been unsatisfactory. Out of 12 batteries in the area listed for attack, 5 have been completely destroyed and 7 have been badly damaged. The army is particularly pleased with these results, for they say that the attack was carried out at the right time before the enemy had completed the concrete casements for the guns. I have directed 4400 tons on the batteries in the area and about 8800 tons on batteries outside it. The bombing has been done mostly by Marauders in daylight and Bomber Command at night. Bomber Command has been particularly skilful and I am very pleased with the results. Of the batteries outside the area 21 have been attacked, 5 by night and 16 by day. On the whole, I think the army will have cause for satisfaction when it comes in. I do not maintain that all the batteries have been silenced, but I shall be surprised if they are able to produce anything like the volume of fire they might have laid on had they been left unbombed.

The Radar position is extraordinary. There is a network of Radar stations all along the invasion coasts, and they are tiny and very difficult to hit. They are an absolute menace because they locate our shipping and our aircraft. Moreover, 5 of the largest Radar stations were discovered by our experts to be unjammable. These I attacked, and they have been completely destroyed. They are the installations holding the giant Wurtzburgs. Many secondary Radar stations still exist, but I think that the enemy Radar activity has been reduced by at least 25 per cent. Finally, two large dumps have been caught by Bomber Command — one at Burg St Leopold and the other at Mailly-le-Camp — and, generally speaking, all the forward camps for enemy troops show no further signs of habitation.

I have not sent my bombers and fighters over the invasion area in greater strength than they have flown over any other area. I did not wish to concentrate too hard on the invasion area for that might have given it away. Consequently, we have not beaten up everything but (and here I go back to Radar), we have done a good deal. There is a major Radar site every ten miles along the coast from Cherbourg to Ostend and these are the outposts of an elaborate inland system. Of the 7 major stations south of Boulogne, 6 have been completely destroyed and 15 more are in a very poor way. I regard these figures as conservative, and I would also refer to another, if indirect, achievement of the attacks. There is good evidence that the morale and efficiency of the Radar crews working the instruments have been considerably impaired. Of late, the fact that they switch off when our aircraft approach them has been noticed. In making attacks on Radar targets, rocket projectiles have proved very useful. A number of attacks remain particularly in my memory. There were the two navigational aid stations attacked by four Mosquitos who placed their bombs within ten feet of the centre of the target. The attacks on the big jamming stations are triumphs of precision bombing, and I should also like to record a word of praise concerning the pathfinders of Bomber Command who have proved extraordinarily accurate. The Radar station near Boulogne, which measures 300 yards by 150 received direct hits at night from 70 heavy bombs.

You will ask me to sum up my general impressions on this, the eve of the battle. To what I have already said I would merely add that the enemy do not seem to know where we are going, and possibly not when. To make it more difficult for them I have today taken out two Divisional Headquarters and four Fighter Telephone Exchanges, besides two main Telephone Exchanges. I have just heard that the lighthouse at Alderney and Guernsey became airborne some time last night or this morning. This seems to me to be of some significance.

When the battle is joined, from an air point of view, if the German Air Force are really thrown into it they will be beaten. I am quite sure of that. They will, of course, do a certain amount of damage; it is impossible to maintain a complete air umbrella. The man determined to throw away his life for the cause for which he is fighting can always do so, but I am quite sure that if they commit themselves to battle they will be virtually wiped out before it is over. In general, I am satisfied with my preparations. My main task has been to delay the movements of the German army in order to prevent it from carrying out that oldest maxim of war — it is the General who concentrates the largest number of men in the shortest possible time at the vital point who wins the battle. I believe that our progress across the beaches will be necessarily slow and I look to the Air Forces to redress the balance which is against us, insofar as the problem of building up is concerned. Normally, with railways and roads to serve him the enemy could reasonably expect to concentrate more troops in the battle area more quickly than we could having to transport them across the sea. It is my object and I shall allow nothing to stand in its way to make it as difficult as possible for the enemy to bring up his troops. As I have just said, I must redress the balance, and I will never be deflected from this purpose. I am going to use all my efforts to delay the German army. Incidentally, I shall make use of fighter bombers for attacks on roads, and these will come into their own as soon as the German army is forced to take to them, not having railways at their disposal any longer.'

Chapter 12
D-Day

At 9.30 pm on 5 June, L-M flew in a Dakota from Northolt to Greenham Common. There he talked to the American paratroops of the 101st Airborne Division. After watching their take-off he flew to Harwell airfield. There he saw General Gale, Commander of the British Sixth Airborne Division, before his glider-borne troops departed. At 1 am in the morning — now D-Day — on 6 June, L-M returned to Bentley Priory and spent an hour in the War Room. So far, there had been no enemy air reaction to the initial stages of the invasion.

By 9 am there had still been no German reaction. Troops were landing in their pre-arranged areas on the beaches: transport aircraft had suffered negligible losses. L-M telephoned Eisenhower's headquarters to report that the paratroop attack appeared to have been successful and that few losses had been reported — and his own fears of heavy losses had not materialised. He followed up his telephone call with a letter to Eisenhower saying that it was sometimes difficult in this life to admit that one was wrong, but that he never had a greater pleasure than in doing so on this occasion. He congratulated Eisenhower on the wisdom of his command decision about sending in the American paratroopers.

The air commanders met at 11 am in L-M's office. Present were Spaatz, Harris, Tedder, Douglas and Doolittle. Their conference began with the usual weather report: it was cloudy but with a chance of the cloud breaking up later in the day. The naval operations had so far gone according to plan. The airborne operation had been unexpectedly successful. Summing up L-M said that tactical surprise had evidently been achieved. He thought this was probably because the enemy had considered it unlikely that the Allied assault would be launched in such unfavourable weather.

After lunch Portal, Chief of the Air Staff, spent thirty minutes with L-M to review the situation in the War Room. At 3.15 pm, the King accompanied by Winston Churchill and Field Marshal Smuts arrived at Bentley Priory and spent an hour with L-M in the War Room. Then, at 6.15 pm L-M chaired a conference to set the specific bombing targets for the night and for the next day. Then he drove to Eastcote to follow the progress of the airborne replacements.

Later he found a few minutes to dictate his diary for 6th June, as follows:

'Yesterday I confess that I was very apprehensive about the American Airborne Division. I felt that they had a task which might be beyond them, and I say quite frankly that I was against this part of the plan. It seemed to me that to fly in so large a force at 500 feet over almost the whole of the Cherbourg peninsula (for they were to come in from the west and the dropping zones were in the east) was extremely hazardous. If the enemy were alert and vigorous it looked as though the American casualties would be far too high and could not, therefore, be justified. You can imagine my relief, therefore, when I heard that their casualties had been light. A chance has been taken and it has come off. I am writing in this sense to the Supreme Commander-in-Chief.'

At this point Saunders asked questions of L-M about the demeanour of the paratroops whom he had inspected prior to their departure. L-M replied:

'I went round to several Groups and talked with them. I would describe their demeanour as grim and not frightfully gay, but there was no doubt in my mind of their determination to do the job.'

Saunders, in conversation with Wing Commander King that same afternoon (who had accompanied L-M to inspect the paratroopers) had been told that the sight from one airfield, where eighty-three gliders and tugs took off, was remarkable. The sky was full of green and red lights, because the navigating lights had been left on. It was like a lovely show of fireworks, though it lasted longer, as the great stream of aircraft moved across the evening sky towards France.

Next morning, 7 June, the Allied Air Commanders met as usual at 11 o'clock — as they were to do for the next fifty-three consecutive days. L-M was in the chair. Reports were heard from all commanders, and air targets were allocated for the night. The main worry was the movement of German reserve forces. The bad weather had prevented British air superiority from delaying the German build-up.

L-M's diary for 7 June says:

'So far the German reaction has not been great, but he is now bringing more troops into the area. He has also moved a number of aircraft to Lorient, which may indicate that he intends to increase his submarine activity from that base and to use the aircraft in conjunction with the U-boats. His reserves seem to me to be coming in to the beach-head area in bits and pieces and it doesn't look as though he can launch a big attack yet.

The Luftwaffe reaction has been exceedingly small. We have attacked them heavily all day today, but I see no prospect of a big air battle as yet. He has, so far, confined himself to tip and run tactics which I expect him to step up. There are signs that he is moving squadrons into the Pas de Calais, possibly to operate against our shipping lanes. The weather has interfered with my air programme all day and is seriously upsetting me. The German army is being reinforced and I cannot bomb the reinforcements in daylight. Night bombers cannot do very much in this direction. You have got to see your targets. I have a feeling we are losing precious time at a moment when the main movements of the enemy are beginning. The work of supplying beaches by the Navy is, I understand, going exceedingly well. One unfortunate mistake is being made by them. They are shooting at our aircraft and are bringing quite a number of them down. This, of course, is very serious. They do not seem to have learnt the lesson of the Dieppe raid in this respect.

Generally speaking, Allied Air Forces are not doing as well against the German army as I had hoped. No effective day bombing has yet taken place, and this is most unfortunate. On the other hand, we have had a very easy run as far as the Luftwaffe is concerned, but I want to knock the German Air Force for six, for then we shall have absolute freedom in the air. It may be that the Hun is trying to lull us into a false sense of security. We shall soon know.'

At the commanders' conference on 8 June there was a resurgence of the old controversy between the British and Americans. L-M said that General Doolittle could, if he wished, produce a scheme for systematic attack on German airfields but insisted that the first essential still must be to hamper German movement in order to lighten the task of the Army. British-American tensions showed. Doolittle suggested that only 10 per cent of the effort of the strategical air forces needed to be devoted to obstructing enemy movement. L-M replied that at least 30 per cent would be necessary. Spaatz said that most movement went on at night and therefore it was useless to employ day bombers. Coningham supported L-M saying he thought that the urgent night movement was only in the tactical area and that long distance movement could be stopped best by daylight action; he was positive that there was no real worry at present from the German Air Force in the battlefield. Tedder sought to smooth over the difficulty by stating that a proportion should be assigned to each task according to the needs of the moment.

At 2 pm L-M chaired the meeting to fix the night's bombing targets. Then he telephoned General De Guingand, Chief of Staff to Montgomery, in which he explained his plans for delaying German movements by cutting railway lines and river crossings. At 6 o'clock there was a conference to allocate targets for the American 8th Air Force bombers.

L-M's diary for 8 June:

'The situation is changing as the German reinforcements come up. The weather is still bad, but our fighter bombers have certainly delayed their movements and I think that the Germans are twenty-four hours behind their schedule. My problem is not targets in the area but those outside. I have sealed the Seine as far as Paris by destroying all communications, and in Paris itself the results of attacking the Ceinture railway have been good. I am quite satisfied with the Seine but not quite so satisfied with the Loire, though 3 bridges over it have gone.

My problem, as I see it, is two-fold. First, to hold the ring outside the invasion area; secondly, to try to stop railway movements towards the area, particularly from the south-east. What I must try hard to do is to stop the trains as far back as possible. The limit I have set at the moment is a line running north of Rennes through Laval, Le Mans, Chateaudun, then west of Chartres and south of Dreux. I want to take the bridges out and thus force the enemy on to the roads. If this succeeds, the rapid movement of reinforcements will become impossible. The German Air Force is beginning to thicken up and about half the fighters in Germany are now, I think, moving against us. I have put the American 8th Army Air Force on to the bombing of enemy airfields. Now is the moment to mess them up, for equipment for the Luftwaffe is beginning to reach them, I am, therefore, going to do an Aunaye attack (by this phrase he meant "a heavy attack" — the airfield at Aunaye had been almost totally destroyed a few days before) on Flers, Laval, Le Mans and Rennes, and for that purpose I am going to use my heavies. I want to catch the German Air Force while they are moving in. At the moment they are very fluid. When they begin to take the air seriously against us they will need dumps, and it is my intention to blow these to hell. The situation is evolving but it is a terrible thing to me to feel all these troop movements going on while I am not able to stop them because of bad weather and low cloud. Never mind, I have a plan and I shall work to it.

The cover for the beaches and shipping has been remarkably successful. Attacks have been very few and all of them isolated. The weather is still lousy; it depresses me, though the met. people say it will clear tomorrow. I doubt this myself. There is another depression in the Atlantic, they tell me, eight hours away but after that they think we shall have a little fine weather. The sea is calming down, there is less wind, but at the moment the weather from the point of view of air operations, is not good at all.'

On the morning of the 9th, it was reported that German air reaction had been less than expected. For future operations L-M said that it was of supreme importance to hold the ring and to interrupt communications across the Seine and the Loire rivers and the gap between Paris and Orleans. All bridges over the Loire and the ten railways leading to the battle area along a line north of Rennes and Le Mans would have to be cut. He also discussed that morning with Generals Doolittle and Anderson about their plan for the Eighth Air Force to attack enemy airfields — and it was being put into execution.

L-M's diary for 9 June:

'I am feeling a bit depressed today. You know the kind of feeling when your instinct is to go out and have several drinks. It seems to me that the German armies are moving up against the beach-head and I am unable to do anything against them because of this perfectly bloody weather. Yet I need not be really depressed, for even with the limited number of sorties which we have been able to fly we have done well. The German armies are not moving up as fast as was anticipated. We have undoubtedly slowed them down in the strategical area, but I repeat, as I have repeated to myself so often, the air is *the* weapon which we must use against the German army to prevent their quick build-up; all the more so because the Germans have not the power to use the air against us. This I am quite clear about, for I am absolutely satisfied with the air defences. No serious damage has been done to ships or military units, and that is a comforting thought.

I have heard several comments from our own army wounded which seem to show that the army is delighted with the RAF and consider that the air cover over the beach-head is marvellous. Admiral Vian has actually gone so far as to complain of the number of British aircraft flying over his ships; I suppose they disturb him in his bath. I'm not sure whether he means this complaint to be taken seriously. Anyhow I don't take it so.

The general situation is about the same as it was last night, except that the Hun has had twenty-four hours freedom of movement under cover of the clouds. He may have got some stuff into the forward area, and if he has it will, of course, split up into small units and be hidden in villages and orchards, which makes the task of destroying it from the air much more difficult. We have been at them, however, since dawn this morning.

My real trouble is a gap of twenty-four hours in the news because the weather is so bad that my fighter bombers cannot operate today, which means that tomorrow I shall have to start all over again and shall be reduced to guessing the probable movements of the enemy for twenty-four hours. The chance of finding his columns on the road is very small in weather like this. They promise me a temporary improvement tomorrow, but I am doubtful.

It is depressing to think that I have, as the PM said, more than 11,000 aircraft and cannot make full use of them, and I confess to experiencing a certain sense of frustration.

I have got my eye on a Hun Panzer Division at Montauban and Toulouse and I am going to despatch some American heavies to give it a good shaking up. I repeat that it is very annoying, when we have reached a stage on land where the army has got enough elbow room to do a proper build-up, not to be able to mount a decent air attack on the enemy's ground forces. I believe that if I had been able to carry out intensive air operations today I could have delayed them at least twenty-four hours and thus increased our own chance of making a successful attack on land. Today seems to me a crucial day and very little has been done in the air. This is, indeed, the first critical moment. Never mind, St George, we shall win all right.'

Next morning, now 10 June, L-M spoke on the telephone to Admiral Ramsay about the shooting down of aircraft by naval anti-aircraft fire. On D-Day the navy had shot down four spotters, several transport aircraft and at the end some Spitfires. Ramsay promised very strong measures to eliminate what was caused by inexperienced people on the ships.

There followed two telephone conversations with Coningham, the usual two conferences, and at 5 pm a telephone call from Tedder:

'The Prime Minister feels that Cherbourg is only weakly held by the Germans; it might pay to switch our air efforts to support an all out air attack.'

L-M agreed to study the idea immediately.

It will be remembered that L-M had had misgivings about the D-Day airborne assaults. He clearly had a special feeling for the airborne forces, having more direct responsibility for their safe arrival on the battlefield than he had for 'ordinary' soldiers. Just before the start of D-Day he had written to Generals Richard Gale and Matthew Ridgway, their British and American commanders. He now received the following replies:

General Richard Gale wrote:

'I received your very nice letter today. We are all in great heart and doing our stuff alright. I and all my Command are grateful to you for all you have done for us. The night of 5/6 was a sticky dark affair over here — but one NEVER to be forgotten. With all best wishes to you personally and to the RAF.'

And from General Matthew Ridgway:

'Your message reached me a few hours before my departure. I value it more than I can tell you, and so will all members of this Division to whom it will be conveyed at the first opportunity. It was a most thoughtful and gracious act. To me it is characteristic of that broad visioned leadership and sympathetic patience with the problems of others which has made my association with you so highly regarded.

With deep respect and warm personal esteem,
Sincerely, Matthew B. Ridgway.'

Chapter 13
First Fortnight

L-M's thoughts and aspirations for the critical period after D-Day are best expressed in the following extracts from his diary.

10 June

'Today has been a grand day and I feel a different man. As I said yesterday, the weather made a complete gap in my information, but things started to build-up early today and movement on the road was noticed from points west of Paris and Dreux. Only a very few trains have been seen. I think they have been clobbered too badly to move much. From the Loire the movement appears to be entirely by road. We pumped stuff into them as hard as we could. I believe that there are no more than 10 German Divisions near the beach-head instead of the 13½ which it was calculated they would have in position there by the end of D plus 2. Of the 10 Divisions 3 are Panzer. It looks to me as though the German build-up is both slow and not very heavy. Train movements are very small near the area. By bombing Amiens, Beauvais and Abbeville I hope to create a bombing barrier round the battlefield, and inside it to reduce and possibly destroy all railway movement. The American heavies have done very well and I have a feeling that there is very little build-up on the enemy's side. There is a possibility that we may get through them with a rush though I am not counting on it.

Bomber Command did good shows last night on railways in Brittany, especially at Rennes, Pontibau, Fougeres, Mayenne and Alencon. My attacks further south are also paying dividends. Things, in fact, are looking much more healthy.

The weather, however, is still not good although it is a fighter bomber day. Cloud on some of the hills is down to 200 feet. Another good sign is that horse transport has been seen on the Breton roads.

The movement of the 17th Panzer Division is being carried out entirely on roads. One of its regiments has been located and is being strafed. As far as I can make out the 21st and 12th Panzer Divisions have most of the tanks; the 3rd is very short of them. A cyclist regiment from Coutances has reached the Germans but it is not in very good strength.

The general situation seems to me to be good. We have slowed up the enemy's movements. Of that there is not a doubt. Dreux is still the centre of them and is being heavily strafed. I think the Hun is getting a trifle windy. My trouble was that gap of twenty-four hours during which he must have received some reinforcements. I cannot but be optimistic today, however, and think that if we break the crust there may not be an awful lot the other side.

Bert's people put up a damn good show last night. Bert is grand and doing frightfully well. The Americans, too, are full out. Luftwaffe is beginning to operate. Contact was made with them this afternoon and there have been sporadic bursts of activity. The Hun is far from dominating the battlefield. On the contrary, he seems scared stiff of poking his nose in. We gave him such a bloody one at Dieppe that I should not be surprised if he has learnt that lesson and is not going to run the risk of the same fate over the Normandy beaches.

11 June

'Not a good day, St George. I made the mistake of not getting to the office until 10 am being over-persuaded to take a bit of a rest. When I got there I found a confused picture, and as I was trying to sort things out I had a 'phone call to say that General Arnold and Admiral King would arrive in five minutes. We waited half-an-hour and by that time my daily conference was due to begin. It was then discovered that these two distinguished Commanders had lost their way. By the time the conference started there was a noticeable lack of bonhomie. The conference was a long drawn out one, and the weather is doing the dirty on us again. The night bombing was again good but the day bombing was bad, and it was a day of great frustration so far as I was concerned. There have been big movements outside the area south of the Seine and the Loire, and we have discovered some big train movements going on which cannot be attacked in this filthy weather. They were found by fighters.

So there we are, St George. The situation is developing and, at the moment, I can do little about it. I am still convinced that the Germans have not got much behind the troops now confronting our armies. More than ever do I want to attack and prevent the build-up but it is very doubtful because of this weather. However, I am certain the German build-up is behind-hand and that he has got only 13 to 14 Divisions in line instead of 16 to 17. Our build-up, on the other hand, is almost up to schedule. It is maddening to think that if we had not had this bad weather we could have clobbered 30 trains, all of which had been discovered moving from the south upwards. There won't be much improvement in the weather tomorrow but it will be a fighter bomber day. Don't think I am depressed however, I am very far from it. The battle is not going at all badly though it might have been a great deal better if the weather had been kind. We are going to defeat the German Air Force, there is not a doubt of it, if they poke their heads up, but it is too maddening not to have been able to bomb those thirty trains. Tonight I am going again for railway targets at Evreux, Massy-Palaiseau, Tours, Nantes, Acheres and Versailles. The railways at Dreux, Nantes and Tours are in a very shaky condition.'

On 12 June, now D-Day Plus Six, L-M told his commanders that it was evident that the Brest Peninsula had been drained of every German reinforcement and that Northeast France now constituted the main reservoir of German reserves.

At lunch at Stanmore Hall, L-M entertained Sir Stafford Cripps accompanied by Sir Wilfrid Freeman and Mr Lennox-Boyd MP. Afterwards he held a small meeting to discuss that evening's bombing targets. L-M commented that information from the Army was so meagre and it came in so late that by waiting for confirmation the air force was liable to be too late to stop enemy movement. Bombing priorities for the next day would be to cut the four remaining rail bridges across the Loire and twenty-nine bridges over other rivers.

Suddenly, a new kind of German attack appeared, in the form of 'pilotless aircraft'. They were popularly but unaffectionately known to the British public as 'buzz bombs' or 'doodle bugs'. The Germans designated them V.1. They were in fact the original 'cruise' weapon. The V.1 system was the objective of the CROSSBOW bombing attacks referred to earlier. They first appeared during the night of 12/13 June between 3 and 5 am. Intelligence reported that the Germans had made this 'a rush job' sending special trains through Lille 'with top priority'. It had been known since 1943 that the Germans were preparing for this. There had been experimental work in the Baltic Sea area, and construction of launching sites in the Pas de Calais area had begun in the autumn.

12 June

'Today the situation is changing and enemy movements are spasmodic. All movement in the Brest area seems to have dried up and there is little forward movement towards the invasion area. The Hun is detraining as far back as Paris. In the Loire area also he is very nearly at a standstill as far as the railways are concerned. It is even possible that he may detrain as far back as Poitiers where he has a Panzer Division. Of course, not all movement has been stopped. A certain amount must have slipped in but I don't think it is a great deal. To prevent shifting of troops down from the north I am going to bomb Amiens, Cambrai and Arras junctions. This will seal off Belgium.

The day itself has been patchy. Only moderate results have been achieved by day bombing but results at night have been good considering the weather. The targets on the Paris Ceinture have been well hit. The attacks on the junctions at Evreux, Orleans and

Nantes I consider to have been good enough; that on Etaples excellent. The tactical area is now bounded by a line running from Vermand through Dreux, Chartres, Le Mans, Laval, Rennes, St Nazaire. In general, I am not dissatisfied. I cannot believe there is much movement in the forward area, nor that the enemy can have got any great amount of stuff into it. The stuff behind, which he must get in to win the battle, is either moving very slowly or not at all. Above all, the Germans want infantry and I don't think they can get them except from Belgium which, as I have said, will be sealed off tonight if the bombing I have laid on is successful. It is towards that country that my main effort will be directed. I shall also attack Poitiers.'

The French city of Caen now became a sticking point for the Allied armies. Montgomery developed a plan involving the British First Airborne Division for a two-pronged attack to the east and the south in order to pinch out Caen. L-M demurred, considering that such an operation would be too hazardous for his aircrews and for the airborne troops. He believed that preparations for a night operation would leave Admiral Ramsay's ships vulnerable to an attack by the Luftwaffe. Monty wrote in fury to his own ADC, De Guingand, that L-M could not refuse him unless he first came out to see him and added: 'Obviously he is a gutless bugger who refuses to take a chance and plays for safety on all occasions.'

De Guingand telephoned L-M in the night of the 12th to say that Montgomery might want him to fly out the next day. However, the eastward thrust of Montgomery's attack failed and his southward movement was forced to retreat. So, next morning at 10.45 De Guingand telephoned L-M again to say that their previous plan had been abandoned and a visit by L-M was not now necessary. In the evening at his home in Stanmore, L-M saw General Browning, GOC Airborne Troops. He explained that Montgomery's plan to encircle Caen had broken down so that the assistance of the First Airborne was not required.

13 June

'A depressing day from the point of view of the air, my dear St George. The weather has been damnable. The army position is improving but they will not be able to do anything until they can clear up Caen, then they may go forward. Material and reinforcements are only dribbling in to the enemy, and this satisfactory state of affairs is entirely due to air attack. At the moment, the Hun is detraining beyond the Seine and Loire areas. There is one railway line working more or less south of Paris, and we should have cleaned that up had not the weather dried up on us.'

Here Saunders noted that L-M laughed and said: 'I sometimes think that the Powers above may have Fascist tendencies, so bad has been the weather.'

L-M continued dictating:

'I feel comfortable about Brittany as far south as Rennes and Laval. They cannot detrain beyond these points, and most of the detraining takes place much farther south. In the north there is no sign of movement and there were good results from our bombing attacks on Arras, Amiens and Cambrai last night. I think, in fact, I may say that I was well satisfied with last night's work. Moreover, we caught a Panzer Division at Poitiers with probably good results. That, at present, is the situation. I hope that by 1900 hours this evening (in two hours from the time this conversation took place) the weather will have cleared sufficiently, in which case I propose to put everything into the air. So far my losses have been light. In the category of fighter bombers they have been exactly what was estimated; they have been far less in the case of fighters; and extremely light in the case of heavy bombers. There has been very little enemy opposition and, from the point of view of the air, the situation looks extremely healthy.'

On Wednesday 14 June the situation appeared to the air commanders to be less satisfactory. L-M told his commanders that movement in the North-west appeared to be frozen. Brigadier Richardson reported to the meeting that the enemy's resistance had stiffened on all fronts. Progress was expected to be slow. But the Allied build-up was considered satisfactory, all being up to schedule.

However, Coningham said that he had been given a rather different picture. He believed the enemy had probably reached Carentan and had launched a serious attack on the far eastern sector. No fresh Allied formations were due to land today or tomorrow, and those fighting now had been fighting almost continuously for a week and were getting tired.

Tedder warned that the present situation had the makings of a dangerous crisis. Enemy build-up was going ahead while ours would remain static for two days. L-M said that the fact that the enemy had avoided big concentrations of troops had added to the difficulty. He would visit General Montgomery in the afternoon.

At 2.30 pm L-M flew from Northolt to Thorney Island where he collected De Guingand. They flew on to Normandy and landed on a newly constructed strip at Bezonville, one mile from Montgomery's headquarters at Creully-sur-Seulles. L-M and Montgomery conferred. L-M offered a heavy air bombardment to clear an opening for the troops: Montgomery liked the proposal. This became 'Operation CHARNWOOD' which was carried out in early July.

Afterwards L-M went on to pay a brief visit to Air Vice-Marshal Broadhurst, now AOC 83 Group, and to other senior air officers in the battle area.

14 June (dictated at 10.20 the same evening)

'The great thing to realise, my dear St George, is that the well-worn platitude "Don't believe a word of what you see in the papers" is perfectly true. The Press takes the biscuit, and the situation given by them, particularly in the evening papers, bears no resemblance to reality. As far as I can see the whole show on land is bogged up. The Hun has kicked us out of Villers Bocage and there is no sign of any big forward movement, or a chance of it. What the Press says, therefore, is simply nauseating. I can't understand the sort of guidance they are getting, or perhaps they pay no attention to it.

I saw Monty this afternoon and he was not in a good temper for I had sent him a signal shooting down an airborne operation which he wanted mounted. When I met him, therefore, he was not very kindly disposed. However, he brisked up a bit when I offered him, in exchange for the operation I was not prepared to carry out, a much more attractive proposal. This I shall refer to after it comes off. When I made it he just swallowed it up, though even now I am not sure that he will choose the right area. We shall see.

Happily, St George, as an airman I look at the battle from a totally different point of view. I have never waited to be told by the army what to do in the air, and my view is not bounded, as seems to be the case with the army, by the nearest hedge or stream. I said as much, though in different words, to Monty and tried to describe the wider aspects of this battle as I see them, particularly stressing the number of Divisions which he might have had to fight had they not been prevented from appearing on the scene by air action. He was profoundly uninterested. The fact of the matter is, however, that we have reduced the enemy's opposition considerably and the efficiency of their troops and armour even more so. In spite of this, the army just won't get on. It looks to me as though if they catch a prisoner or see a tank belonging to a particularly enemy Division they at once assume that the whole of that Division is intact and moving against them. I may be doing them an injustice, but they don't appear to me to realise that, due to our action, that Division has certainly been disorganised and is probably very much below strength.

So we have a bog, but I hope my scheme will unstick things. Nevertheless, the fact remains that the great advantage originally gained by the achievement of surprise in the attack has now been lost. I hope my scheme will loosen things up, but I can't be sure.'

Next morning in London, L-M was able to report to his commanders that he had seen Montgomery and he believed that the appreciation given the previous morning by Richardson was a truer picture than the more alarming one given by Coningham. Montgomery was looking for assistance from the air forces to loosen up the static situation around Caen. In the afternoon Tedder telephoned L-M from France to give the results of the planning for the bombing of Caen.

15 June

'The air war is going quite well and German communications are in a hell of a mess. Evidence of this is piling up. The German Air Force is now showing signs of getting together to put up a defence in the area of Paris — Beauvais — Evreux — Dreux. This is their main operating theatre and we shall fight them in it if they poke their heads up.

The British army is static but the Americans are pushing on north of Montebourg and west towards Piconville. A stage has now been reached when the first flush of excitement, so to speak, is over. We have got the air battle well in hand and now I must sit back and be content to watch the situation for the next day or two. My immediate plan is to go for the enemy's dumps and when they are destroyed he just won't be able to get himself supplied.

As for the army, I am being more and more driven to the conclusion that Monty won't move unless he has everything on a plate. He has got much of his army tied up on Villers Bocage. However, I may be wrong. We shall soon see.

My own opinion is that if he has not cleaned the situation up and begun an advance in the next 48 hours he will have to wait at least a fortnight before trying to do so. Then my problem will be how to keep the enemy off him all that time.

To sum up the general situation, I would say that the Air Forces have set the arena for the army. They have dislocated the enemy's supplies and thrown him out of his stride, but I don't think the army has taken advantage of this situation or made enough use of it.

I was particularly pleased with the attack by Bomber Command on Le Havre last night. It was colossal and we are going to get a very big dividend out of it. I repeat that the enemy is in such a mess that it is difficult now to find a place in which to hurt him for he has been pinched all over, but I expect to do so, and if his Air Force reacts we shall go on fighting it till it ceases to exist. Once more the air is the dominant factor.'

16 June

'The army is still very sticky and I am beginning to be afraid that we may miss the boat. The German Divisions seem to me to be filtering in, getting together their little bits and pieces, and trying to sort themselves out after a rough journey. Their heads are, so to speak, joining up with their tails.

The weather, from the point of view of the air, is bloody, though last night Bomber Command did a good show. The trouble is I can't get proper reconnaissance and without it I am beginning to lose the threads. It is reconnaissance deeper into France over the back areas that I must have.

In general, the Hun is in a bad way. His movements have been crippled. I seem to be saying this a lot but it is true, and I can cripple him further if the weather would only let me. The American 8th Air Force bombers did a very good show yesterday. They attacked bridges over the Loire and destroyed the whole lot. One photograph I saw showed a lump of bridge sailing through the air. These were all railway bridges, but one road bridge not included in the programme went for six by mistake. I haven't bombed Chartres, St George, though from a strictly military point of view I should have done so for there is railway movement through it which ought to be stopped.

I know now that the Hun Divisions moving up from Poitiers had hell. We clobbered Angouleme and made a great mess of it. We put much of the SS Division out of business, and some of the 2nd Panzer Division is still tied up in Cambrai. The anticipated bombing, which I ordered when I knew where these Divisions were, was very good and the attacks on Arras, Amiens and Cambrai were made just at the right moment. I think I tied up the northern Divisions while they were in process of getting into their trains, and I believe it may be another five days before they are able to make any move.'

The Germans had kept up a continuous attack of flying bombs, also known as 'pilotless aircraft' and as 'Divers'. On the 16th, L-M went to the Air Ministry at 6 pm to discuss what more to do about them. It was reported that 554 had landed and had exploded in the London area. L-M believed that anti-aircraft gunfire probably did more harm than good against these weapons because it hindered our own planes: he believed that fighters were the real answer. That night there would be a heavy attack on their launching sites in the Pas de Calais area which were codenamed figuratively 'No Balls'. The counter-operation was codenamed 'CROSSBOW'.

Next day an analysis showed that in the previous six nights, 714 Divers had been plotted on radar — of which 510 had crossed the coast. British fighters claimed to have destroyed 81 and anti-aircraft batteries claimed to have destroyed another 55.

17 June

'The situation on the British front is still static but the Americans are improving their positions and seem to me to be making a move. From the air point of view the weather is still very doubtful.

I am being somewhat diverted from the battle by having to deal with Crossbow (the sites from which the German pilotless aircraft were being launched). I haven't quite got the measure of them yet to enable me to do what I think would be really effective bombing. I am not certain whether I should obtain good results because their exact location may not have been pin-pointed in all cases.

Generally speaking, my programme for freezing the enemy's communications is progressing steadily but more slowly than I should like, again because of the weather. Undoubtedly, however, bombing attacks, especially on railway centres, have got on the Hun's nerves and I am, in effect, making him think that we are going to attack in other places by means of other landings. A very good thing to make him think this, even though in actual fact we are not going to do any such thing. Still, when all kinds of railway centres get bombed he never knows and is certainly being kept guessing.'

During the night of 17/18 June an estimated 145 German 'Divers' crossed the English coast. Two of these flying bombs fell within half a mile of L-M's house but he and Doris were lucky not to have any damage caused by them.

On Sunday 18 June, Eisenhower attended L-M's daily morning conference. He told them that OVERLORD operations were going well on air, land and sea. In the afternoon L-M flew to visit American fighter stations in the New Forest area near Southampton and then on to Normandy to visit a Ninth Air Force fighter-bomber base.

His diary for 18 June was terse:

'Nothing to report. Waiting on events. The British army is still static.'

On the 19th the Under Secretary of State for Air, Mr Balfour, visited Stanmore and lunched with L-M.

18 June

'Everything today is perfectly bloody, St George, and from my point of view there is nothing good. A German Division has moved up from Bordeaux through Santes. We have known that for the last two days but we just cannot bomb them because of the weather, and now it looks to me as though they will slip through. I am without photographic reconnaissance and am helpless. I must have it.

As to the situation in the bridge-head. The Americans are putting up a good show and doing well. Our own attack in the Caen region has been postponed another twenty-four hours. I confess to being very much disappointed by the army. I don't say that another Anzio is probable but it is certainly possible. They cannot expect the air to do everything for them, and on dud days like this when the weather is bad it is up to them to push forward. I know that the opposition against them is not great. They must get on. I am still being troubled by having to divert bombers against Crossbow.'

On the 20th L-M chaired his regular conference of commanders at 11 am. He was surprised to have a discussion about a proposed daylight attack on Berlin on the 21st with 2000 heavy bombers. Just before the conference he had been agreeing bombing targets in France. It emerged that Tedder had authorised the raid without consulting L-M as a retaliatory attack on Berlin in order to reduce German morale which had been raised by German 'Divers' falling on London. Next morning, Doolittle reported that 1311 Allied bombers had dropped 2315 tons of bombs on Berlin during the previous night.

L-M lunched with Browning and spent the afternoon discussing future airborne operations. At 3.30 pm they both met Eisenhower at SHAEF headquarters.

After several blank days, air reconnaissance was now reporting a good deal of enemy movement in North France and in Belgium. The targets chosen for bombing were rail marshalling yards and 'Diver' launching sites.

20 June

'A better day today. But what we suffer from is a lack of information. In the last day and a half I have lost track of the general movement of the enemy. Now I am just beginning to get scraps of information and I hope to get a lot more tomorrow morning from the Photographic Reconnaissance Unit. Weather is improving, but it is not so good over in France as it is here, but the prospects are better for the next day or two so the Met. tell me, and I hope therefore to get better results.

There is little doubt in my mind that one German Division had got through during the bad weather period, but in what kind of shape it is I do not know.

The Americans are going on very well, and there is a reconnaissance report to the effect that they are fighting on the outskirts of Cherbourg. I think the Hun is short of ammunition in that port, but has plenty of petrol. He is also short of food, and I don't think Cherbourg will bother us very long. It wouldn't surprise me if it fell very quickly. There is just a chance that the Hun might attempt to evacuate some of his troops by sea into the Channel Islands and Brittany. I hope to God they do, and so, no doubt, does the Navy. Their morale is pretty low, for they're not good troops, and it is just on the cards that they may chuck their hands in.

As far as build-up is concerned the British are behind for lack of good weather; on the other hand, Dick O'Connor, commanding the 8th Corps has now arrived. He is a tower of strength, and when he gets cracking I should not be surprised at anything. It is even possible that the Hun might crack completely. He is still behind-hand with his build-up, but not so much as I had hoped. He is undoubtedly very short of supplies, and the moment he cracks I shall throw in every aircraft I can lay my hands on, especially fighters, to shoot up everything they see.

Generally speaking, the picture today is better, but I am still suffering from lack of really good information. The pilotless aircraft are being coped with fairly well today. There were only six over us, of which five were shot down. The fighters have got everything well in hand at the moment, but the weather is good.'

21 June

'Here is the situation. After having been starved of information for some days I got lots of photographs yesterday, and I am digesting what they brought me. As I see it, there is a good deal more movement far away from the battle area. Indeed the enemy appears to be shifting stuff from Norway into Denmark, whence it will doubtless move South via Holland and Belgium to Northern France. I have therefore laid on a heavy bombing programme and am going principally for the rail centres at St Omer, Hazebrouck, Lille and Armentieres. I had a great deal laid on for this afternoon, but much of it had to be diverted against 'Crossbow" targets. One hundred Lancasters of Bomber Command were going to Bethune to bomb it in daylight, but the weather died on us and the operation had to be scrubbed. I shall do it tomorrow morning if the weather improves. It is still lousy on the other side, but I'm told that it may clear this afternoon. The build-up is still clogged because of high seas, but the Americans are nearer Cherbourg than they were.

Today I had a long discussion with the Supreme C-in-C about future airborne operations. I put several projects to Ike and I am going to start planning them immediately. We found ourselves in complete agreement.

Yesterday was a good day from a bombing point of view. We got a German Division in the Soissons/Rheims area. Good targets were found and quite a lot of damage done. It was a fighter-bomber day again, the weather being bad for heavy bombers. Results were good both to the East and West of Paris, and I am clobbering that area again today as hard as I can. "Crossbow" has interfered but not very much. Now that I have got some information I can begin to use my medium bombers once more in the main task, which is to delay the enemy's build-up by disrupting his communications.'

On the 22nd L-M gave a lunch at headquarters for the commanders of the Polish, French, Norwegian, Belgian and Czechoslovak air contingents. In the evening at 11 pm he welcomed Mr Herbert Morrison, Minister of Home Security, who wanted to discuss flying bombs before making a speech in the House of Commons.

22 June

'I have just put our Allies into the picture. Their eyes were fairly popping out of their heads.

L-M (*left*) with Tedder and Montgomery at a briefing being given by General Eisenhower. (*RAF Museum, Hendon*)

General Eisenhower (*seated centre*) photographed before D-Day with General Sir Bernard Montgomery (*right*) and ACM Sir Arthur Tedder. L-M back row second from right and Admiral Sir Bertram Ramsay third from right. (*Popperfoto*)

Relaxing before D-Day . . . (*RAF Museum, Hendon*)

L-M addressing American airmen before the invasion of France.
(*RAF Museum, Hendon*)

An official portrait of L-M in his office at Stanmore taken shortly before the
D-Day landings. (*RAF Museum, Hendon*)

A view from one of the troop transports showing Jeeps and men landing on the French coast, June 1944. (*Hulton Picture Company*)

The 'Battle of Britain' Class Locomotive, *Sir Trafford Leigh-Mallory*. (*British Rail*)

Today the situation is one of great interest. Yesterday the weather permitted me to get some indication of the German moves, particularly in the Pas de Calais area and to the south of the bridge-head. Movements have certainly been made into the Pas de Calais area and are now, I think, being digested. After the process of digestion has taken place they may move on down into Normandy. This I am trying to prevent by bombing and I hope to achieve some success.

Yesterday the weather was lousy and I was therefore unable to bomb the targets which I told you about — Armentieres, Arras, Hazebrouck, St Omer and Lille. They are being bombed today. The Germans are undoubtedly making use of the Meuse railway system and the lines running through Rheims and Chalons. I was always doubtful about that area because I could not induce the American Eighth Air Force to bomb it in sufficient strength. I don't think they have done the job properly for they sent over penny packets instead of large forces. Now we are doing our best to catch up on this situation. Laon and Rheims will be bombed tonight and the Americans will bomb Epernay by daylight and also take out a number of bridges in the area. I am convinced that there is very little railway movement west of Paris.

What I am now searching for are detraining points in the area east of Paris. I have found two — one at Brie Conte Robert and the other at Tournan. Both are being bombed. Poiters is also showing signs of considerable activity and I shall probably have to bomb that as well. There is also congestion at places like Creil and Beauvais, and they will certainly have to be attacked. Incidentally, we have discovered a Depot of the pilotless aircraft at Nucourt, South of Beauvais. That is being attacked. I am not, however, allowing the pilotless aircraft to interfere with my main strategical direction of the battle. I have no doubt that the Germans would like me to use big bomber forces on the sites launching pilotless aircraft, and they may even have begun to bomb London by this means in order to get me to do so, but I refuse to be diverted from my purpose. I shall wait for a day of fine weather and then I shall plaster them, but I am not going to attack them now, not while all this railway movement is taking place. That must be stopped in the interests of the battle, and if it means that London gets 40 or 50 pilotless aircraft shot at it, it must just take it, as I am sure it will.

For several days now, as you will have doubtless perceived, the weather has been fairly good in England, but it has been bad on the other side, both South and over Pas de Calais and Belgium. It has remained stationary there and is only just beginning to break up. I am not really happy as yet because I still have not go enough information. The weather has prevented photographic reconnaiss-ance on the scale I want, and I am still only getting little bits and pieces. This means that all I can do is to choose what seem to me to be the most likely targets and hope for the best.

So far the weather has held up the passage to the bridge-head of the Guards Armoured Division but there is a chance they may get over today. 'Monty' won't attack until they are there.'

Chapter 14
23–30 June 1944

While L-M was getting good news on the war front, there was sad news in the family. On 23 June, L-M replied to a letter from his daughter-in-law Jeanette, who had written to tell him that she and his son Tom were splitting up. He wrote:

'I am very sorry not to have answered your letter sooner, but with operations constantly in progress I just don't seem to have time for anything.

I had some idea of what you wrote about and suspected that ICI's action was connected with it, but Tom always swore that his personal behaviour had nothing to do with his removal from Aylesbury.

I have had several talks with Tom in recent months and hoped that he would realise how foolish he was being but you probably realise just how far one gets. Tom is now 27 and one can only advise and try and guide him, but I am afraid that my efforts — similar to countless episodes in the past when I have tried to make Tom realise how unreasonable and stupid his actions are and how damaging to himself — have really no effect. One would think that he would learn by experience that certain things just don't pay.

He is a pathetic figure looking for a job now as he is definitely finished with ICI. He has had some splendid chances, first Imperial Airways and then ICI but I cannot really recommend him again, because it lets down the people who are good to him on my account.

I am very sorry for you and only hope that you will be able to start your life again with a more fortunate choice.'

But the war continued. Once again L-M's own words tell the story:

23–24 June

'Crossbow pilotless aircraft are becoming more and more tiresome, and the Government are beginning to get jumpy about them. The Cabinet is nervous and repeatedly calling for action. "Crossbow" has always had high priority, and I have now detailed 200 aircraft of the American 8th Army Air Force to be kept at immediate readiness to attack "Crossbow" targets whenever they possibly can. At the first sign of really fine weather I shall lay on a maximum effort, and bomb them with everything I've got. I am not going heavily for storage sites yet, for I have not got enough intelligence about them.

The 2nd Army is still static, but the Americans are making progress in front of Cherbourg. It looks to me as though the Germans could not last out very long in that port, for our reconnaissance machines were not fired at to any great extent, except for one place in the town. North of the beach-head the German movements died down and there was much less railway activity in the Rheims/Chalons area.

There was also very little movement North of Paris. This I attribute to the successful bombing carried out during the previous day. On the other hand, two German Infantry Divisions were moving up from Toulouse and the Pyrenees, last night Saintes and Limoges, through which they must pass, were both bombed by Bomber Command.

The weather yesterday (23rd) was bad, so bad indeed that even the bombers could not do anything. The heavy bombers bombed on instruments. I directed the fighters to the area NE of Paris, Beauvais, Soissons, Compiegne and also to districts South of the Loire. They have orders to watch for any train movements and attack them.'

24 June

'The Americans are still not yet in Cherbourg. There are rumours that German resistance is hardening, but I still do not believe that it can last much longer. The morale of the garrison is low, for quite a high proportion of it consists of foreign non-German troops who don't want to fight. As I believe I said a day or two ago, they have plenty of petrol but are short of ammunition.

General Montgomery's drive to the South has temporarily been cancelled. The Guards Armoured Division is over the water, but is at the moment in reserve, for I believe that not all its tanks have yet been landed.

Today the weather is much better; it will be very good for bombing this afternoon, tonight and also, I think, tomorrow. Therefore I am going to make a big effort against the pilotless aircraft. But I must emphasise this. I have no intention of allowing pilotless aircraft to occupy too large a share of the general picture. I am only bombing them heavily at this moment because there is a general lull in the movement of the enemy, and it is therefore easy to give them a packet without letting up on targets of direct military importance.

The most important enemy movement is South of the Loire, and against this I have directed the fighter bombers. They have special orders to attack 4 de-training points which have been discovered. The American 9th Army Air Force has done particularly well. It got some very good train targets yesterday South of the Loire, and the 8th also did well, and got a number of locomotives.

An interesting phenomenon is the slight but indisputable rise in German air resistance. They are putting more fighters up now in an endeavour to defend some of their more important rail movements. They are also using minelaying aircraft to an ever increasing extent against our cross-channel convoys, and I have therefore allocated the highest priority, as far as bombing is concerned, to the airfields from which these aircraft set out. I am also initiating a big rail, road and bridge programme for the daylight bombers.

The bombing in the Laon/Rheims area was good. The attacks on bridges are being carried out in the most scientific way, the targets being chosen by railway experts who have to explain the reasons for their choice.'

His daily conferences continued at Norfolk House. An interesting account was published in the *Daily Mail*:

'The preliminary conference enables the Commander-in-Chief to fix in his own mind the plans he will put forward at a momentous conference of air chiefs which begins at 11 o'clock every morning.

It is a large assembly. It is also a gathering of celebrities. It is held out of reach of enemy bombs. Air Chief Marshal Leigh-Mallory presides. The Deputy Supreme Commander of All Forces, Air Chief Marshal Tedder, sits on one side of him, with the Deputy Air C-in-C, Major-General Hoyt Vandenberg, USAAF, on the other. The last named came into the Invasion picture late replacing another American general.

The blunt, ever-successful Air Chief Marshal Sir Arthur Harris of RAF Bomber Command, comes to the big conference. So does the enigmatic Lieut-General Carl Spaatz, Commanding General of the US Strategic Bomber Force. So does gay, gallant and beloved Major-General "Jimmy" Doolittle, who leads the US Eighth Air Force heavy bombers. Lieut-General L. "Keep Mobile" Brereton, commanding the US Ninth (Tactical) Air Force, is there, together with several other American air generals. Air Chief Marshal Sir Sholto Douglas, under whom Leigh-Mallory was serving as a Fighter Group commander less than two years ago, attends as the present Air Officer Commanding RAF Coastal Command. If he is not with General Montgomery in France, the famous Air Marshal Sir Arthur "Maori" Coningham, commander of the Tactical Air Forces, will be present, and in numbers of aircraft engaged, will assume responsibility for a major part of the day's operations.

Dozens of other Staff officers crowd in — there are representatives of all three Services, political advisers, the civilian Railway Adviser, meteorological officers, scientific advisers, Intelligence officers, and any other experts required.

The conference usually begins with the "met. man" giving a forecast of the weather ahead. A naval officer will report on current operations at sea. A soldier will give an appreciation of the ground position on all fronts. Every aspect of air operations, current and planned, is outlined. Then Air Chief Marshal Leigh-Mallory sums up and a general policy, which will embrace every one of thousands of sorties to be flown by aircraft of every type, is laid down for the next 24 hours.'

On 27 June, L-M decided that it was now vital to cut the two routes from Germany to the West through Strasbourg and Saarbrucken. Priority targets for bombing would continue to be rail marshalling yards.

25 June

'A day's holiday yesterday being Sunday. The weather yesterday was not as good as had been expected. I had hoped to direct a big effort against the pilotless aircraft, but it turned out to be a comparatively modest show. The day heavies did not get a good run at it.'

26 June

'Today Monty's attack has started, the object being to move SW of Caen then turn left-handed to capture the high ground South of Caen. This, if successful, would force the enemy to withdraw. The attack, owing to the vile weather, is getting very little air support. I don't know its outcome, and personally I have a feeling that it won't amount to much, and I have considerable doubts about the success of the Army. They may be able to do it.

My mind is very clear on one point about which I feel very strongly indeed. It is that we must be prepared to use every bit of air we've got, every single aircraft, in order to unstick the Army if, as I fear, it gets bogged.

Look at this photograph. (Here the AOC-in-C produced a large photograph showing the damage caused by one night attack by 100 heavy bombers on a small aiming point. The point and the area around it for a distance of roughly 1000 yards across was completely obliterated.) I am convinced that we could do this sort of thing to eight different points along a battle front.

It was Napoleon who said that the man who concentrated the greatest force at the right time and at the right place, won the battle. That is what we should do with our air weapon. We would never have attempted the invasion of the Continent without overwhelming air power, and it was because we had that power that the initial assault was successful. We must use air power to get the Army forward if they can't do it on their own, and I repeat, it looks to me, unfortunately, as though they can't. I proposed to use it in this way. We can find 6–8 "blobs", that is to say, battery positions or strong points, along the edge of the assault area. This can be done at first light by heavy bombers. Then an immediate follow up should be an artillery barrage covering the first 1000 yards in the depth of the area to be attacked. When that was lifted I should put in my medium bombers to clobber in front of the advancing Infantry up to a depth of from 1000 to 4000 yards. I am convinced that the moral effect of this triple form of assault would be terrific.

Finally, I should put the day heavy bombers on to more distant battery targets. If this be done, I truly believe that it would have the effect of getting the Army through. If it is not done, then there is, unhappily, a great chance that the Army will continue to stick. Those are my own views, and, as I say, I feel very strongly about them. The Deputy Supreme Commander, however, does not share them. He feels that the Army should be left to act on its own with the ordinary air support it has hitherto been getting. Naturally his views are shared by the supporters of strategical bombing, who are only too glad to get away from the battlefield and bomb distant targets. I foresee a first class row on this issue, but I am prepared for it. When I originally propounded this scheme of full air support to the Army, Air Chief Marshal Tedder was not present, but General Marshall was. He thoroughly agreed with it. If the present attack on Caen is not successful then I shall raise the scheme a second time, and I believe that Ike will back me. After all, as elaborate a plan as this was adopted and put into practice for the actual assault on the beaches, and I cannot for the life of me see why it should not be adopted again now that the second phase has been reached, if the Army sticks. It seems only logical and commonsense to do this, and I feel I shall get my way.'

27 June

'We had practically no operations yesterday, and no reconnaissance owing to the weather. On the other hand, it was ideal for the German pilotless aircraft, and the show they put up was really a pitiful effort. They only succeeded in pooping off 130. I think, however, that the reports that the people are getting windy are probably true. All the stuff put into the Press designed to calm the populace is of definite assistance to the enemy who can gain more than a hint of our counter-measures. I would much rather nothing whatever was given out. But there it is. I think we have got to make up our minds to put up with this weapon until the war is over. It will fluctuate in intensity, and possibly the Hun is now using prototypes, and has something larger up his sleeve. He may find it possible to launch this weapon from sites farther back than those he is using at present, of which we have knocked out 25 in the last few days. Some of these unfortunately were not operational, but that is not our fault. We covered the ones we were told to cover.

As for the Battle, the weather in France is bad today and is not likely to be operational from an air point of view, except for some fighter bombers. It is also very doubtful whether the night bombing programme can take place tonight or the day bombing programme for tomorrow. This is particularly unfortunate for I had detected certain very important moves. Rommel knows his Monty, and he is beginning at last to take a personal interest in the battle. At least I think so. He is now building up his armour in the Evreux/Dreux region, and I believe he is waiting for Monty to stick his neck out. Unless I am quite wrong, Rommel has a very shrewd idea of how to fight the battle and has good information. For example, he chose to obstruct, by means of poles, areas that I had selected to land gliders on, only a few days before the show. There is no doubt in my mind that he is keeping his armour back and will hit Monty on the flank with it when he moves and wherever he moves. If Monty turns right-handed and makes for Brittany his left flank will get it. If he turns left-handed towards the Pas de Calais, it will be his right flank. I am not saying that Rommel is going to succeed or that Monty is not aware of this, but I have a feeling that it may cramp his style.

Things are now eggbound and they may well become glacial. What we are now doing is paying for the American failure to bomb the railways in the Moselle and Metz area in accordance with the plan that I had drawn up for the battle. I am sure that if we had gone for those railways in the same way as we went for the others, the German rail movements would not be nearly so considerable as in fact they now are. There are heavy train movements through Metz, Vitry-en-Artois and also South through Blaireville. The vital spot is Vitry-en-Artois where the railways converge. It was to be bombed last night but the weather was so bad that we could not do so. It is down to be bombed tonight and again tomorrow by the American 8th Air Force. Today it is, I hope, receiving some attention from fighter bombers, but it really seems as though the Powers above are playing into the Germans' hands with this vile weather.

Other targets, all connected with this rail movement are Strasbourg and Saarbrucken still further to the East. What I must first do is stop movement at Vitry-en-Artois which will have the effect of slowing everything up, and then go for other targets further to the East. There are indications that the Germans may be moving as much as four divisions out of Germany into France, and even depleting their Russian Front in order to do so.

I have always said that the Germans will take a big risk in order to push us into the sea; that is the only hope they have of forcing a stalemate, and I repeat that our bombing of railways in the Northern Area (Northern France and Belgium) was good, but we are paying for our failure to bomb adequately in the central district.

The weather has been so bad that I have only just had photographs of the main German rail centre near Paris at Vaires.

(Here the AOC-in-C produced an air photograph showing the marshalling yard at Vaires, congested with railway traffic.) This is the first picture I have had of this place for a fortnight. It has been bombed but they have repaired it and I am told they had 5000 men on the job. If it is humanly possible Bomber Command will go there tonight and clobber it, but I am not at all certain that they will be able to do so.

The Met people hold out no hope of better weather conditions within the next two days.

The movement I mentioned of Infantry Divisions up from the South of France has now stopped. I don't think a very great deal got into the battle area. As for Monty's attack, it has not gone very well, but it may still be all right. He has had atrocious luck with the weather, for about midday yesterday not ordinary rain came down but a tropical downpour, turning roads into rivers and fields into lakes and swamps. This held him up.

I repeat that my main preoccupation is to stop railway movement from the East so as to prevent Rommel from building up. At the moment he has dispersed his tanks and he won't concentrate them until he is ready to fight.

The Americans are a strange lot. They are still obsessed with the notion that to bomb Germany in daylight is the proper course. I have to humour them, and this I explained to Tedder. If I let them go off and bomb some German target very heavily, then I may induce them next time to put a really big effort on to some railway target instead of merely attacking it with a dozen aircraft or so. The Americans don't like being under the command of an Englishman, and that is a fact which I have to face.'

28 June

'Operations are completely dead owing to the weather, which is frightful, but last night, thank God, Bomber Command got to Vaires and also to Vitry-le-Francois and did a good show. There were explosions at Vaires which seems to indicate they must have hit some ammunition. I feel somewhat relieved about this for they were the two most essential targets. Four de-training points have been discovered West of Paris, and I am going to clobber them as soon as I possibly can. For tomorrow I am promised weather very much like today, but a little better than today, with alternative sunshine and showers, but there seems little immediate prospect of settled weather.

As for the pilotless aircraft, I frankly do not understand why the enemy has not made far greater use of this weapon than he has. Assuming that he has 25 sites available (that may be an underestimate, for we have certainly not attacked all his modified sites), and assuming that he can let off two flying bombs an hour, he could put 600 on to London or the South of England in 12 hours.

In actual fact he has only put over about 120 in 24 hours, and of these about 70 have reached England and 25 the London area. This is all the more incomprehensible since the weather conditions for this form of attack are ideal and have been so for some time. I am forced therefore to the conclusion that if this is their idea of an intensive effort, it is a pretty poor one.

As far as military operations are concerned, my impression is that the Army is inching forward. This is how I would describe it. They've got a bridgehead over the Odon which they established last night, and the 2nd Army are going through it tomorrow.

Since operations have died on me I have turned my thoughts to administration. I have just held a conference concerning the re-equipping of squadrons with new types of aircraft, a matter of very great importance. I held a second conference to discuss the structure of this Headquarters, and to decide whether or not to reduce the staff to a nucleus. At present it numbers more than 400 officers, and it may be more satisfactory to reduce this number to a hundred whose duty it would be to co-ordinate the work of the subordinate Commanders, in addition to the normal operational work. I have had a talk with Tedder concerning the future, and he is very strongly of the opinion that my main Headquarters should remain here. I think on reflection that he is probably right. It is easier for me to fight a strategical battle in close and immediate touch with the "powers that be" than to do so from France. I shall, however, establish Advanced Headquarters in that country and make a practice of going there two or three times a week. You must help, St George, to find me a little pleasance over there.'

29 June

'Today was the first day when it has been possible to use bombers and fighter bombers in daylight, for some considerable time, owing to the slight but definite improvement in the weather. I suppose, however, that it was for this reason that the American 8th Air Force with all its fighter support and two Groups of the American 9th Air Force, chose to go to Leipzig and bomb aircraft factories. This they did without reference to myself. I cannot but regard this as serious, for I wanted to attack without delay the big railway movement East of Paris. To do so today, I have had to take squadrons from the Tactical Air Force, though they are committed to a big programme of immediate support to the Army by bombing enemy movement in the area West and South-West of Paris. However, there it is. The Americans have gone off and I can do nothing about it.

Today I have not had all the Air Forces that I should have had to carry out what, in my view, is my essential task, to help the Army to win their battle.

The fact is that the Americans have no idea of balance. They want to attack aircraft factories, come what may, so they attack them. It is a childish attitude, for the Luftwaffe is for the present at any rate, no sort of menace, and the German Army is. Although the papers talk of a 7-mile advance by Monty, I cannot myself make it at most more than 8000 yards. Moreover they are already beginning to talk about enemy counter-attacks, and this does not seem to me the right way to refer to an all-out offensive. If they are talking about enemy counter-attacks already, then it looks to me as though they are not too happy. I hope to God I am wrong, but I have a dreadful feeling that if the weather and American insouciance allow the German Army build-up to continue too long, it may prove very difficult to break out of the beach-head, and another Anzio may be created. That is what I am frightened of. It seems to me that the Army has had every opportunity, despite the bad weather, to exploit the initial surprise and therefore success of the landing, and they haven't taken it.

As for the air, it is not a good day for medium bombers but they will do something, but the conditions are good for fighter bombers. Last night, thank heaven, Bomber Command attacked Metz and Blainville and this relieved my mind a lot: they are very important train centres at this moment, when the enemy is engaged on using the French Eastern network of railways.

The attack on Vitry-le-Francois of the night before was not bad but not terribly good, but together with the attack on Vaires it has, I think, sufficed to hinder the train movement in that area quite a lot.

I am feeling slightly frustrated and have the distinct feeling that the Army is becoming more and more sealed in. I hope and pray that I am wrong.'

On the 30th the Duchess of Kent visited the AEAF headquarters. L-M showed her round the War Room.

30 June

'Not as good a day as it looks for air operations. The weather is bad for bombers but all right for fighter bombers. I have at last got some reconnaissance which has revealed a very interesting situation. You remember that Bomber Command attacked Vitry and Blainville. The result has been to stop railway movement in the Metz area and the Germans have had to shift their stuff further south, quite a long way south, towards Mulhouse. I am therefore beginning to clobber in that direction. The fact is that we are forcing them constantly to shift their railway movement, as more and more railway centres get attacked.

I don't think the public realise how much the air has done in this battle. In fact I am sure they don't. For example, the three attacks carried out by Bomber Command last week on Vitry, Vaires and Blainville in execrable weather have had the exact effect that I hoped for. The German movement has been stopped. It is becoming more difficult for the enemy to bring up his reinforcements, and he can of course make use of none of the railways near the battle area. Tonight Bomber Command are going for Vierzon to interfere with this new southerly train movement which will be more difficult to stop because there are no big bottle-necks to attack. The railways are more spread out. That is why I am going to send out fighter bombers to plaster railway lines, sidings, bridges, anything they can see. I have put the American 8th Air Force on to the job but it is a bit volatile in temperament, and I am not certain that they will bomb the railway targets SE of Paris that I want them to. I shouldn't be surprised if they went off elsewhere, but somehow I don't think they will and I daresay they will do very well. Whenever they buzz off to Germany they take all the fighters with them and consequently my effort is greatly reduced. That is why the attacks made by Bomber Command are of such great importance.

The Army has called for the assistance of heavy bombers, which I am going to give them, and they are going to attack what is thought to be the main Panzer concentration at Villers-Bocage.

I am still very preoccupied by the attitude of the general public towards the air. They are not seeing the picture in the proper perspective. It seems to me that the Press and the wireless are concentrating on the Army and neglecting the air. I don't say this because I want publicity but because I think the public ought to know the truth, and I am convinced that the truth is that the air has done more to wage this battle and will have done more to win it than either of the other two arms. If it had not been for the air attacks by bombers, fighter bombers and fighters delivered before D-Day and immediately afterwards, it is my view that the Army would have had double, if not three times the amount of resistance which they have in fact encountered.

As it is, the Germans in front of them are short of petrol and ammunition and are in a generally poor state. This is due to air attack.

Aren't the Russians doing well? That is where the real victory is going to come. I believe they will be inside Germany within two months.'

Chapter 15
1–10 July

Cold, overcast, and every airfield socked in — that was how July began. There was even a fire burning in the grate of L-M's office that day as he dictated his diary.

1 July

'Today has been a very depressing dud day. In the morning there wasn't a single airfield operational. I could do no bombing, and the air effort was reduced to a minimum.

Yesterday we had some slight success against the railway movement SE and S of Paris. The fighter bombers of the 8th Army Air Force went out and cut a number of railway bridges, hit quite a number of trains, and to judge from the explosions, one or two of them must have been carrying ammunition. I hope therefore that I have slowed the enemy's movements in that area, and I am promised sufficiently good weather to be able to do it again this afternoon.

The attack by Bomber Command on Vierzon was good, but not that on Villeneuve, where the weather was bad. There are no prospects of being able to carry on the air war tomorrow at all. The weather is completely u/s!* (unserviceable), and I cannot plan air operations on this sort of basis.

The Army I can only describe as stagnant. The expected German counter-attack was duly delivered at 09.45 hours this morning, but very soon petered out, and that I think is undoubtedly in part due to the success that Bomber Command had in plastering Villers-Bocage.†

At any rate the Army were ready and longing for the German attack. What I don't understand, however, is the sequel. I should have thought that having beaten off the counter-attack with considerable ease, the Army would then have pushed on, thrusting with all its armour, and seen the Hun right off. But it doesn't look to me as though they have done this, or are about to do so.

---

* Unserviceable — usually applied to aircraft. In this case meaning 'unfit for flying'.

† At this point, Saunders noted: That morning in the C-in-C's conference, Air Chief Marshal Sir Arthur Harris, when asked about the attack on this place, said that preliminary photographs showed it to have been quite successful and then added dryly . . . 'In fact, Villers-Bocage can be said to have been thoroughly liberated.

Personally, I should have thought that this was the moment to fling in all the armour. How well I remmber the way it was done on August 8th 1918, beyond Amiens. Then the Army put in 450 tanks, all they had, and scored what was the beginning of a decisive victory. Now, with three times that amount, they seem to be marking time waiting about, and of course the Hun can take the opportunity of reorganising in this vile weather, for we cannot do much to stop him from the air.

The situation regarding the pilotless aircraft seems to be getting better from the Germans' point of view. They are putting more of them into the middle of London and seem, therefore, to show a slightly increased efficiency in aiming. The weather of course has been perfect for them and will continue to be so as far as I can gather. In the past 24 hours they have made what has been up till now their maximum effort, and we have been unable to do much to stop them. Nevertheless, in the first week the defences accounted for 25 per cent of the flying bombs sent over, and in the second week, 35 per cent. Whenever the weather breaks, the percentage of 'kills' rises sharply. The fighters are out against them, especially the Tempests, operating under frightful weather conditions.

Spaatz is all lined up to bomb them with everything he has as soon as the weather clears, and so is Bomber Command. But the fact is, my dear St George, the Hun has had a double slice of luck. The weather has made it possible for him, not only to carry out railway movements which he could never have done in decent weather, but also to maintain his pilotless aircraft attacks. I suppose the ultimate solution is for the Army to capture the Pas de Calais, but it doesn't look as though they are going do to that in the near future. The sites are extremely well camouflaged, which makes hitting them a matter of considerable difficulty.

2 July

'The main news today is of more German Army movements up from the South, from Bordeaux through Saintes and Angouleme. The weather is completely dud and I cannot operate from this country at all. The conditions are a little better in the Cherbourg Peninsula, and I am hoping that three Groups of P.38s will be able to take off and attack these movements. They have orders to smash up trains, to create road blocks, and do everything they can to impose delay on the enemy.

SE of Paris there is also some movement, but we have had some movement, but we have had some success at Joigny on the railway to Dijon, which we have blocked. There are indications that trains are moving up through Nevers and Bourges, and when the weather changes we shall have to attack these centres.

To the North of France in the Cambrai — St Quentin are, a good deal of canal traffic has been observed. It may be that the Germans are bringing up construction materials and supplies for the sites of the pilotless aircraft by this means.

There was no bombing last night, and as far as I can see there will be none tonight. As for the Army, it can only be described as static. Monty appears to be waiting to be counter-attacked, but not to intend to attack himself. I confess frankly that I cannot understand it, for he has a superiority of at least three to one in tanks and from three and a half to four to one in men, and I should have thought that after the failure of the German counter-attacks yesterday, if he used his armour vigorously he could clean the Hun right up. In regard to that we can only wait on events.

A plan is brewing about which I shall speak tomorrow when I have considered its full implcations. On first sight I don't like it much, but I will talk about that in due course.

3 July

'The plan I referred to yesteday has not yet matured, so I shall not describe it today, beyond saying that frankly I think it to be a perfectly bloody one. It misses the boat in every possible direction, and will I think, it adopted, sow discord between us and the Americans. It also makes the 2nd Army look deplorable. We had our chance in the early days and missed it.

The conditions in the air are simply frightful, but yesterday the Tactical Air Force did some good work in the battle area. Last night Bomber Command were unable to attack Villeneuve because of weather conditions.

Railway movement East of Paris has died down, and there are indications that he is trying to get trains up through Orleans and Villeneuve, which will be dealt with.

I was fortunate enough to get some reconnaissance in the South West, from which I have discovered that the trains to take the two Divisions up to the battle area are moving East, indicating therefore that they will pick up these troops in the South of France, possibly near Marseilles and bring them back again to the Bordeaux area to be thence brought up to the battle. This will give us a certain respite. I shall not, therefore, clobber Angouleme tonight, but I shall wait until it is packed with enemy troops, then I shall hope to do them the maximum amount of mischief. I shall wait therefore until the day after tomorrow. I have ordered the Tactical Air Force to give the fullest support they can to the 1st American Army, while the American 8th Air Force is to take on what we call the Paris gap, though targets East of Paris remain their final priority.

I have discovered that Mosquitos are good at attacking railways at night, and I am therefore going to send two Mosquito Squadrons to roam wide over France attacking any railways they can find.

Looking back on everything, despite the unspeakable weather, the main offensive that I have launched against the railways has paid an enormous dividend. I have secret information that as far back as 2nd May last the Germans were no longer able to use the railways in the Northern Area and were trying to base their plans on using only the South and East.'

4 July

'Yesterday was the worst day we've ever had, because of the weather. My operations were practically nil. The Army advanced almost imperceptibly but in one place got 2000 yards ahead, and this morning two brigades advanced two miles in the direction of Caen. Then they appeared to pack up for the day. Why, I don't know.

Yesterday, too, we walked into a village on the western side of the bulge and, finding some mines in it, retreated, and the Germans are now in it. I confess I don't understand this hesitation. I should have thought that when you are attacking, the thing to do is to attack. The involved explanation published today in *The Times* concerning the strategy employed, made me laugh. But, seriously, it is pitiful.

As far as the air is concerned, those two Hun divisions down in the South are getting ripe to bomb and may be attacked this afternoon, weather permitting. Tonight Bomber Command goes to Orleans and Villeneuve.

There has been considerable rail activity in these places, and I am fed up with them. They are going to get a good clobbering. The railways SE of Paris are also pulsating with activity, and I shall try and attack them if I can. They haven't been reconnoitered for a week. The weather, however, is still not settled, and another depression is on its way.

This morning I had a meeting with Generals Doolittle and Brereton and Air Marshal Coningham, with Tedder to act as a sort of referee. I put the proposal before them that when the Army is engaged in actual battle the Tactical Air Forces must be used to assist it, and their strategical tasks must therefore be taken over by the 8th Army Air Force. I explained that this meant that the 8th could not be used against Germany, but would have to attack the strategic targets in France behind the enemy's front, of concern to the battle. They all understood this, but it is possible that, on occasions, the Americans may ask to go to Germany. If I don't want them to do so, I may say so, and if they still press their wish then it will be for the Supreme Commander to decide between us. That seems a fair enough arrangement and we had a perfectly amicable meeting. Indeed, the set-up seems to be beginning to work. But until the Army moves and we get a little decent weather, I shall have no "hot news".'

5 July

'Everything is perfectly bloody. All the bombing in daylight was abortive though they bombed through the overcast, but there was quite a lot of good work done by the Tactical Air Force in the battle area. Very fortunately Bomber Command was able to attack Orleans and Villeneuve last night with, I believe, good results. Moreover, they also got one of the main dumps of the pilotless aircraft, and did what I also believe to be a good show there.

The fighters of the 8th Air Force did some very good work SE of Paris, getting 80 locomotives and 140 railway trucks. Right down South, near Bordeaux, not much was discovered except two trains loaded with lorries, which were attacked. The Mosquitos had a field day, or rather field night. They went all over France clobbering trains and railway engines, and had a lovely party. The weather was bad for bombing this morning, and no one saw anything. It was bad at middle day, but I am told it may clear this afternoon.

I have now received extremely good evidence that Germany has not been able to use the railways of Northern France and Belgium for a considerable time. A prisoner taken recently, stated he had moved from Holland to Normandy, but to get there he had travelled via Alsace Lorraine and all around France. Some of the German divisions now moving towards the battle area have had to detrain as far East as Bar le Duc and complete the rest of the journey by road. In one case, a division travelled by road the whole way but its tanks were sent by rail. The division arrived before the tanks, which were in poor shape.'

6 and 7 July

'There is too much controversy going on for my liking. Yesterday was a disappointing day and results were patchy. The Tactical Air Force, however, did well, and the Americans had at last a clear day to bomb the pilotless aircraft sites, of which they attacked between twenty and thirty, including some big sites, and I think did some good.

I sent the Tactical Air Force further afield. Today (7th) the weather was bad over here and in France, but good in Germany, so I allowed the American 8th Air Force to go to that country, more particularly as the Army is static and I did not therefore need them. I pushed the Tactical Air Force to the South of the Loire and the fighter-bombers have been at it today, while Mosquitos will take up the task tonight. They will also go to South and South-East of Paris.

As I say, I have had no help from the 8th today because they wanted to go to Germany, and I didn't see why they shouldn't. Yesterday (6th) the 8th were sent into targets South of the Loire and took a route which brought them fairly near Paris, where they were heavily engaged by fighters, had to fight a battle, and expended so much ammunition that they had to turn around and come home before reaching their objective. I have urged them, when next they go out to that area, to route themselves over Brittany where there is not much opposition.

Tonight Bomber Command will attack Nantes and will go again to Vaires. There will also be attacks on flying bomb bases, and a biggish effort made to help the Army. I am a bit doubtful about it as I don't think the plan is a very good one, but it may do some good, but I have a feeling they are wasting our air effort.

The 8th will attack Angouleme and Belfort. The bridges across the Loire at Tours and Saumur were attacked yesterday, and if it has been found that they were not destroyed, they will be attacked again.

Yesterday I got a great deal of reconnaissance, and found that the area bounded by the Seine and the Loire is generally very quiet with very little movement. I think this means that what movement there is takes place at night. I get increasing evidence from POW reports of the extra detours that the German armies are having to make in order to reach the Loire. Some of them have had to walk from South of the Loire. They have tried to use bicycles, but a great many of these have gone u/s through punctures for which they have not got mending outfits.

Over here, there is a very sharp division between myself and some other people over the full application of our air effort. I want to help the Army all I can, because that is what I am convinced the Air Force should now do. I have always been of that opinion. We should never have got the Army to France at all had we not had overwhelming air strength, and having got them there we must do our utmost as an Air Force to give them every possible assistance and to try and unstick them. I am not yet going to talk about the plan that I have mentioned. It is quite possible it may not come off.'

At last, L-M was able to look further ahead. But he was finding it difficult to obtain information from Eisenhower's headquarters. He decided to move an echelon of his staff to Forward SHAEF in the tent city at Portsmouth. On the 7th he had to write formally to Eisenhower

'to request that I now be given some indication of the policy regarding the probable scope, strength, and location of future airborne operations . . . this information will be particularly helpful to me in deciding the future airfield disposition of troop carrier forces in this country which has now become a matter of urgency.'

Later the same day two waves of heavy bombers with a fighter escort carried out an hour's heavy bombing on the northern outskirts of Caen. The purpose was to destroy strongly defended localities, reportedly some including concrete, to ease the advance of our forces. It provided a considerable uplift in morale for the Allied troops — but pilots reported doubts as to whether there really were any German defences to be hit, and instead the large bombs cratered the roads and held up the advance. Nevertheless Montgomery was pleased with the air support and told Major-General Frank Simpson at the War Office:

'We must definitely keep Leigh-Mallory as Air Commander-in-Chief. He is the only airman who is out to help us win the land battle and has no jealous reactions.'

On Saturday 8 July, L-M flew to Normandy. There he discussed future operations with Montgomery, and afterwards visited some US airfields. He asked pilots whether they felt the German air force was showing a more aggressive spirit but they ridiculed the idea. Then he gave a press conference from which *The Times* reported his view that air supremacy had now been achieved over the Luftwaffe. Everything that had happened since the invasion of France had started had proved conclusively that the policy of bombing railways and all other communications in northern France and Belgium was absolutely right. He dined with Broadhurst at HQ 83 Group and afterwards talked with General Dempsey.

Next day, Sunday the 9th, he visited more US airfields, lunched with General Omar Bradley (Commander, 1st US Army) and General Quesada (Commander, 9th Tactical Air Command). He returned to Stanmore in the evening, bringing back a message from Montgomery expressing the Army's appreciation of the efforts of the Allied Air Forces.

8–10 July

'First the general situation. There is very little to say. The weather makes air operations on a large scale impossible. There are signs of railway movements SE of Paris and again through Vitry. Bomber Command will attack that railway centre, if weather conditions permit. South of the Loire the two divisions I spoke of are beginning to move up, though in what condition I cannot say.

On the battle-front itself the situation is not yet good enough to make targets for the Air Force.

Today, I want to talk about general matters but, in passing, just let me say what a grand time I had seeing the fighter pilots in France, getting their reactions to the battle. People down "the hole"* moan sometimes about the possibility of German fighter strength. That is nonsense. Our fighter pilots will see them off any and every day of the week. In wet and bloody circumstances they are as full of guts and fighting spirit as they can possibly be.

I have come back feeling thoroughly truculent, and I am going to speak my mind. I have been in a difficult position for the last four

---

* The underground Operations Room.

weeks or so. I have always taken the view that the Army must be given all the air support it desires. After all, it is a citizen Army, composed for the most part of men belonging to every walk of life, to whom soldiering is neither natural nor easily learned. Moreover, brave though they have shown themselves to be, they are for the most part untried troops who have never been in action before, with the exception of one or two divisions who thought they had won the war in Africa, and don't feel at all inclined to start winning it all over again in Normandy. The men they are fighting are the finest soldiers in the world. To them soldiering is a profession, whatever the means they used to earn their livelihood in peacetime might have been, and they are in a desperate way. They are up to all the tricks, they know how to fight, and if they fail in their duty they're shot.

All this by way of background. What I have been up against more or less since D-Day is the school of thought which takes the view that the air support given to the Army should be the minimum rather than the maximum, on the principle that if you give the Army an inch it will take an ell. This school urges as a principle that really heavy Air Forces should not be employed on the immediate battle-front but elsewhere, beyond and outside it.

I maintain, and always have, that heavy bombers can produce a concentration of high explosive infinitely greater than any which can be produced by any other means. Look, for example, at this photograph of Aulnay.' (Here, the C-in-C produced a photograph showing an area of complete and annihilating devastation a thousand yards across.) 'Such a result as this was achieved by Bomber Command in twenty minutes, and to be able to produce this when and where it is needed is, in my view, a prime factor in the winning of a land battle by the type of troops under Montgomery's command.

I talked to Monty about a month ago on the subject of air co-operation and told him that he should have every machine he wanted. To this course he agreed, and I at once sent over planners to him to fix up the details of the immediate operations he wished laid on. On my return from seeing him, I rang up Air Marshal Coningham. He was out at dinner and I could only get his deputy, Strafford, to whom I explained the ideas of Monty and myself. My views were communicated to Coningham late at night when he returned from dining, and he at once made immediate arrange-ments to go over to France the next day with Air Chief Marshal Tedder, the Deputy Supreme Commander. They did so, and agreed between themselves that the Army should be supported only by the Tactical Air Force and not by the rest, and that as far as the operations of the Tactical Air Force were concerned, Monty should make his requests through Coningham to me. This was arranged by the Deputy Supreme Commander and there was nothing that I could do except acquiesce or clear out. For the moment I did nothing, but I soon found that requests from the Army reached me too late to be able to deal with them properly. A bombing operation is a complicated business, and such questions as the effect that certain types of bombs may have on certain types of targets have to be carefully considered. It is no use, for example, creating a vast wilderness of craters in front of a Division of tanks. They can't move over them.

I soon found out that I was not being given time enough adequately to consider this and similar problems. I was therefore in a very awkward position but, as I say, I decided to sit tight, for I felt quite sure that the plum would one day fall ripely into my hand. Now, as the result of my talks in France yesterday and the day before, I feel sure that it has. The policy of double-dealing, the effect of which has been to deny the Army what it wanted in the field, has failed. Monty wishes to deal in future direct with me, and we have told Eisenhower so. Eisenhower has agreed, and the reason that he has done so is that Monty is to be put in command of all the armies in France. This means that I am going to put Air Marshal Coningham where he ought to be, in charge of one tactical branch of the General Air Forces, and I am going to take command of their dispositions myself. If he does not like the situation, he will have to clear out. If Tedder does not like it, then he or I will go. My mind is now fully made up. Either I am to be allowed to direct, if necessary, the whole Air Forces available to the full and immediate support of the Army, or I shall resign on that issue.'

Here Saunders intervened to remind L-M of the school of thought in the Air Ministry which took the view that to be the servant of the Army in war would mean continued subservience in peace. L-M's response was: 'Yes, I am well aware of that school of thought and believe it to be very narrow-minded. I know quite well that in all probability an effort will be made when this war is over to suppress the Royal Air Force, and this attempt will follow the lines of that made after the last war. But to show independence at this moment and to go ahead without reference to the Army is, in my considered opinion, a very short-sighted policy. How much stronger the Air Council will be when peace comes if they can say, when maintaining the necessity for a strong Air Force, "Well look, in war it went wholeheartedly to the help of the Army and gave it whatever it wanted".

There it is. I think — I hope — I have pulled it off. Some of the younger American Generals won't like it but they will have to lump it, for Eisenhower is behind me.'

Saunders expressed his opinion that Coningham would do his duty however much he personally might feel upset by the new development. He was a patriotic man, just as was Harris, who was now fully co-operating with L-M despite the early differences of opinion between them. L-M nodded agreement and continued:

'I am very glad to hear you think so, and hope and believe you are right. We shall soon know. My relations with Monty have always been cordial. It was agreed at the outset that he would have to work through Coningham, but he expressed the desire to see me occasionally and talk over the general course of the battle. Now I hope we shall have an opportunity of even closer collaboration. In fact I'm sure we shall have, for I am determined on it.

Let this be my last word: I shall give the Army all the support for which it asks.'

Meanwhile, Portal wrote on the 9th from the Air Ministry to the Secretary of State for Air: the topic was the new appointment to AMP*. He named seven possible candidates —

'but after long consideration, I think the choice really lies between Slessor and Leigh-Mallory . . . Of the two I am not at all sure that Leigh-Mallory would not be the better choice. His chief failing is as a judge of men, but you do not make important appointments on his advice alone, and I think that with the help of VCAS and CAS any serious mistakes will be avoided.

Leigh-Mallory's assets are his operational reputation, his great energy and ability and, above all, his fair-mindedness which, I think, is recognised throughout the senior ranks of the service, and on the whole I believe he would be the better choice.'

Portal offered the job of the South East Asia Command to Peter Drummond — but on the 19th July the latter turned it down, something that turned to L-M's apparent advantage.

---

* Air Member for Personnel.

Chapter 16
11 to 26 July

Tuesday 11 July was L-M's birthday, his fifty-second. It was marked by an argument with Air Chief Marshal 'Bomber' Harris at the regular commanders' conference. L-M said he was pleased with the success of the railway plan: movement across the River Seine had stopped although supplies were still coming into the enemy by other railways: the enemy was now using Paris as their main unloading and distributing centre.

But Harris questioned the value of continuing to attack the rail marshalling yards. He said that they had been attacked since April and, as far as he could see, they might go on for ever without achieving any decisive result. The cost to Bomber Command had been too heavy, he said. It was three and a half months since they had attacked Germany yet it had been estimated that five months would be enough to put Germany back to full production again. In his opinion, attacks on bridges were a surer way of achieving dislocation.

Tedder intervened to support L-M over the value of attacks on the marshalling yards in the Paris area. He also recommended attacks further east and in Germany itself. When Harris asked what priority was now envisaged to challenging the German Air Force to a battle, L-M replied firmly that this now had lower priority.

Next day, L-M gave lunch to representatives of the Air Forces of Poland, France, Belgium, Norway and Czechoslovakia followed by a talk on the war situation in the War Room. But let us return to L-M's diary, for further insights of the progress of the Battle and the development of his Command relationships.

11 and 12 July

'First, operations: I have come to the conclusion in the last two days that the unceasing bad weather we have had since D-Day has made it possible for the Germans to infiltrate, not only in the bridgehead, which I know about, but also in the Paris area, which I am now convinced has become the focal point of their supply system. I am therefore determined to attack the three main railway centres at this city, Noisy-le-Sec, Vaires and Ville-Neuve. Our railway expert, Brant, is of the opinion that Noisy-le-Sec has already been so badly clobbered that it is not in use. About that I am inclined to disagree with him, for we have had no reconnaissance photo of it since 4 June. Anyhow, the other two are going to be attacked. I shall get a double dividend from such a move. Not only will all the stuff, of which a great quantity must have accumulated, be destroyed there, but also the whole supply organisation will be disorganised if the attacks are satisfactory. Otherwise, with this vile weather, I have had no reconnaissance, no bombing, no nothing!

Now about the matters of which I spoke at our last meeting. Yesterday I saw the Chief of the Air Staff (Portal) and we had a partially acrimonious interview. He was very angry at the interview which I gave to Press Correspondents on the other side. I told him that I was extremely sorry, but that I was under the impression that the ban had been lifted since one of my staff — to wit yourself St George — had given the Press certain facts about air operations prior to D-Day, and that as far as I was aware, no objection had been made. He then simmered down and we were soon on our usual terms. I complained frankly of the whole of my set-up, and told him how I was placed. He did not by any means disagree, but was somewhat startled when I told him what I proposed to do*, and still more startled when I said that I did not intend to inform Tedder that I was going to see the Supreme Commander-in-Chief, but would tell him after I had done so. I explained that in my view Tedder had not been open with me over the role which Coningham should play in his estimation, and that in any case I was perfectly entitled to go direct to Ike. Things then became more cordial and we had a good laugh over Bert (Harris) and his operations, particularly on the point of how strange it was that the very things he said his Command could never do, they were now doing to such good effect and that he was so pleased about it. Our interview ended in an atmosphere of bonhomie.

I then went over to see Ike at SHAEF and told him that Monty had given me to understand that he was to be Commander-in-Chief of the Allied Armies in France, and that that being so I must work closely with him. Ike seemed worried at this statement and hummed and hah-ed. Eventually, he said that he had agreed to such a step but that it would not be a final one. "At the earliest opportunity" said Ike "I will have two Commanders-in-Chief in France, one British and one American, and that will happen when the American Army Group is formed. I shall then take control myself, as Supreme Commander-in-Chief."

My own feeling is that he won't ever really take over, but will continue to leave things to Monty while affecting to consider that this is a purely temporary arrangement. I went on to tell Ike that Monty and I had talked over the whole question of how we could best play ball together, and I outlined my ideas about taking a larger proportion of control over the situation, and of putting Coningham in his proper place as Commander of the 2nd Tactical

---

* L-M was referring to the plan outlined in his diary for 8–10 July.

Air Force. Ike was inclined to agree with me — at any rate he saw my point. I urged that the battle was not strategical and tactical, but a single problem in fact, and to be dealt with as such. I ended by informing Ike that I was going off to see Tedder and tell him the situation.

Off I went to do so, and Tedder and I had some very plain speaking. I said that everyone seemed interested in seeing that I had nothing to do, and I pointed out that as far as I could see, Tedder was doing everything through Coningham. Tedder argued that he had been given control, or rather supervision, of air strategy by the Commander-in-Chief. In so doing, he was acting in a manner in which the Chief of the Air Staff would normally act, but the responsibility for the strategical movements of the Air Force had been handed over to SHAEF, and Ike had asked him, as Deputy Supreme Commander, to handle it. The conversation, having started somewhat acrimoniously, presently reached quite an amicable level. I had obviously shaken him a bit, and he certainly shook me, to such an extent that I am still thinking over the question whether to decide at once to take more control. This attitude of mind I explained to him, pointing out that it would be very difficult for me not to take more control when we go over the other side, but I added that I would turn the problem over again in my mind, and if I took a decision in accordance with my present intention, then instead of Tedder barging in on strategy he would have to give way to me. At any rate, if that happened we could try out the whole system for a month, which would prejudice nothing. This does not seem to me to be unreasonable and I think he agrees with me. I am still thinking the matter over.'

13 July

'It gets worse and worse.* The weather is absolutely frightful. The Army is inching forward in one or two places. Poor devils, the mud must slow them up. Bad show, and not their fault. As far as the air is concerned, there was very little activity yesterday, but what there was was very good indeed. The Tactical Air Force found trains south and west of Paris and did some excellent work. There were a number of fights and about twenty German aircraft were destroyed. Bomber Command, too, achieved two successes against the marshalling yards at Tours and Culmont-Chalindrey. The other two places which they were detailed to attack, Vaires and Revigny, were covered with cloud and they brought their bombs back. Today a certain amount of activity has been laid on, but the prospects of carrying it out are nil, at any rate as far as this country is concerned. The weather is vile in the bridgehead, but south the

---

* L-M was referring to the weather. Rain was streaming down from low remorseless clouds as he dictated this passage.

clouds are breaking and may lift enough to allow something to be done.

Here I am with the biggest Air Force the world has ever seen, and I do not think more than 20 per cent of it has been in operation since the start. I would put it indeed at not more than 15 per cent. As for the Tactical Air Force, I shall quietly take more and more control. I shall attend their meetings and gradually assume direction. I propose to do nothing violent, but they will get used to it, and one day, quite soon, I hope I shall have created the situation I want.'

On the 14th Kingston-McLoughry and Zuckerman returned from Caen. Their report was that 'troops had been surprised at such a heavy attack in that particular spot. There was no evidence of concrete strong points in the bombed area and no sign of dead Germans.' The area to be bombed had been selected by the Army who had told L-M that it included concrete pill-boxes.

14 and 15 July

'Here is the plan — Monty's famous plan which I said I would outline when the time came. When it was first outlined the Germans were nearer the coast than they are now, and their line ran well north of Caen through Carentan to the coast. I should have thought that the way to have dealt with them in view of the overwhelming forces at our disposal would have been to have driven one wedge southwards, using the American troops, in the general direction of Lessay, and another one, using British troops, south-east of Caen, towards Falaise. That would have meant that the enemy would have been cut up and could have been destroyed in detail.

Monty, however, had quite a different plan. His idea was that the British Army with enormous forces of tanks should do three things:

   (i)   Sit tight where they were.
   (ii) Suffer no reverses (fancy that!)
   (iii) Move eventually and take Caen.

In the meantime, while they held firm and occupied the enemy the Americans were to sweep on to Caumont then to Vire and finally to Laval, detaching a Corps to capture St Malo and Rennes. That was the plan, but it seemed to me to ignore the fact that the Germans were massing reserves west of Paris, and that even if the advance were successful the only result achieved would be to have driven the German Army back on to those reserves. In fact however, the object was not achieved, not even by the British forces, who failed to hold off the German advance in front of them, while two Panzer Divisions slipped away, right-handed, and appeared against the Americans. The plan, in fact, has gradually petered out.

The next plan evolved seemed to me to be even worse, for it did not contemplate that the British Army should cross the River Orne but should proceed down its left bank, using it to guard its left flank. Plans are now brewing about which I will speak in due course. The air operations of yesterday were very limited, and I am now told by the Met. that the biggest depression we have yet to encounter is on its way and should be here by midnight. It appears to cover the whole of the Atlantic. After that, when it clears off, it is said we may have some better weather. Despite the bad weather of yesterday, Bomber Command did a good attack on Ville-Neuve but failed to bomb Revigny where there was 10/10ths cloud. Fighter-bombers did good work on railways and trains.

You remember the interesting controversy which has been going on concerning the use of heavy bombers in support of the Army? When I was last in France, I spoke to Monty on the subject and also to Coningham, and left no doubt, especially with the latter, as to the nature of my views. Now large scale plans are being made which all depend for a great part of their success upon the use of heavy bombers in close support. Coningham has changed his attitude. At this morning's conference he laid before me in detail exactly what the Army wanted, and then left it to me to take the necessary steps. Tedder listened and said nothing. I think he has been told by Ike to leave things to me.'

16 July

'Air operations have gone phut, except that last night Bomber Command's attack on Ville-Neuve was good. Attacks at Chalons and Nevers were also satisfactory and I am very pleased about them. The weather was so bad that the fighter-bombers lost their way and didn't know where they were, but this didn't prevent them from shooting up a number of trains which they came across more or less by accident. The Leigh-Mallory plan*, is coming to fruition. I have always maintained that accurate bombing by Bomber Command was a winner. Its full application, I hope and believe, is about to come. In using this arm I have emphasised certain essential principles. Any strongpoint, for example, that has been really heavily clobbered must be by-passed, for it is impossible to get tanks or even Infantry over it. But at the spots where the Army must go around, the air form of attack must be such as to leave the ground uncratered. Medium and light bombers must be used for this purpose to quell the immediate defences. I am glad to say this principle has been accepted, together with the other equally vital principle by which the Army must follow in the immediate wake of the bombers. They must not wait an instant. All this has been agreed, and I hope that we shall see a spectacular show. There are

---

* See last paragraph of Diary for 14/15 July.

people in a higher quarter who won't be sorry if it does not succeed. But it is equally true to say that there are others who wish it every success.

On the whole, the position regarding the weather is more cheerful. It might clear up and become quite decent. I have a strong feeling that the Army is at last beginning to feel that it must get on, and that to help it to do so the air has a very important part to play. There is no doubt that air assistance has a tremendous moral effect. I think the Army is going to be all right, for once they get going they will gain confidence and the thing may well go with a swing. It is up to us to help give them that confidence by handing out the biggest measure of support we possibly can.

Incidentally, I had a friendly argument with Tedder on the subject of Dieppe, which he, wrongly in my view, said had been an easier battle to fight. It was, in fact, much harder than this present battle for we were operating at the extreme limit of fighter range with far smaller forces than those which I have under my command today, against a Luftwaffe very much more powerful than it is at present.'

Next day, the 17th, at the 11 o'clock morning conference for air commanders there was a sharp dispute between Tedder and Doolittle concerning the failure of the Americans' 8th Air Force to carry out their obligations to attack CROSSBOW targets. It was a symptom of Doolittle's general reluctance to bomb targets outside Germany or which he had not chosen himself.

That afternoon L-M flew to Normandy to watch the air offensive, which was to be the prelude to Monty's ground offensive scheduled for the following day. This, which had Eisenhower's full support, was to be a repeat of the failed exercise of 7 July, in order to break into the area SE of Caen. Despite all this activity, L-M managed to write a quick note to Jeanette, his daughter-in-law, who had sent him a birthday present.

17 July
'The glass is going up but there has been thick fog on the other side.
The prospects, however, are better.'
Saunders noted that L-M touched his portable barometer and frowned on seeing it fall.
'There was quite a lot of air activity last night, though none which can be described as spectacular. A number of very useful targets were hit and bombed with great effect, mainly railways. I am now getting daily reports concerning the number of trains clobbered, lines blocked, etc., and the evidence that the attacks are good, and have been so for a long time now, is increasing. For example, the attack by Bomber Command at Nevers was extremely successful. One photograph shows no less than sixty engines mashed up. The attack on Culmont-Chalindrey was also extremely good.'

L-M showed Saunders air photographs which the latter found particularly impressive: they showed the complete destruction of three lines of railways, converging so that they resembled nothing so much as a ploughed field.

'I confess I am in a great state about the weather. Is it going to play? If it does we are on the eve of a decisive battle. The whole Army is on tenterhooks. I shall be going over tomorrow to watch, I hope, the first stages of what I should like to call the air blast battle. I am having, as usual, some trouble with the Americans. I strive to be philosophical and I hope that I am being successful. I think I am, for otherwise they would at times drive me mad.

For example, yesterday for the first day for weeks there was fine weather over the "CROSSBOW" sites in the Pas de Calais. But though these targets are first priority with the Americans and they are supposed to have two hundred bombers at instant readiness to attack them, they went off almost everywhere except there. It appears that what happened was that when we laid on the plans in the morning, the Met. people said the weather would be bad in the Pas de Calais. In the afternoon, however, they changed their minds and said it would be clear. Whereupon Spaatz, instead of ringing me up in which case I should have at once altered the targets in order to allow him to send bombers to the Pas de Calais, rang up Tedder instead and said he didn't understand the lay-on. The net result was that the Americans did not bomb the CROSSBOW targets.'

On 18th July *The Times* reported the attack across the Orne river in north-west France:

'. . . the stupendous air assault that preceded the attack and closely supported it through hours of heavy fighting. Nothing comparable has ever been achieved before in direct support of an army in the field. Operation Clobber — to "clobber" a target is one of the newest verbs in air force language — will long be remembered. In record time, plans devastating in their simplicity had been completed. After several hours of deluge it could be recorded that AEAF has fulfilled all its obligations to the minute. As a private soldier said: "The chief thing about a raid like this is that it's on our side." Sir Trafford Leigh-Mallory himself flew into the battle in an unescorted aircraft to direct the offensive. When he returned to London last evening he was well satisfied. General Montgomery sent a message of thanks to Air Chief Marshal Sir Trafford Leigh-Mallory: "The tremendous weight of air attack inspired the troops and had a decisive effect." '

On that day over 7000 tons of bombs were dropped on the outskirts of Caen. But, once again, there were only marginal gains due at least in part to staunch resistance by the German army. Eisenhower and the staff at SHAEF were furious with Montgomery. L-M told his commanders on the 18th back in Stanmore that he had discussed future command arrangements with Montgomery because there was a belief that Eisenhower might take direct control of the Allied armies.

L-M told Montgomery that he 'would set up his caravan at his (Montgomery) headquarters and maintain a sort of formal echelon there, paying visits himself at frequent intervals. As long as he (Montgomery) was Commander-in-Chief of both armies, he would concert plans with him.' If and when General Eisenhower took command of the armies and General Montgomery became GOC British Armies, then it would be appropriate for Montgomery to liaise with Air Marshal Coningham while he, as Air C-in-C, would have his formal headquarters alongside the Supreme Commanders' Headquarters.

On 19 July L-M told his commanders that 'at the Prime Minister's conference yesterday evening, the amended defence plan was approved'. He now directed Bomber Harris to divert his attacks from railways to fuel and ammunition dumps instead and to industrial targets in Germany, something which Harris had been longing to hear.

L-M met General Bradley about a controversy of whether or not to bomb. Bradley preferred to have no bombing as it impeded the advance of his tanks. Afterwards L-M wrote to him: 'It was very good of you to come over today. I was more than sorry that I had to rush off. I had made an appointment with CAS before I knew you were coming and it was the only possible time that week.'

L-M also wrote to Montgomery saying that he was sorry that Bradley would not allow him to use Bomber Command: 'It looks like being an almost 100 per cent American show, which is a pity in the circumstances.'

19 July

'It was a classical battle on Tuesday. The plan was a good one and the air could play its full part because we knew where the defences were and the bombs fell on them. The whole thing went very quickly up to 11 am. Then something seems to have happened and progress slowed down, and in the afternoon the Hun made a counter-attack though without success. The visual control post in a tank called up some Typhoons who went at once into action and knocked out sixteen German tanks with rockets. The bombing of Bomber Command at first light was extraordinary. Aircraft were spread out in a great fan in the red dawn, coming in over the sea. It was an incredible sight. Soon there was nothing but a pall of dust and smoke and I could see but little from the Storch* in which I was flying. I must say that the air side was tremendously successful. The Army had been unable to move in the Caen area for three weeks and we got them unstuck in three hours. The Army were particularly cheerful to see the bombers going straight on through

---

* Fiesler Storch — a German light aircraft. This one had been captured in North Africa and commandeered by Broadhurst, who in all probability was with L-M on this occasion.

the flak undeviating towards their target. Occasionally one would go down in flames, but the others pressed on and never wavered. It was a magnificent sight.

About half past ten I saw Monty and we had a long talk during which we decided to deal together as long as he was in command of the armies. We would do all the broader planning, and in settling the part to be played by the air we felt we must co-operate to the full.

I then went on to see Dempsey who was surrounded by the fog of war. It was then about two in the afternoon and he had not got much news. This did not worry him however, because he pointed out that chaps frequently forget to send reports back as the battle develops. I hope he was right, but I believe the real reason for the lack of reports was because by then the Army was not making much progress. He, and others, were very appreciative of what had happened in the air. I made Monty realise that all this air show had been organised and laid on by AEAF and he afterwards made some very correct references to it.

I got back to Headquarters that evening. The next day I was beginning to feel bitterly disappointed, for it does not seem to me that the breakthrough which we produced has been exploited and pressed to a conclusion. There we were, having helped the Army over all the preliminary gun positions of the enemy, but it was a disappointment to the Air Force that they didn't go further. After all, they must expect to be shot at a bit. They now appear to be tied down again and merely seem to be mopping up certain strong points which were apparently left behind. The Press seems to me to be completely misrepresenting the battle. Now we shall have to wait until we know exactly where the new targets are and this will not be so easy, for without precise targets Bomber Command are useless. If the Army can't get through now, I just don't know what the prospect is for the future. It is, of course, conceivable that the Germans may collapse and pack up, but as yet there is no indication of this. On the contrary, the German Army has fought very well, and unfortunately the vile weather of the last weeks has enabled them to bring up a certain amount of stuff, of which they are making the maximum use.

The country in which the Army has now to fight is very difficult, for it's so close with so many hedges, streams, etc., and with the roads running all along the ridges. In the American sector, General Bradley refuses to allow the villages to be flattened out by bombing, because he is of the opinion that to do so would impede his advance. I fear, therefore, that he will find them more strongly held than would have been the case if I had been able to flatten them out. We are doing what we can with light bombers, but I cannot use Bomber Command.

I talked with the CAS yesterday who was very pleasant: we discussed the battle and he was not very happy. The fact is we are paying now for not getting on with the job in the early days. We have broken the crust but it may form again. One good thing: the morale of our pilots is terrific, and their performance most inspiring.'

Next morning, 20 July, L-M's conference discussed the new German jet-propelled Me262 — none of which had yet been seen flying. By contrast, production of an American jet-propelled aircraft was said to be 'not very far advanced'.

He lunched with the Air Council in London. This was when L-M may have learned of his possible next appointment — in South East Asia with Mountbatten. Cross was now serving as one of five directors under Portal in the Air Ministry: he recalls Mountbatten coming back from Asia. Cross and others were asked to produce a short list for a new air commander for Mountbatten. L-M was not on it but a few days later Mountbatten came into their office, rubbing his hands with glee and said 'I've got L-M.'

21 July

'The weather is simply indescribable in the beach-head. In spite of that, the Army might have attempted to make use of our medium bombers, but they never asked for them. They could have attacked the little villages which are holding up the advance. No request, however, reached me. It is just monstrous. I don't believe it to be malice on the part of the Army, but merely stupidity. They have to be taught how to use the air, or rather what the air weapon means. The impression was given at the outset that we had broken the crust and that we were streaking through. That was true, but only for a few hours. The Hun then counter-attacked and back went the Army, then it went forward again, but it has still not reached the line on which it halted after the first assault.

The fight has now degenerated into an infantry battle, and the Army is stuck again. The position is very serious indeed. I cannot help feeling that they had a priceless opportunity and if only they had pushed really hard we would have got through, for they reached an area in which there were only scattered gun positions and no really organised defences.

There it is. What annoys me is the way in which the operation has been misrepresented by the Press. They have been quite wrong, and it looks to me as though the presentation of what happened can only be described as an immoral piece of bamboozling of the public. A resolute push would have inflicted a major disaster upon Germany. As it is, they have just held.

Now what to do? I haven't got the weather or I would destroy those gun pockets with my medium bombers. It is maddening, and all because the Army pays lip service to the Air Force, but when it comes to the point they seem to be quite unable to appreciate the situation from an air point of view. To such an extent does this seem to me to be so, that now I make up my own mind what targets to attack after having appreciated the situation for myself.

As for the specific task of the Air Force, it has been virtually accomplished. The railways, S, SE and E of Paris are in a state of paralysis. Everything on them has been wrecked and there is no movement at all. The only movement is coming from Belgium and last night (20th) I heavily clobbered Courtrai, and I am going for Cambrai tonight. We found a number of their entraining stations, and thoroughly beat up the Hun Army as it was getting into the trains. The Air had a great day, and pilots reported seeing numerous Germans leaping from the trains and running for their lives.

The only things now left to bomb are the marshalling yards at Rheims, and I have also given Bomber Command a list of dumps to destroy.

The Tactical Air Forces are doing extremely well in the tactical area. Movement around Amiens is being successfully dealt with and, in fact, the Germans are in a bad way. They are living in fact on what they succeeded in getting up during the bad weather.

Now there is another bad day. Almighty God is batting on Hitler's side. The Russians continue to pour westwards. I am told that Germany is playing rather a subtle trick on them. They have withdrawn a few troops from Normandy and set them against the Russians, instructing some of them to allow themselves to be taken prisoner in the hope that the Russians will deduce from this fact that Germany thinks nothing of the Allied push in the west — so little indeed that they have actually taken troops away to reinforce the hardpushed Eastern Front.'

L-M was now absent more often from the daily conferences at his headquarters. On the 24th he was away in Normandy, where he talked with Montgomery and stayed the night in his own caravan there before flying back to Stanmore next morning.

Operation COBRA started on 24 July — during which there was some 'short' bombing before the bombers of the American Ninth Air Force could be recalled. There was more the next day: an American general, McNair, was killed — and was buried in great secrecy. This unfortunate episode would have done nothing to improve air/ground relationships.

25 July
'We tried to lay on a battle for the 24th, for the Met. said there was more than a 50/50 chance of it coming off. The Commander of the 8th American Air Force agreed with ill grace, but at the very last moment the weather died on us, and as far as I can see we shall say goodbye to any decent weather for at least three or four days.

There is an enormous depression in the Atlantic and others are following behind. In fact, from a weather point of view, conditions are absolutely frightful.

I went over yesterday and had a word with General Bradley who is extremely worried. I eventually got him to postpone his attack for a little time and the bombing which preceded it did not take place until 10 o'clock today (25th) and his infantry went in at 11.

I also saw Monty yesterday, who told me his plans for the next week or so. They are pleasantly aggressive and he aims to keep the Hun busy along the whole front. He was very frank about the whole situation. I think it is time that I had a representative at his Headquarters to deal with the strategic planning of the air side, and I am thinking of sending Air Commodore Kingston McCloughry. This is becoming more and more essential as the war evolves.

I fancy that we shall soon get Ike settled over there, more or less permanently, and then we should get a proper set up. That will be an excellent thing. Spaatz is proving rather troublesome and went up in the air when I urged him to support Bradley, for he complained that the operation had been wrongly planned and was taking place at least two hours earlier than it should. However, he was soon seen to be completely wrong and gave way.

Speaking generally, I have the impression that the War will soon be over. I shouldn't be surprised if the end of September saw its end. I base my opinions on the advances of the Russians, which are tremendous. I think they will be in Germany by the end of August, if not before, and then anything may happen.

It is for this reason that I believe we should hit the Germans very hard at this moment, and if the 8th Air Force wish to do so I am not going to stand in their way. On the contrary, I shall encourage them, though I shall reserve everything else for operations in aid of the Army as and when necessary.'

On the 25th L-M was at his headquarters, taking the chair at the 54th Allied Air Commanders' conference. Later he drove to Uxbridge to Advanced HQ AEAF and sat in on Coningham's daily conference. He decided to attend Coningham's conferences more frequently in future, in order to keep himself fully up to date in the tactical developments of the air war and to prepare for the time when Advanced HQ AEAF would cease to exist. L-M said that he agreed fully with the view that the strategic air forces should be used as far as possible for targets in Germany except when he had a particular target for Bomber Command. He now saw his function as being more and more the direction of the Tactical Air Force.

On the 26th L-M held the usual conference in his office at 9.45 in the morning. Then he flew to Portsmouth to confer with Eisenhower. For L-M this was a momentous meeting; there was a good deal of plain speaking on his side and some heated argument with Tedder. Eisenhower said that he wished AEAF HQ to be alongside SHAEF when SHAEF moved to the continent. L-M said that at present he felt that he should deal with Montgomery as the C-in-C of the armies, and he felt it desirable to have a representative at his HQ.

Tedder thought that Coningham was the person to represent L-M at Montgomery's HQ. L-M disagreed and felt the time was near when Coningham should revert to his original role as Commander of 2nd TAF. It would move to France the next week when HQ 21 Army Group moved across, and that might be a suitable moment for Coningham to take over 2nd TAF. When Montgomery reverted to the position of C-in-C 21 Army Group, he would deal with the Commander of 2nd TAF direct, but as long as Montgomery was C-in-C of the combined armies in France, the planning should be on a higher level and in collaboration with himself as the Air C-in-C.

L-M flew back to Normandy at 2.30 pm to talk to General Bradley (US 1st Army) and General Quesada (9th TAC). In the evening he dined at Montgomery's headquarters together with a deputation of Russian generals who were visiting the front.

That day, Captain Harry Butcher, the US Navy aide to Eisenhower, wrote in his diary that 'Ike wrote to Portal the other day saying that Leigh-Mallory had developed into a good co-operator and had a fighting heart. Portal replied with similar magnanimity and so L-M's stock has been improved by his action.'

Chapter 17
A New Horizon

L-M's diary continues:

27 July
'Yesterday I went to France and saw General Bradley. The American battle is going well, and our bombing has had a big effect. A lot of Germans have surrendered as a result of it. General Bradley was pretty pleased with himself, and I don't blame him. But he hadn't yet realised the amount of strategical assistance he could get from the air until I told him.

I was then going to see General Dempsey but I was delayed, and when I was ready one engine of the aircraft wouldn't start, so I cut out Dempsey and went to see Monty instead, only to find that Monty had gone to Dempsey so that we could all three of us meet and talk matters over together. However, I eventually saw Monty. He had a Russian Admiral and four Generals dining with him. After dinner, we got down to business and the results of our planning will, I hope, appear in due course.

My caravan is settled there, and some kind of set-up on the other side will soon be established. I had a long talk with Broadhurst of a very satisfactory kind. It becomes more and more obvious to me that I must deal direct with Monty, at any rate as long as he is in command, and I have no reason to suppose that he will not continue to be there. I have sent Kingston-McLoughry over there to stay with him. He will be going to and fro.

As far as the battle is concerned the British Army has bogged down, but the American push is going very well. The British are meeting very stiff opposition SE of Caen and it is obvious that the Germans are determined to prevent any advances in that direction if they can possibly do so. That means that, the first plan not having been successful, we must think again.

It is, however, encouraging to know that the Americans are pushing right on and that things look decidedly hopeful on their part of the front. At first their offensive stuck a bit, but then it gathered momentum, and that is a very good sign.

As for the British Army, I think we haven't been too clever, but the air side has done everything it could. In fact, the air assault preceding the Caen push was a classical application of air power, and the only thing which went wrong was that the Army did not make full use of it. Perhaps they did not realise how effective the air assault was going to be. At the moment the vile weather has cancelled air operations, which are altogether stagnant except for fighter-bombers who had a good day yesterday. Today things will be bad again because of the weather, though it may clear this evening.'

28 July

'The Americans are going well but, as usual, the weather as far as air is concerned has been indifferent. There has indeed been nothing doing except for the fighter-bombers. That, however, is not so bad for they are just the aircraft now wanted in the battle.

The Germans are beginning to crack on the Normandy front, and the Americans are more or less through. It is a very good show. While the American front is in a state of action, the British front remains in a state of inaction. I should like to see both fronts moving and a general attack launched all along the line, but nothing like that is happening and this situation, from the British point of view, is, in my judgement, disastrous. I would attack, attack and attack again; they must get on.

As far as I can gather the Americans made their plan themselves, and are pushing resolutely ahead. The fault with us is — basically — generalship. We moved all our stuff east of Caen, then we had a check, and at once changed all our plans and shifted everything back again in order to attack in a different place. Such a move takes a week to complete, and in the meantime the battle continues. Foch, I am sure, would have behaved differently and would at this supreme juncture have attacked all along the line. I hope that the British will move, but I doubt it. Action on their front is at present conspicuous by its absence.

As far as the general set-up of the high command is concerned, it seems to be creaking along, but to be going quite well. There are increasing signs of co-operation. I am hampered a bit by being responsible for the measures taken against the flying bomb, though all the practical part I hand over to Roderic Hill. The fact that the Germans may launch their new rockets* is a possibility I cannot ignore. They are not just a bogey of German propaganda and they may poop them off — how and when I do not know.'

On Sunday 30 July, for the first time since before D-Day, L-M did not hold a morning commanders' conference.

31 July

'We had the usual bloody meeting on Saturday, but there was no open quarrel. On the other hand, in the afternoon the Army plan for the next day's battle (Sunday) arrived. It contained no specific

---

* This is a reference to the V.2 ballistic rocket.

targets, and the advance was to be made over extremely difficult country. I therefore had to make guesses as to the whereabouts of the enemy, since no one could tell me positively exactly where he was, I chose a number of aiming points, and I am glad to say that from results it would appear that I chose well, for prisoners of war report that the bombing was singularly successful.

After that I relaxed and went to Lord Kemsley's* for the weekend, where I played a little bridge and some childish games and met Lord and Lady Linlithgow†. It did me a lot of good, and I thought the conversation intelligent and useful.

Despite bad weather, Bomber Command has of late been bombing in daylight from 1500 feet, and preliminary reports show them to have been very successful. At any rate, at the least it heartened our chaps in the Army and disheartened the enemy.

I have now arranged my set-up in France. Advanced Headquarters will proceed there this week with Air Vice-Marshal Strafford from Uxbridge. Over there the two Tactical Air Forces will be kept separate. Strafford's Headquarters will be close to the Americans and I shall regard them as my own and go over there frequently to preside over the meetings. I shall be there, in fact, three or four days a week. A time will come when the Supreme Commander will go over, and when that happens, which will be presumably in the beginning of September, I shall move my Operational Headquarters, and the centre from which I direct the battle will be shifted from England to France.

As far as the general situation is concerned things seem altogether to be going well. Though I hesitate to say, I believe anything may happen. The Army situation is beginning to look a lot healthier. Perhaps the American example is infectious. Anyhow, the Army is beginning to realise that the Hun is not invincible, and morale is consequently going up. Possibly, the Army is beginning to feel it can see the Hun off at any moment, and when it becomes sure of that it will, I am sure, do very well. It all boils down to a question of morale.'

1 August

'I am now reaching a position when I can afford to sit back. My main business was organising this show and getting things going. I had to fight all the preliminary battles behind the scenes. Things are now in running order and are proceeding, on the whole, very reasonably well.

My main job is to watch developments and to intervene only when necessary. The strategical part of the show is over. The

---

* Lord Kemsley (1883-1968) was chairman of Kemsley Newspapers and at the time was Editor-in-Chief of *The Sunday Times* newspaper. His son was killed in action in 1944.

† The Marquess of Linlithgow (1887-1952) had been Viceroy of India, 1936–1943.

railways in France are in a bloody awful mess and are, for all intents and purposes, "out".

That means that I have, at the moment, only the tactical side of my job to think about. Last night for example, the only "fruity" target which Bomber Command could find was the railway engine yard at Laroche, which they pranged heavily, with so far as I know at the moment, very good results.

The battle in Normandy was fog-bound until an hour ago. This means that neither tanks nor aircraft could operate. The weather is now getting clearer and I have hopes that something will be done this evening.

The general set-up is working far more smoothly now I am glad to say. Everything is much easier. Notably, I have no more troubles with the Americans who are co-operating in every way, though that does not mean that they may not slip some champion double cross over me at any moment. However, I hope they won't.'

At the commanders' conference on 4 August the military intelligence report was given by Lieutenant Colonel Heathcote-Amory (who subsequently became Britain's Chancellor of the Exchequer in 1958). Next day, at a meeting Brigadier Mann, Chief of Staff to the Canadian General Crerar, explained the plan for Operation Totalise to push through the Falaise Gap. He said that captured orders showed that the Germans now always expected a delay of one and a half hours between preliminary bombing by the Allies and their actual attack. Therefore in this operation, the troops would advance at night at the same time as the bombing was being carried out on their flanks. The first of two phases would start at 2300 on 7 August.

It was agreed that as Bomber Command could not be available for both phases, all the bombing would be given to the American Eighth Air Force under Doolittle.

Back to L-M's diary:

4 to 6 August

'I am afraid my diary may be a bit scrappy because I have so much to do. I went over on Friday last (4th) to see, among other persons, General Crerar, commanding the Canadians, and we discussed his next battle.

I missed seeing General Dempsey. I then went on to Monty who talked a little. On the morning of the next day I went to see Bradley with Monty. We held a three-cornered conference in an orchard near St Lo, the staff officers being bidden to withdraw out of earshot. At that conference we discussed the general lines of the battle, which is designed to roll up the German Army in France. The atmosphere was one of the greatest bonhomie. I think the plan evolved there was very good indeed. I shall not go into details, beyond saying that the idea is for the combined armies to pivot with the British Army holding the left flank near Caen, and then move in a great swing towards the left. I particularly admired the crafty manner in which the Americans were induced to capture the town of Vire.

Our main pre-occupation of course was to deal with the air side of the battle, and that I was enabled to do on my return to England.

I arrived at 6.30, went straight down to the War Room and had a two-hour conference, laying on the next battle. On Sunday the 6th, I had another conference to fix the final details, and then I took a small holiday after lunch and played tennis.

I am glad to say that General Spaatz now realises that the immediate object, which may well prove to be the final object, is to destroy the German Army in France. To achieve that end, he is prepared to make every possible contribution. He won't be required to bomb in the immediate battle area, but he will deal with the immediate strategical area.

The Hun is beginning to show signs of cracking, I think. The moment that is definite we shall get cracking and throw everything in we possibly can.

That evening I had a little trouble with C-in-C Bomber Command, who had not got his co-ordinates for the targets he was to bomb, but I got them for him by 8.35 the same evening. The weather doesn't look at all good and can only be described as doubtful. It is of course a vital factor in the general situation.'

On 8 August L-M flew to France in the morning to watch the second stage of Operation Totalise at 1300. The initial dropping of markers by the American Eighth Air Force was extremely wild and went among Canadian troops, causing their bombers to create about sixty casualties among Allied troops. Near the end another bomber formation bombed the southern outskirts of Caen causing another three hundred casualties among Allied troops.

After watching the bombing from the air, L-M landed and suggested to the Canadian General Crerar (GOC 1st Canadian Army) that the bombing should be carried out again by Bomber Command.

Next morning Doolittle admitted to L-M that 'stupidity' had played a large part in the American failure to bomb the right targets. L-M recommended to the Air Ministry that no official report should be made 'in the interests of Allied co-operation'.

Afterwards L-M gave a Press conference. His written draft started in an unusual style:

'My motto in this great battle, as in all others in which I have been engaged is this: "'Tis not in mortals to command success; but we will do more Sempronius, we'll deserve it." '

Next day he gave an extended talk to a number of journalists. On 10

August *The Times* had quoted L-M as saying that the Luftwaffe had shot its bolt and would not be able to stage a comeback.

But on 13 August Portal wrote L-M a personal letter. He said he noted that L-M's talk had evidently created a very good impression. However one remark caused him some surprise, namely: 'If we could cause the German army to break and try to get away the Allied Air Forces would be able to turn the retreat into a rout and bring about its destruction.' Portal said that this was a most dangerous prophecy. Similar optimistic forecasts by senior officers in the past had seldom been justified and they were thus brought into disrepute:

> 'I am told that the statement quoted above was contained in the draft of your address which was submitted to the Air Ministry. The Air Ministry deleted this paragraph and substituted an innocuous alternative. I am therefore puzzled to understand how this passage came to remain in the text which you gave.'

L-M wrote back to Portal:

> 'I always think it is colourless if one reads a document out to people, and it does not get the stuff over nearly as well as if one talks to them. Consequently, I talked to the Press rather than reading out the actual paper, but I think I managed to stick very closely to what was in the paper. I cannot remember exactly what I said in my concluding words, and I am sorry if I painted too strong a picture.'

9 August

> 'Crerar was as sick as mud with the American bombing, which was frightful. So much of it fell in the wrong place that it wasn't really any good. I am now talking of the battle that opened two days ago in the Caen area.
>
> On the other hand, Crerar had nothing but praise for Bomber Command. The markers came down to the exact minute and to the right targets, and the bombers came straight on to the markers. No bomb fell anywhere near our troops. Some of the American bombing, however, was as much as fourteen thousand yards from the target. Two packets fell just past me when I was turning back from flying over Caen. They were two lots of twelve which bombed Caen by mistake. The American bombing (8th AAF) began by being very scattered, but they eventually hit the first two targets. I watched the second wave come in, however, and I could see no bombs at all in the target area, but a good many fell far away to the West of the Orne. Succeeding waves, seeing where the bombs were falling, went in and bombed there as well. Then the markers, seeing what was happening, rushed off and poured marker flares down on the right targets so that the latter end of the attack put their bombs in the right place, but I reckon that out of 390 aircraft laid on, not more than 150 dropped their bombs anywhere near the target.

As for the contention that smoke and dust obscure targets in daylight so as to make it impossible to see them — I don't believe it. I kept a careful eye on the Caen/Falaise road, which is absolutely straight for miles. It was completely free from obscurity and visible for a very long way. In fact I could see every yard of it.

As for the battle in itself, the Canadians, as the result of the failure of the American daylight bombing, were held up yesterday afternoon after having captured all their first objectives, very largely because Bomber Command had done such a good job.

On the whole however, I believe the situation to be good. The Huns are fighting extremely hard. Our hopes must be centred on the right flank, and we will trust that the Americans there will go forward very quickly. That is the main thing. The German counter-attack of 4 Panzer Divisions made it possible for the Air to put up a wonderful show. A certain number of the leading German tanks penetrated quite a long way, but their rear echelons were so heavily attacked from the air that they were bashed up and utterly unable to get forward.

It is my considered opinion that the air attack broke up that German counter-attack. Had the rear echelons been able to push on to reinforce the forward elements there would have been a nasty mess, but they were quite unable to do so because of the air attack. I think we have got a chance of putting the German Army "in the bag". I have given strict orders that when the first sign of the cracking comes I am to be informed, so that I can throw every available aircraft into the battle.

I believe our chances are 6 to 4 on of destroying the German Army in the next fortnight. It depends on two things — weather, and the behaviour of the Americans on the right flank. If they push ahead, all will be well. My own personal view, but I am not a General, is that the armour should be taken away from Caen and pushed in en masse on the right flank in the American sector, and that the Poles should also be put into the battle there. They would go through anything.

To revert to the last Caen battle, the Canadian plan, which you will remember I told you was a good one, would have been first class had Bomber Command been able to carry out the whole bombing programme. Owing to fog on airfields however, it was thought that it would not be possible to turn them around quick enough, and in order to make sure that there would be proper bombing by day, the daylight part of the programme was entrusted to the American 8th Air Force. As luck would have it Bomber Command could have carried out the whole programme for they had 800 aircraft ready, bombed up and waiting, but by that time the 8th had been laid on for the job.'

On the 10th L-M held his first commanders' conference at the new Advanced HQ at St Saveur Lendelin, north of Coutances. Next morning he left Montgomery's headquarters at 9.30 and returned to Stanmore.

11 August

'A good meeting yesterday, with Bert Harris full of co-operation. Jimmy Doolittle produced a long apology for the bad bombing by the 8th, which I myself had seen. He was full of excuses but I cut him as short as I could, and did not reveal that I knew just where the bombs had in fact fallen.

My conference in France next day with the Tactical Air Force took place near St Lo, after a long and dusty drive. It was very satisfactory. I then returned to Headquarters and dined alone, afterwards seeing Monty. We ran over the general situation together. He is going for complete encirclement and if he succeeds he may do the RAF out of a job. By this I mean of course, he will have won the battle since he will have cut off the German Army, and we shall not therefore have any more targets to pursue along the roads. We shall be able to do a certain amount of bombing on the trapped troops, but not nearly so much as would have been the case had they been streaming back to their frontiers.

However, I am not one to complain. My conversation with Monty really confirmed our previous plans. My relations with him are cordial, but I cannot pretend to like him. As a General he is one of the luckiest that there has ever been.

At the moment the Germans are trying to reinforce their front, and yesterday we even caught at least a division on the move in daylight, near Compiegne. Strafford's forces went for them.

I also talked with General Crerar. His battle is not going too well and he may want help. I also had a row with the 8th Corps because they called for Marauders to help them, but gave no targets or aiming points, merely indicated a vague stretch of open country. They do not yet appear to have got it into their heads that air forces
have got to be used with precision, if they are to be any good.

This morning I arrived a little late for the conference because I had wanted to take off at 9 am but the port engine wouldn't start for half an hour. At the conference Spaatz was full out to give every help he could — which was satisfactory.

I have no illusions however as to what the Americans will do as soon as the fighting is over or virtually over. They will return to their zone and have nothing more to do with me. It is for that reason that Spaatz is setting up his headquarters as close as possible
to SHAEF at Granville. I don't mind, for by that time the war will have been won.'

12 to 14 August

'The battle is going well, but it looks as though the Air Force will be robbed of its chance of finishing off the German Army, because the neck of the bag between Argentan and Falaise is drawing closer and closer. The fact of the matter is they won't come out.

Yesterday, everything was laid on to bomb them to pieces and I had hopes of being able to smash them, but they just daren't face the roads — that's the long and short of it. I had every aircraft I could, waiting and ready, and by the night before last they had already smashed the roads to such an extent that our Mosquitos at night saw the lights of German vehicles full on in the tactical area. All they did however was to move two Panzer Divisions to Argentan to try to stop the Americans. I think those divisions are actually in Argentan, but the Americans have got two places — one on each side of it — so that the town is not much good to the Huns.

The crossings over the Seine are being dealt with by Bomber Command, and the American 9th Air Force have gone for roads very successfully. My own view is that the chances of the Hun getting out have now gone. Inside of course he is being harried by the fighter-bombers which have clobbered and clobbered and clobbered. But the opportunity of wiping out the German Army as they streamed back over the roads in headlong retreat doesn't look as though it will come my way.

It is possible that they might last inside the pocket for as much as a week or ten days. They are almost surrounded. When that army in the pocket has gone, what can the Hun do? He will, I suppose, try to hold the Seine for a short time but he has no more troops, or certainly none of any value, and with the large forces at our disposal, we shall be able to continuously outflank him.

I had my usual talks with Monty and Bradley which were quite satisfactory. The heavy attack today by Bomber Command in support of the ground forces on the Canadian front resulted in some bombs falling among our own troops, one quite near Air Marshal Coningham, who has just been on the phone to me about it.

I also attended the opening of the Malcolm Club and this was quite successful. The Minister for Air was there in good oratorical form. I left before his 50th and final speech.'

On 15 August — which was D-Day Plus 70 — L-M decided to discontinue his personal diary of the battle. He regarded the air campaign in France and Western Europe as won. His thoughts were turning to his next responsibility, in the Far East where he would soon be going for the battle against Japan.

Chapter 18
Preparing to Leave

On 16 August L-M chaired the commanders' conference at Stanmore then flew to France to his Advanced Headquarters. In the evening he dined with Montgomery at the Army HQ near Vire.

On the same day Portal wrote to the Secretary of State for Air:

'Since I last spoke to you about Leigh-Mallory's future the following developments have occurred. Mountbatten, with Portal's permission but on his own initiative, approached Eisenhower and asked whether he would have any objection to him applying for Leigh-Mallory as Air C-in-C South East Asia. Mountbatten then approached Leigh-Mallory and L-M "jumped at the idea" of relieving Peirse. Eisenhower reacted saying that his early doubt about Leigh-Mallory had been completely erased and that he was giving excellent service.'

On the 17th L-M spent an intensive day of visiting British airfields in France. He lunched with Coningham at HQ 2nd TAF near Bayeux. In the evening he met Eisenhower to discuss the future set-up and location of headquarters. He dined with Montgomery and General Dempsey at 21 Army Group HQ.

Early next morning he met Montgomery again and agreed to suspend bombing of bridges because the Allies would now need them for their advance. Instead the bombers' targets would be in Germany. The German forces were apparently encircled in Normandy. L-M told his commanders that, now at the end of the first phase of the battle for France, the main German strength in the west had been destroyed or seriously mutilated. In the air it was now a fighter-bomber battle and it was hard to find targets for medium or heavy bombers.

McEvoy praised L-M's leadership:

'In Ops in France, we usually lost more planes than we gained as we were over enemy territory. The Wing Leaders felt this was unfair and they blamed L-M. But after every single Op. L-M had a conference to which all Wing Leaders and Station Commanders came, some still bleeding, "hot from the battle". As a result of what he learned, L-M adjusted the tactics for the following day. L-M always turned up himself. He always encouraged people to speak up and he was good at accepting criticism from his juniors.'

That same day Paris rose in revolt — and six days later the city was liberated from the Germans.

L-M's job was effectively completed. Now began the preparations for the Far East. On the 22nd L-M officially informed Eisenhower that he had been designated as Air Commander-in-Chief South-East Asia. He asked to be relieved of his command by 1 September. He also informed Montgomery and returned to Stanmore the following evening.

L-M made farewell visits to the American airfields which had been under his command. In the afternoon of the 29th he met first Portal and then the Prime Minister. The following day he told his air commanders that their most important task was now to prevent the Germans getting their strength away to the east and using it to fight another battle. The main effort would be the employment of fighter-bombers against trains and railway tracks. Then he started a round of farewell visits to the British airfields which had been under his command.

L-M moved his operational headquarters to France. He held his final commanders' conference at Stanmore on Thursday 7 September. He read out a letter from the Air Council expressing their appreciation of the efforts by the Allied Air Forces against the enemy's flying bomb organisation.

On Friday the 8th L-M's mother wrote to his sister Mary:

'I heard from Trafford this morning. He was just going off with his HQ establishment to France yesterday. Only had two there until now. What a crowd there will be with all the other HQs as well, and what scenes there will be in Brussels, especially when Queen Wilhelmina returns. Wasn't it horrid of the Germans to set fire to the beautiful Hotel de Ville — wretches!'

That same day L-M held his first commanders' conference at his new headquarters with FORWARD SHAEF at Granville, north of Avranches on the Cotentin peninsula. He announced that these meetings thereafter would only be held twice weekly, on Tuesdays and Fridays.

News now came in that the Americans were refusing to accept any British successor to him as C-in-C AEAF and furthermore agreement to his new appointment in SE Asia had not yet been received from General Arnold, the American Chief of Staff in Washington. Consequently, he was asked to carry on at least until the end of September and possibly halfway into October. He agreed to do so, although it meant greatly reducing the period of leave and rest which he had been granted.

On Sunday, L-M was in Brussels for meetings with Coningham of 2nd TAF and then at Advanced AEAF. He was accompanied by his personal assistant, Flight Officer Lady Freeman, and by his Staff Officer, Group Captain Loel Guinness. Guinness had joined L-M shortly before D-Day: he had previously been a Station Commander at Exeter. Guinness liked L-M enormously. He told the author: 'He was full of guts and drive, and a gentleman too with good manners. He was awfully pleasant to be with.' Guinness was subsequently Member of Parliament for the City of Bath.

On Monday L-M conferred with Lieutenant General Bedell-Smith. Next day he met his commanders at FORWARD SHAEF at Jullouville. The following day he was back at Stanmore. On Friday he met his commanders at Versailles, where his headquarters were in Marshal Petain's house near SHAEF in the Trianon Palace Hotel.

With the drive continuing successfully towards Germany, L-M told his team that 'the main function of AEAF is now to act as a link between the Army and the Strategic Air Forces.'

On 21 September he was at HQ SHAEF at Versailles where he attended a meeting chaired by Bedell-Smith with Tedder and others. He asked his driver, Sergeant Cockings, to check up on the exact location of General Spaatz's headquarters 'somewhere down in Chantilly' because they would be driving there that evening. Much amused, Cockings replied to L-M that he already knew exactly where Spaatz's headquarters were — because two American soldiers wearing helmets were standing publicly on guard outside the building! L-M pointed this out to Spaatz, and next day the soldiers were moved inside.

Meanwhile Doris wrote to her sister-in-law Mary on 24 September from Montrose House, Stanmore:

'My dearest Mary,

I daresay Mother will have told you that Trafford has been chosen to command the air in SE Asia with Louis Mountbatten — I always thought this would come because he told me at his farewell party that directly the European campaign was over Trafford was to join him — and we laughed then, but it has come to pass — I have decided to go with him and run his bungalow which will be always full of people coming and going etc. The Air Council gave me a passage by air and I will fly out with him in his own Dakota. It is all rather an upset somehow — too much to see and "clothes" — this is where I want your help. The headquarters are at Kandy, Ceylon — lovely climate 75 degrees on the average — you know Ceylon, Mary, and what one wants. I believe it's beautiful and they say the Air C-in-C's bungalow has a gorgeous view and is very nice.

I don't imagine the dressing up which a command like that would be in peace time, will be on the same level — but I presume I have to look nice and be able to visit the Governors in India, Ceylon etc which means a lot of frocks. Does one take one's fur coat, woollen dresses and underwear? Can one get shoes made there? And can one get silks and cottons for copying frocks? Stockings? I imagine the prices out there are very high. I believe I shall get special coupons and must see about that at once.

I shall value your advice so much Mary — and remember that all the luggage except perhaps a trunk of linen and silver which may be able to come on a transport plane will come on the Dakota with us. We shall have plenty of room and Trafford says can take a lot — the crew consists of two pilots — one the ADC, four crew, Osbourne, Trafford and I and perhaps a Staff Officer.

It is rather sad having to leave the old people — my mother will feel it very much — but I always feel my place is with Trafford and that's where I should be. Jacqueline will eventually go to America and anyway she goes back to her flat tomorrow. Tom is settled and my sister is near Mother so there is nothing to keep me. I shall love the scenery there, I believe it is quite beautiful, and will paint — I do hope I'll find a kindred spirit! I can't believe the war in Japan will take many years — one or possibly two.

Trafford is home today and goes back tomorrow — his headquarters are in Versailles — a beautiful house that was all furnished up for Petain and he is very comfy. He has had a cold at the moment and we are doing every kind of quick cure with good results — but I'm afraid he'll be very tired when the cold leaves him. He is (at the moment) going to leave Eisenhower on October 15th, take one month's leave, and we go on November 15th — but every day for the last three weeks the plan is different, so anything may happen — but I'll have to get my clothes together!

My love to you, from Doris.'

L-M had to plead by telephone from HQ SHAEF for information about the Arnhem operation — which was intended to capture and hold a bridge over the River Rhine behind German lines. The problem was that SHAEF was left completely uninformed about operations in Holland. The failure of the Arnhem operation meant a considerable slowing down of operations against Germany.

L-M told 2nd TAF at Brussels on 27 September that for them the air battle against Germany would now take priority. He then travelled back to his Versailles headquarters in order to deal with fighter direction and airfield allocation.

21 Army Group asked for the cutting of the Walcheren dyke by air attack in order to see the result which could be achieved by flooding. However, a SHAEF conference on 29 September decided not to attempt a deliberate breach of the dykes but to inform the political authorities that in the course of the bombing the dykes might incidentally be broken. Immediately after the end of the meeting Montgomery sent a written demand for the flooding of the island. But L-M demurred, asking whether the operation had yet been cleared by the politicians.

The question was resolved on 6 October at a Versailles conference chaired by L-M at which Eisenhower decided that the next three days' effort would be directed against oil targets: the Ruhr would be the target of next urgency: there would only be a limited effort against Walcheren.

On 4 October, Radio Moscow broadcast a decree signed by Kalinin, President of the Supreme Soviet, that the Order of Kutusov First Class had been conferred on L-M 'for outstanding leadership in the invasion of France'. In view of L-M's high opinion of the Russian contribution, this must have given him great pleasure.

The 11th October was his final day in command of the Allied Expeditionary Air Force. L-M sent out messages of 'profound and sincere' thanks to all his commanders.

On 15 October AEAF was officially dissolved and L-M was released from his responsibility as Air C-in-C. He left SHAEF on 16 October. It was no longer necessary to replace him with an American or a Briton because there was less need now for fine timing and coordination between large masses of aircraft and ground force units. Thereafter Coningham officially reported to Tedder who took over from L-M the coordinating of air operations.

After relinquishing his AEAF post, L-M gave a Press conference on 16 October which was extensively reported in the next day's newspapers. Then he planned a few weeks of rest and recuperation — partly at home in Stanmore and partly, he hoped, in Marrakech.

The *Sunday Dispatch* newspaper carried a profile of him. He told them that the assault on Europe had come off with uncanny regularity. True, he had slightly over-estimated the requirements for fighters in Normandy, so that a little pruning had been possible in July. But, on the other hand, the Luftwaffe might have been more forceful. True, there had been a short period of anxiety when it was found that the air filters for the Sabre engines on the Typhoons were inadequate. But the correction had been quickly made. True, he blamed himself for anticipating that the German Seventh Army would try and run from France, and be slaughtered by air, whereas much of it stayed and was slaughtered on the spot. Apart from these points the air war had developed so exactly as he forecast that it was like seeing a film run through twice.

The newspaper described L-M as having
'a shy manner. He speaks quickly and eagerly and carries conviction. He is at his desk at nine sharp every morning and if he is called away to afternoon conferences he will be at it again till midnight. His personal assistant and his clerks work in shifts to keep pace with his late working-hours. They find him considerate and kindly — provided that nobody has moved any papers from his desk. For while it is permitted to tidy his desk, no paper or file may be removed without his instructions.

He is a steady pipe smoker and he enjoys his ration of sweets. He likes his tea very hot, strong, and sweet — real "sergeant-major's tea".'

★　　★　　★

But instead of enjoying a holiday, L-M fell ill. Only two weeks later on 30 October did he feel able to reply to a letter from his daughter-in-law:
'By way of having a really good leave I have just had a week in bed with bronchitis and am just up again. I must spend this week getting all right again, next week preparing to go and the following week off.

As a result of all this my arrangements have been thoroughly upset. I will however try and suggest a time to meet sometime before I go as I would like to see you.

Tom seems much quieter at the moment. He is enjoying his job and there don't seem to be any external attractions. I do hope things go all right for him, but I don't much like leaving him for so long.

I am much looking forward to my new job and shall be thoroughly thankful when I get there. All this finishing up and preparation is very wearing. Mummy is coming with me and we are flying out together.'

On 31 October Portal wrote to L-M to ask a favour:
'I understand you will be travelling out in your own York, and I wonder if you will do me a very great favour by offering any spare seats you may have in your aircraft to my brother, Admiral Portal . . . now going out to a new job in Ceylon.'

L-M immediately got in touch with Admiral Portal. He found that the latter could not be ready to leave before the 17th, and so could not accompany L-M.

On 3 November L-M flew to a French airfield near Paris which had previously been used as a German fighter station. There both he and Bomber Harris were decorated by General Eisenhower with the Degree of a Chief Commander of the Legion of Merit medal. Sholto Douglas was also awarded the same medal but it was reported that bad weather had prevented him from flying in from Paris to receive it.

On 6 November Doris wrote to her daughter-in-law Jeanette from Dorney Wood, at Burnham in Buckinghamshire:
'I wonder if it's going to be possible to meet before we go on the 14th? (This date is a secret.) I was going to have fixed a day or a night to see you last week, but Daddy was in bed, and we were both quite ill with the inoculations that they pump into you that I seemed only able to cope with the current affairs. It is all very sad that you have drifted out of the family and it's difficult for us to realise that it was necessary, but there it is, and I daresay you are both happier and will make more of your lives — Tom is all alone — the original girl that he met in Aylesbury is quite a thing of the past, and there is no baby. I expect you know all this — whether there ever was, I am not quite sure, but I don't think she was much of a person — and traded on Tom's "nuisance" shall we call it! It's all such a pity — Tom is working very hard at this motor business and making quite a good thing of it.

We are leaving Jacqueline at Hendon still, with her flat in London where she and Tony occasionally meet. They see very little of each other and their lives are very difficult. Lets hope the war may soon be over and they can start their lives over in America.

I am torn between being very excited at going and wanting to get there and starting this new life, but it's difficult to re-adjust oneself at this time of life and I'm leaving behind so many I love. Still I can look after Daddy when he's with me and I know there will be plenty of "welfare" for me to do when I get there.'

The next day Doris wrote to her sister-in-law Mary from Montrose House, Stanmore:

'We did so enjoy seeing you on Friday, it was so kind of you to have us and make us so comfortable. We went on to Dorneywood and had a very restful weekend, a little golf, and billiards and conversation with the dear old man.

I am now really getting down to my packing up — what a business! How maddening about the gas stove — I saw it in the boot of the car and said in both Trafford's and Ralph's presence — "don't forget the gas stove is there"! We will get it to you somehow.

I will certainly write and tell you all I can about the great adventure. We leave from Northolt at 9 am on the 14th — Tom and Jacqueline will be there and crowds of people seem to be coming — I shall be thankful to be off now. These last days are very trying in every way!'

On 8 November, L-M went to see the King at Buckingham Palace. Next day there was an official reception at the Dorchester Hotel in honour of the departing Leigh-Mallorys.

On Friday 10 November he saw Saunders, his historian, for a final talk. L-M told him that he was very happy about the set-up in South East Asia Command, that he was going out there as Air Officer Commanding-in-Chief both of the British and American Air Forces, and that he had won his main point which was that all subordinate commanders of both countries should take their orders direct from him. He said more than once that he had insisted upon this, as his experiences as Commander-in-Chief of the Allied Expeditionary Air Force had shown him clearly the difficulties of trying to carry out any other arrangement. He added that sometimes his position when commanding the Allied Expeditionary Air Force had been so difficult that he had been on the point of resigning but had refrained from so doing because he hoped that his duty lay in doing his utmost to make the system work. But he added — 'I am not going to have any more of that sort of nonsense in my new Command.'

Trafford and Doris spent that evening with their old friends, the Dodgsons. It was described afterwards in a letter, dated 11 November:

'Trafford picked us up at 6 o'clock in his enormous car with Jacqueline, and we sailed down to Stanmore, and after Doris had said we'd only have a scratch meal as everything was packed up, when Osborne and the other man heard we were coming they put on a dinner party — all the silver got out, and it <u>was</u> fun. Tom turned up unexpectedly. <u>Drinks</u> just took our breath away. Usual cocktails with heavenly pure grapefruit juice (America!). Chateau Lafitte which always used to head the wine list, the most sought after burgundy and it certainly was gorgeous. Given to Trafford by one of the Guinnesses who has a flat in Paris and the old caretaker hid it away during the occupation and Guinness got away 12 cases of it home. Port wine and then Jack disappeared during coffee, and arrived down with a bottle of Chartreuse her Tony had brought back from Paris. Xmas present to Trafford, but she felt this was the occasion to open it! <u>and was</u> it good. Jack and Tom looked quite sozzled (but actually were sober) both very tired and the boo<u>z</u>e gave them a comfortable sleepy feeling. I have underlined the "z" in booze as you put "s" in your letter!'

Traf. in frightfully good form and <u>thrilled</u> with his new undertaking. They have a 4 engine "York" plane to take them over (one day next week) absolutely super affair. 1st night they land and sleep in Italy — next night sleep in the air and land at Baghdad, spend the day there, cruise the next night, day and night, and arrive for breakfast at Bangalore. (I wonder if Guy will hear of their arrival and be there to meet them?) Wash and brush up there and arrive all clean and tidy at Kandy 2 hours later.

Isn't it all staggering and Arabian Nightish dream! Doris is feeling a bit apprehensive, and longs to have a female with her I'm afraid it may be lonely for her in Kandy — when Traf goes off to Burma and India. He will take the 2 ADC's and man servant, and she'll be left with the crowd of black servants! Which she doesn't much fancy. Pity Jac couldn't go with her. I think if she had not married she might have gone as another ADC!

Their York has 24 passenger accommodation, crew of 8. So they have plenty of room to take <u>all</u> their luggage — plate, linen, golf clubs, tennis rackets, fishing rods! As Doris says the inside of the plane will look just like a jumble sale — and crowds of big bugs to see them off, so it will be a real pantomine! <u>and</u> 2 Squadrons of Spitfires with them the whole way over, they will be handed over from one area to another, so at the changing of the guard there will be 4 Squadrons. We <u>did</u> laugh about it all — and you can imagine how funny they are about it. Doris saying <u>quite right</u>, she didn't want to be chased by Jap planes, and Traf saying <u>quite ridiculous</u>, he didn't want the Spitfires!! Well, well, I think that's about all.'

Trafford wrote a final letter to his sister Mary:

'Thank you so much for sending us a book for the journey; it will help to while away some of the time. We did so enjoy our night with you and Ralph, thank you so much for having us. What a tragedy about the stove. Unfortunately I had not arrived home when the car was packed and never noticed it when I was unpacking the plants. If I can I will get it flown down to Odiham and you can collect it from there.

Please tell Ralph that I have sent the letter on to the bank. I have had a terrible rush seeing everyone and packing. I have a very full day tomorrow and then off.

Very much love

Your loving brother

Trafford.'

Next morning, 14 November 1944, Trafford and Doris departed from Northolt airport, never again to be seen alive.

This book began by enquiring 'who was L-M?' It is to be hoped that by now the reader will have discovered quite a lot about him as a man and what he achieved. Noel Baker thought he was a great man and a great commander. He has been described as pompous, energetic, shy, ambitious, charming, human, dedicated to the RAF and his country and, by Portal as a poor judge of men. Despite Portal's judgement, he certainly seemed to know who to listen to — to name a few: Bader, Broadhurst, Cross and Johnnie Johnson. And his First World War protégés, Haslam and West were not exactly failures, either.

Perhaps the words of Johnnie Johnson, Britain's top scoring fighter pilot of World War II, make a fitting conclusion to this, the closing chapter of L-M's life.

'Underneath his rather pompous manner, I though L-M was a very human, if shy, man. As a Commander-in-Chief he was excellent. He was an outstanding organiser and very firm, but not to the point of inflexibility. He was very much aware of the changing nature of air operations, and was always on the lookout for new ideas. When I had the Kenley Wing in 1943, whenever we had had a particularly successful outing, he would always phone me direct to offer his congratulations. He invariably ended by asking me if there was anything I needed to keep up the good work. I think he appreciated that the best ideas, in a rapidly changing situation, would come from the sharp end rather than from the staff.

One instance of L-M's responsiveness was in June 1943. At that time, the enemy were avoiding combat until we were at the limit of our radius of action, so forcing us to disengage and go on the defensive before we had well and truly clobbered them. I suggested to L-M that if I had another Wing under my command, to stay out of the initial battle and remain intact to cover the withdrawal of the first Wing, I could be much more effective. I got the extra Wing and it worked out fine.

L-M was very much a "fatherly" figure and at his best when he held conferences with his young "wing leaders", because he did not pretend to know about fighter tactics and relied on us to keep him up to date.

L-M, of course, never had the "right" job. Sidelined at 12 Group in 1940: Fighter Command in 1943 when the short range of our Spitfires prevented any real offensive work — and, in 1944, the wretched, unwanted AEAF.

I thought he was a "good" man, not a conniver, and we all had a soft spot for him and regretted the manner of his death.'

Chapter 19
Postscript and
Unanswered Questions

The Leigh-Mallory plane left Northolt on 14 November — and disappeared.

Seven months later, in June 1945, it was reported as having been discovered. The wrecked aircraft was lying on the side of a French mountain in the foothills of the Alps at a height of about six thousand feet. There were no survivors. Why did the aircraft crash? In September 1984 the author found some of the remains of the aircraft still on the mountainside, forty years after it had crashed. The wreckage lies on the southern slope a few hundred feet only from the summit although there is a higher peak beyond. The valley itself is surrounded by mountains on three sides. The aircraft may have left the plains near Grenoble and flown up the valley as a route through the mountains. There are several valleys leading up to the mountains. It was the wrong valley.

At the end of this particular valley a plane would come up against a mountain. There is no way through. The pilot appears to have turned the aircraft to the left and northwards in an attempt to escape — but just failed to clear the summit. An inhabitant of the nearest village commented that there had been a snowstorm and that he had heard the noise of a plane pass over and then go back again.

Blame cannot be apportioned now. The pilot, Squadron Leader Lancaster, possessed considerable experience of flying Sunderland aircraft in Coastal Command. But he had not completed a full training course on a York. Lancaster had wanted an opportunity to take a trip in a York to Algiers as a second pilot. But the special training course laid on for him only gave him total flying experience of nine hours forty minutes in a York.

The plane's flight plan had been to fly at a height of seventeen thousand feet over the mountains. But at ten o'clock in the morning, soon after departure, it was sighted by a passing Dakota between Granville and Laval (in north-eastern France) in appalling weather conditions and flying at only 1500 feet. The crew's watches were found to have stopped at 12.35 pm.

L-M's funeral took place on Friday, 15th June 1945 in the tiny village below the site of the crash. The village is Le Rivier d'Allemont. All the plane's occupants were buried in its walled cemetery.

Their names and ranks are inscribed on simple headstones. From the left they lie:

Lady Leigh-Mallory
L-M himself, age 52
Leading Aircraftsman J. C. Burnett RAF
Squadron Leader C. G. D. Lancaster DFC and Bar, Pilot,
    age 32
Corporal J. E. M. Burgess RAF
Sergeant H. J. Chandler RAF, age 42
Flight Lieutenant K. A. Mooring RAF, Navigator, age 24
Flight Lieutenant Peter Chinn, Pilot, age 20
    (L-M's personal assistant)
Flying Officer A. J. Enser, Flight Engineer, age 29
Flight Lieutenant J. A. Casey, Royal Australian Air Force
    age 29

Among the people present at the funeral was L-M's son-in-law, Tony Doherty, who wrote his own account immediately afterwards:

'I have just returned from Grenoble and I will try to tell you about the funeral. It was, I know, just as you would have wanted it to be. More respect or sincerity couldn't have been shown if it had taken place at the Abbey. Everything possible was done and the Service was beautifully carried out.

We reached Rivier d'Allemont a little after two, an airman parked our jeep and we went down to the Graveyard. It is located a little distance below the village on a small bluff with a small orchard behind it. Far below can be seen the river and its muted roar is faintly audible. The cemetery itself is very tiny, only slightly larger than a tennis court, and surrounded by a stone wall. In a space in the centre the ten caskets had been placed side by side. Actually there were two rows, one of six and one of four, because of the limited space. On either side of them were banks of flowers, on the south side were wreaths from the RAF, USAAF, French and others. On the north side were a large number of bouquets of wild mountain flowers gathered by the school children of the town that morning. On the north side behind the flowers was a company of about 100 RAF Airmen, on the east a like number of Americans. On the west side above the graves was an RAF firing squad. Behind them was a squadron of the French Air Force. Behind them and up the hill in the orchard was a band of a French Chausseur Mountain Regiment in their Alpine boots and berets. On the south side was another group of RAF Airmen. The Principal Party followed and the Chaplain to the south side in front of the Americans.

The Service started with the band playing a piece. After this the Chaplain gave the service. Three volleys were then fired by the Firing Squad, the echo of their fire rolling down the valley. An RAF Bugler played "The Last Post". The notes ended by a salute of the grave by the individuals of the Principal Party. The band played while the Services filed out.

While I waited for them to leave I had a chance to talk to Group Captain Moon who was in charge of all the arrangements. He told us of the deep feeling of sorrow throughout the village and their desire to do everything possible to help. He said that at the scene of the crash the villagers are building a stone cross on a little grassy slope.'

There was a Memorial Service in Westminster Abbey on Thursday, 28 June 1945 for the passengers and crew of York MW 126. Curiously the list of casualties for the service omits one, Sergeant Chandler. L-M's son Tom was kept away by illness.

But that is not quite the end of the story. Questions remain unanswered.

A curious coincidence had been pointed out in a letter to *The Times* by a prominent mountaineer, Geoffrey Winthrop Young in December 1944:

'It would seem strangely to have escaped notice that Trafford Leigh-Mallory, the Air Chief Marshal, was the brother of George, the mountaineer, whose name a few years ago was in all our minds as three times the spearhead of the assaults on Mount Everest, and who was last seen disappearing through cloud upward towards the summit. Thus these two brothers, as unlike in themselves and their careers as in the forms of high and dangerous adventure they severally pursued, vanished similarly out of life, while leading in their maturity supreme but very different undertakings of their countrymen.'

A very different question was raised just after the war. Two men visited the chauffeur Cockings. They asked if he could remember whether or not L-M's briefcase had been loaded onto his aircraft with him. His briefcase and its contents had not been found in the wreckage although many of the plane's contents had not been destroyed by fire. L-M's family silver had not been found either. The French villagers claimed not to have found the wreckage until June 1945 — so where was the briefcase? Presumably it had contained secret details of his future responsibilities. Was it found before the end of the war? Was the plane itself found earlier than seven months after it crashed? If so, what happened to the secret papers?

Another question is Spiritualism. L-M's daughter Jacqueline was snoozing on her bed in her London flat at the time when L-M's plane crashed although of course she did not know it. She insists that he appeared in the flat and told her that her mother had died and then left again. L-M's son Tom attended a seance with a famous medium named Estelle Roberts in 1945. The inconclusive results, in which it was claimed that L-M returned to speak to his son, were published in the *Sunday Pictorial* newspaper of 7 October 1945.

Another unanswered question. Both of L-M's two children, Tom and Jacqueline, developed the incurable disease of Multiple Sclerosis after the crash. Experts say that the disease does not run in families. Its cause is not known. Possibly intense shock or bereavement has a part to play.

But the unanswered question above all is: why is L-M not remembered? He was the most senior member of the Royal Air Force to be killed in the Second World War. The villagers did not build their promised stone cross on the mountainside above Rivier d'Allemont. There is no statue of him in England as there was to Montgomery and other survivors of the war. Perhaps it is because survivors can write their own memoirs. They can justify themselves against those who cannot answer back.

L-M's only memorial is a stained-glass window in Mobberley village church, near to his brother's memorial window.

Perhaps L-M would not have wished for a public memorial. Knowing the man, he might have been content to be known as having done his part, and done it magnificently. He helped Freedom prevail over tyranny. 'Never was so much owed by so many to so few.' L-M was a leader of the Few.

Index